# ENVIRONMENTAL LAW

# MAN AND THE ENVIRONMENT INFORMATION GUIDE SERIES

Series Editor: Seymour M. Gold, Associate Professor of Environmental Planning, Department of Environmental Planning and Management, University of California, Davis, California

*Also in this series:*

AIR POLLUTION—*Edited by George Hagevik**

ENVIRONMENTAL DESIGN—*Edited by Wolfgang F.E. Preiser and Steven Parshall**

ENVIRONMENTAL EDUCATION—*Edited by William B. Stapp and Mary Dawn Liston*

ENVIRONMENTAL ECONOMICS—*Edited by Cleve E. Willis and Barry C. Field**

ENVIRONMENTAL PLANNING—*Edited by Michael J. Meshenberg*

ENVIRONMENTAL TOXICOLOGY—*Edited by Robert Rudd**

ENVIRONMENTAL VALUES, 1860-1972—*Edited by Loren C. Owings*

NOISE POLLUTION—*Edited by Clifford R. Bragdon**

WASTEWATER MANAGEMENT—*Edited by George Tchobanoglous, Robert Smith, and Ronald Crites*

WATER POLLUTION—*Edited by Allen W. Knight and Mary Ann Simmons**

*in preparation

---

The above series is part of the
# GALE INFORMATION GUIDE LIBRARY

The Library consists of a number of separate series of guides covering major areas in the social sciences, humanities, and current affairs.

General Editor: Paul Wasserman, Professor and former Dean, School of Library and Information Services, University of Maryland

Managing Editor: Dedria Bryfonski, Gale Research Company

# ENVIRONMENTAL LAW

## A GUIDE TO INFORMATION SOURCES

*Volume 6 in the Man and the Environment Information Guide Series*

**Mortimer D. Schwartz**

*Professor of Law and Law Librarian*
*University of California, Davis*

*Gale Research Company*
*Book Tower, Detroit, Michigan 48226*

**Library of Congress Cataloging in Publication Data**

Schwartz, Mortimer D
    Environmental law.

    (Man and the environment guide series ; v. 6) (Gale
information guide library)
    1.  Environmental law--United States--Bibliography.
2.  Environmental law--Bibliography.  I.  Title.
KF3775.A1S35           016.344'73'046          73-17541
ISBN 0-8103-1339-1

# VITA

Mortimer Donald Schwartz is a law librarian and professor at the School of Law, University of California at Davis. He received his J.D. and his LL.M. from Boston University, School of Law. In 1951 he completed his M.S. from Columbia University School of Library Service.

Schwartz belongs to numerous professional organizations including the American Association of Law Libraries, American Society for Information Science, International Institute of Space Law, and the American Association for the Advancement of Science.

In addition to having numerous articles published, Schwartz has written STATE LAWS ON THE EMPLOYMENT OF WOMEN (coauthor) and THE POLLUTION CRISIS, volumes 1-3 (coauthor).

# CONTENTS

# Contents

# FOREWORD

The rapidly expanding scope and sophistication of literature in the area of environmental studies has created the need for an authoritative, annotated guide to the range and quality of information sources. New legislation, publications, developing techniques, and increasing levels of public involvement in environmental issues have created a need for government, industry, organizations, and individuals to seek more authoritative information on man-environment relationships. This information can be used to rationalize proposed public or private actions, resolve issues, and measure the impact of past actions on man and the environment.

The objective of this series is to provide an authoritative and systematic guide to significant information sources on selected topics for use by scholars, students, scientists, reference librarians, consultants, professionals, and citizens. The scope and scale of each volume are directed toward accommodating both the immediate and continuing needs of users in addition to establishing a chronological benchmark of the literature on each topic.

This series is concerned with the cause and effect relationships of man's impact on the urban and natural environment. It emphasizes the human problems, issues, and implications of these relationships that can be used to study or solve environmental problems. The series is intended to be a primary reference for people not familiar with the location and organization of information sources in the general area of environmental studies. It should also serve as a basic reference for advanced students or professionals who need an annotated and selected sample of the current literature.

Each volume is prepared by a noted authority on the topic. The annotations and selection of references have been carefully reviewed to present an objective and balanced array of thought and practice. The organization of each volume is tailored to emphasize the way information is organized in this multidisciplinary and rapidly evolving field.

This volume is the most authoritative, current, and comprehensive reference work on environmental law available. It brings together a diverse set of information sources from the physical, social, and natural sciences in the legal

# Foreword

context of the environmental planning and management process. The scope, historical perspective, and current focus offer an annotated guide to the literature that is based on important or representative legal decisions in current practice.

This volume presents a compendium of reference material, legal cases, and ideas valuable to the legal scholar and practitioner. It contains a selected collection of periodical literature, government documents, professional journals, and teaching materials on the rapidly evolving field of environmental law. The introductions, annotations, and sources have been carefully written to give the reader a technical and pragmatic grasp of this fundamental aspect of man-environment relationships.

The scholarly nature of annotations, classification, and cross-referencing of materials presents an integrated view of time, space, values, and events that is not common to other reference works in this area. The author has made a very technical and unorganized subject accessible to practitioners and students by his clear and concise organization of a wide range of sources.

This is a major contribution by a noted authority on the literature of the field. It should help to improve the science of environmental planning and management. Environmental law has become a critical dimension of living in a world of limited resources. This volume contains a blend of legal insight from professional practice and scholarly thought that can help to create and preserve a quality of life and environment still possible on Spaceship Earth.

As the sixth volume in this series, ENVIRONMENTAL LAW continues the standard of scholarly excellence and problem solving usefulness that will be followed in six additional volumes now under contract. When the entire series is completed in 1978, it will represent the most authoritative and comprehensive guide to the man-environment literature ever published.


Seymour M. Gold, Series Editor
February 1977

# PREFACE

This volume deals with environmental law as a field intended to protect, preserve, or rehabilitate the physical environment. The extent of this field can be seen from the table of contents. It can be further defined by noting what areas have been excluded. Among the excluded areas are medicine; population control; water resources development; water rights, irrigation flood control, and reclamation (except where relevant to watershed protection or soil conservation); hunting regulations; mining rights; oil and gas conservation laws; food purity; government research, reports, and purely investigatory hearings (however, if hearings or reports relate to proposed legislation, they are included); fisheries, except where specifically relevant to species preservation rather than to commercial or territorial concerns; highways and transportation; urban renewal; and weather modification.

Some of these excluded topics are simply too vast to be considered for this Guide, while others are of peripheral relevance. Moreover, some of the excluded topics are already treated in other bibliographies or are suitable for such separate treatment.

The materials reflected in this volume are mainly English language books; government documents, both federal and state; and proceedings, papers, and other such products of conferences and symposia. Bibliographies are included and usually appear at the beginning of each subject area treated. Periodical articles are generally not included because this vast resource can be easily tapped by consulting both the INDEX TO LEGAL PERIODICALS and the SOCIAL SCIENCES AND HUMANITIES INDEX, starting the search under the topic heading "Environmental Law." However, periodical titles and other frequently issued publications, such as loose-leaf services, devoted entirely or substantially to environmental law have been included. A selected list of periodicals can be found in the last section of this volume.

Works dealing with more than one subject have been listed under only one of the subjects. In many instances, the title of the work so treated will reveal the extent of its coverage as to other subjects. The index should be consulted also for possible cross references.

A unique feature of this volume is that almost all items listed have been held in hand by the author and their contents examined to verify the nature and extent of the work. In some instances, it was not possible to obtain a particular publication for actual examination but its inclusion in this volume appeared to be obviously appropriate from a description in a publisher's circular or some similar source. In those instances, the title has been listed but without comment. Most of the materials listed in this volume have been published within the past five years since those dates seem to be the most relevant.

## BIBLIOGRAPHIC NOTE ON LEGISLATION AND COURT DECISIONS

This bibliography contains mainly books, in the form of monographs and treatises, and government documents in the form of congressional hearings, reports, and studies. Not included is the "law" in the form of a huge body of legislation and court decisions. Such materials are available in several sources. Two excellent sources are the ENVIRONMENT REPORTER and the ENVIRONMENTAL LAW REPORTER, described in the first section of this bibliography, "The Legal Process." Two other useful sources are CASES AND MATERIALS ON ENVIRONMENTAL LAW AND POLICY by Eva H. Hanks, A. Dan Tarlock, and John L. Hanks (St. Paul, Minn.: West Publishing Co., 1974) and CASES AND MATERIALS ON ENVIRONMENTAL LAW, 2d ed., by Oscar S. Gray (Washington, D.C.: Bureau of National Affairs, 1973). These latter two volumes are designed for classroom use in law schools, and, therefore, are most likely available in law school libraries, or for purchase through law school bookstores. The first two publications mentioned above can probably best be located in large law libraries, mainly those referred to in Appendix B, "Selected List of Law Libraries," in this volume.

## FOREIGN GOVERNMENT PUBLICATIONS

The number of U.S. government documents listed in this bibliography reflects the wealth of information being generated through official sources, as well as indicates the thinking of the federal government about environmental law problems. Most of these publications and subsequent ones similar to them are listed in UNITED STATES GOVERNMENT PUBLICATIONS: MONTHLY CATALOG (Washington, D.C.: Government Printing Office). Great Britain and several other countries produce comparable catalogs for their government publications. In May 1974 the Environmental Protection Agency commenced publication of its monthly SUMMARIES OF FOREIGN GOVERNMENT ENVIRONMENTAL REPORTS, available on subscription. The Environmental Protection Agency is developing a collection of environmental reports issued by foreign governments and international organizations. The monthly SUMMARIES OF FOREIGN GOVERNMENT ENVIRONMENTAL REPORTS lists items so received and includes descriptions of their contents. Information about starting a subscription may be obtained from Managing Editor, Summaries of Foreign Government Environmental Reports, National Technical Information Service, 5285 Port Royal Road, Springfield, Virginia 22161 or by telephone to (703) 451-4468. Direct assistance in researching with government documents, both United States and foreign, can best be obtained by consulting the government documents librarian in a law library, a university general library, or in the larger public libraries.

In structuring this volume, the attempt has been to offer the interested reader a threshold approach to an important subject and to preserve an historical perspective of an especially significant time span. In working on this volume, I have been fortunate in having the dedicated help of Gregory O'Leary, a student at the School of Law, University of California, Davis, California.

Mortimer Schwartz

# Section 1

# THE LEGAL PROCESS

Dickson, Lance E., comp. LAW AND THE ENVIRONMENT; AN ANNOTATED BIBLIOGRAPHICAL GUIDE TO MATERIALS IN THE TARLTON LAW LIBRARY. Austin: Tarlton Law Library, School of Law, University of Texas, 1973. 42 p.

Durrenberger, Robert W. ENVIRONMENT AND MAN: A BIBLIOGRAPHY. Palo Alto, Calif.: National Press Books, 1970. 118 p.

Works on environmental law are not organized in one section but some may be found under relevant topic headings, e.g., land use.

THE ENVIRONMENTAL LAW DIGEST. Washington, D.C.: Environmental Law Institute, 1970. 80 p.

ENVIRONMENTAL LAW REPORTER. Washington, D.C.: Environmental Law Institute, 1971- . Monthly, loose-leaf.

A news and analysis service divided into the following sections: Summary and Comments, which reports, analyzes, and recommends actions by legislatures, agencies, courts, and litigants; Litigation, which reports current court decisions; Administrative Proceedings; Statutes and Regulations; Articles and Notes; Bibliography and Facsimile Service.

ENVIRONMENT REPORTER. Washington, D.C.: Bureau of National Affairs, 1970- . Weekly, loose-leaf.

A news and reprint service detailing environmental developments in federal and state legislatures, administrative agencies, courts, private industry, and public organizations. A separate loose-leaf volume reports the full texts of court decisions of environmental importance.

Grossman, George S. BIBLIOGRAPHIC CONTROL IN LAW AND ENVIRONMENT--SURVIVING AN EXPLOSION. A PAPER PRESENTED AT THE 1970 ANNUAL CONVENTION OF THE ASSOCIATION OF AMERICAN LAW SCHOOLS. Council of Planning Librarians Exchange Bibliography no. 334. Monticello,

III.: Council of Planning Librarians, 1971. 27 p.

> A description of many useful publications, some of which are often overlooked.

_____. LEGAL BIBLIOGRAPHY: A CRITICAL OVERVIEW FOR ENVIRON-
MENTALIST. Council of Planning Librarians Exchange Bibliography no. 366.
Monticello, III.: Council of Planning Librarians, 1972. 21 p.

Kerbec, Matthew J., ed. YOUR GOVERNMENT AND THE ENVIRONMENT:
AN ANNUAL REFERENCE. Arlington, Va.: Output Systems Corporation,
1971- . Annual. Illus.

> Contains information about technical, legal, administrative, and
> enforcement aspects of air, water, solid wastes, radiation, and
> noise pollution. Volume 2, 1972, is entitled YOUR GOVERN-
> MENT AND THE ENVIRONMENT: AN ENVIRONMENTAL DI-
> GEST.

## LITIGATION AND THE COURTS

ALI-ABA Course of Study on Environmental Law, Washington, D.C., 1971.
ALI-ABA COURSE OF STUDY C/S 3018: ENVIRONMENTAL LAW; STUDY
MATERIALS. Philadelphia: Joint Committee on Continuing Legal Education
of the American Law Institute and the American Bar Association, 1971. Var.
pag.

ALI-ABA Course of Study on Environmental Law, Smithsonian Institute, 1972.
ALI-ABA COURSE OF STUDY: ENVIRONMENTAL LAW--II; STUDY MATERI-
ALS. Philadelphia: Joint Committee on Continuing Legal Education of the
American Law Institute and the American Bar Association, 1972. 220 p. Illus.

> Study materials for a seminar on developments in environmental law
> during 1971. Included are addresses and outlines of relevant top-
> ics; discussions of leading cases, standards, and regulatory agency
> activity; a bibliography of articles on NEPA; and articles on pros-
> pects for the future.

Axtmann, Robert C., ed. RESCUING MAN'S ENVIRONMENT: NINE ESSAYS
ON ENVIRONMENTAL REFORM. Princeton, N.J.: Princeton University Council on Environmental Studies, 1972. 235 p.

> One essay on the law: O.S. Gray, "Legal Issues in Environmental
> Action."

Baldwin, Malcolm F., and Page, James K., Jr., eds. LAW AND THE ENVI-
RONMENT. New York: Walker and Co., 1970. 432 p. Map.

Brecher, Joseph J., and Nestle, Manuel E. ENVIRONMENTAL LAW HAND-

BOOK. Berkeley: California Continuing Education of the Bar, 1970. 343 p. Illus., forms.

CIVIL DISOBEDIENCE, 1969-1970. LAND AND THE ENVIRONMENT, 1970-1971, A COMPILATION OF THE ORIGINAL DICTA PUBLISHED BY THE VIRGINIA LAW WEEKLY. Charlottesville, Va.: 1972. xxiv, 248 p.

Consumer Interests Foundation. DO CITIZEN SUITS OVERBURDEN OUR COURTS? A CASE STUDY OF THE JUDICIAL IMPACT OF STATE ENVIRONMENTAL LEGISLATION. Washington, D.C.: 1973. 14 p. Pap.

A short evaluation of conditions in Connecticut, Florida, Indiana, Massachusetts, Michigan, Minnesota, and California.

Estrin, David, and Swaigen, John, eds. ENVIRONMENT ON TRIAL; A CITIZEN'S GUIDE TO ONTARIO ENVIRONMENTAL LAW. Toronto: Canadian Environmental Law Association and Canadian Environmental Research Foundation, 1974. 409 p. Photos., tables.

Florida Bar. Continuing Legal Education. ENVIRONMENTAL REGULATION AND LITIGATION IN FLORIDA. Tallahassee: 1973. 636 p. Illus.

George Washington University. The PTC Research Institute. SPECIAL CONFERENCE OF INVITED EXPERTS ON AIR AND WATER DEPOLLUTION: ROLES OF INDUSTRIAL PROPERTY, INNOVATION AND COMPETITION. Washington, D.C.: 1970. 135 p.

Two presentations on the antitrust aspects of cooperative pollution control enterprises among corporations.

Grad, Frank P. ENVIRONMENTAL LAW: SOURCES AND PROBLEMS. New York: M. Bender, 1971. Supplement I, 1973. 104 p. Supplement II, 1975. 183 p. Loose-leaf, illus.

Gray, Oscar S. CASES AND MATERIALS ON ENVIRONMENTAL LAW. Washington, D.C.: Bureau of National Affairs, 1970. 1,252 p.

Gregory, David D. STANDING TO SUE IN ENVIRONMENTAL LITIGATION IN THE UNITED STATES OF AMERICA. IUCN Environmental Law Paper no. 2. Morges, Switzerland: International Union for Conservation of Nature and Natural Resources, 1972. 28 p. Pap.

An exposition of the federal law of standing.

Hasset, Charles M., ed. ENVIRONMENTAL LAW. Ann Arbor, Mich.: The

Institute of Continuing Legal Education, 1971.  195 p.

> Proceedings of a conference including presentations on new direc-
> tions in the law, injunctive and declarative relief in private suits,
> private damage suits, public suits, legislation, the AEC, local en-
> forcement, industry's response to new law, and problems of litiga-
> tion, regulation, and enforcement.  NEPA, Michigan legislation,
> and a model complaint also included.

Jaffe, Louis J., and Tribe, Laurence H.  ENVIRONMENTAL PROTECTION.
Chicago:  Bracton Press, 1971.  702 p.

> Explores the legal and political questions relevant to the structure
> of environmental protection programs and to policy determination.
> Separate parts are "Introductory Materials" with nine different dis-
> ciplinary perspectives on environmental protection; "Automotive Air
> Pollution" with studies of U.S. vs. AUTOMOBILE MANUFAC-
> TURERS ASSOCIATION, The General Motors Proxy Fight, 1970-
> 71, administrative standard setting and urban transportation; "Water
> Quality Management" with emphasis on the Delaware River Basin
> Commission; "Carcinogens," which focuses on DDT; and "Ways and
> Means," a study of litigation and administrative programs.

Landau, Norman J., and Rheingold, Paul D.  THE ENVIRONMENTAL LAW
HANDBOOK:  THE LEGAL REMEDIES IN EXISTENCE NOW TO KEEP GOV-
ERNMENT AND INDUSTRY FROM DESTROYING OUR ENVIRONMENT.  Foreword by Ralph Nader.  New York:  Ballantine Books, 1971.  496 p.  Illus.,
forms, map.

LAW AND THE ENVIRONMENT:  SELECTED MATERIALS ON TAX EXEMPT
STATUS AND PUBLIC INTEREST LITIGATION.

> See U.S. Congress.  Senate.  Committee on Interior and Insular
> Affairs, below.

Law Society of Upper Canada.  Department of Continuing Education.  POLLU-
TION:  ENVIRONMENTAL LAW REFERENCE MATERIAL.  Rev. ed.  Toronto:
1972.  176 p.  Pap., oversized tables, bibliog.

> A collection of materials used at a conference including papers on
> the significance of environmental problems, use of experts as wit-
> nesses, noise pollution, air pollution, common law remedies, pol-
> lution as a crime, American environmental law, and summaries of
> twenty-three pieces of Canadian legislation.

Longgood, William.  THE DARKENING LAND.  New York:  Simon and Schuster, 1972.  572 p.  Bibliog.

> A study of the earth's damaged and endangered life-support systems
> and the social, political, and economic influences thereon.  In-
> cludes a short section on legal action.

MacDonald, James B., and Conway, John E. ENVIRONMENTAL LITIGATION. Madison: Department of Law, University of Wisconsin Extension, 1972. 438 p.

> A discussion of the procedural and substantive rules used in environmental litigation. Emphasis is on remedies, standing, causes of action, and procedural defenses.

Meyers, Charles J., and Tarlock, A. Dan. SELECTED LEGAL AND ECONOMIC ASPECTS OF ENVIRONMENTAL PROTECTION. Mineola, N.Y.: Foundation Press, 1971. 410 p. Illus.

Practising Law Institute. ENVIRONMENTAL LITIGATION. Criminal Law and Practice Course Handbook Series, no. 39. New York: 1972. 112 p.

> Materials used at a seminar, April-May 1972. Includes outlines and papers on discovery, standing and jurisdiction, actions under criminal statutes and the Rivers and Harbors Act of 1899, defense of private damage suits, NEPA, and proof.

_____. LEGAL CONTROL OF THE ENVIRONMENT. Criminal Law and Urban Problems Course Handbook Series, no. 21. New York: 1970. 399 p.

> Nineteen papers presented at a 1970 lawyers' workshop to study available legal controls and litigation techniques. Wide range of topics covering common law precedents, types of controls, current legislation, aspects of litigation and procedure, administrative practice, and future governmental directions.

_____. LEGAL CONTROL OF THE ENVIRONMENT--2d Criminal Law and Urban Problems Courses Handbook Series, no. 22. New York: 1970. 168 p.

_____. LEGAL CONTROL OF THE ENVIRONMENT--3d Criminal Law and Urban Problems Course Handbook Series, no. 30. New York: 1971. 204 p. Illus.

_____. POLLUTION LITIGATION. Criminal Law and Urban Problems Course Handbook Series, no. 26. New York: 1970. 240 p. Forms, map.

> Presentations on jurisdiction and standing, experts as witnesses, air pollution case preparation, sample complaint, sample pleadings--water pollution, pleading theories, presentation of the case, sample requested instructions, sample charge to jury, administrative proceedings and sample acts. Most papers employ air pollution as the case example.

Reitze, Arnold W., Jr. ENVIRONMENTAL LAW. 2 vols. Washington, D.C.: North American International, 1972.

Research and Development Corporation, ed. ENVIRONMENTAL LAW. Greenvale, N.Y.: 1970. 307 p.

A collection of eleven law review articles dealing with aspects of environmental law and litigation including private rights and air pollution, remedies, aircraft noise, oil pollution and international law, class actions, antitrust implications of industrial cooperation, and use of witnesses.

Rosenfeld, Martin J. OUTLINE OF ENVIRONMENTAL LAW. Irvington-On-Hudson, N.Y.: American Legal Publications, Blackstone Law Summaries, 1973. 91 p. Pap.

Chapters on the problem, private remedies, legislation, water pollution, air pollution, solid waste, radiation, noise, land use, public trust and condemnation, recurring legal issues, and new developments.

Sanders, Norman K. STOP! A GUIDE TO DEFENSE OF THE ENVIRONMENT. San Francisco: Rinehart Press, 1972. 160 p.

An activist's guide which includes the chapter "Offensive and Defensive Environmental Law," pp. 49-64. Selected national legislation included.

Sax, Joseph L. DEFENDING THE ENVIRONMENT: A STRATEGY FOR CITIZEN ACTION. Introduction by George McGovern. New York: Knopf, 1971. 252 p.

The author, professor of law at the University of Michigan, explores institutional factors that reduce the effectiveness of regulatory agencies and presents a strategy for the assertion of citizens' rights to environmental management through the court system. Most chapters deal with litigation and legal theories. A model law is appended.

Thompson, William N., and Smith, Bradley F. STATE ATTORNEYS GENERAL AND THE ENVIRONMENT. Kalamazoo: New Issues Press, Institute of Public Affairs, Western Michigan University, 1974. 92 p. Pap.

Tucker, Edwin W. LEGAL REGULATION OF THE ENVIRONMENT: TEXT, CASES AND PROBLEMS. St. Paul: West Publishing Co., 1972. 245 p.

Introductory and intended to acquaint the reader with governmental responses to a variety of specific environmental problems. The study treats legislation, constitutional restraints, the administrative process, and significant court decisions.

U.S. Congress. Senate. Committee on Interior and Insular Affairs. LAW AND THE ENVIRONMENT: SELECTED MATERIALS ON TAX EXEMPT STATUS AND PUBLIC INTEREST LITIGATION. 91st Cong., 2d sess. Washington, D.C.: Government Printing Office, 1970. 43 p. Pap.

Follows suspension by the IRS of the tax-exempt status of charitable organizations involved in environmental litigation. Includes documents relevant to the role of private litigation in environmental protection and to issues raised by the IRS.

Yannacone, Victor J., Jr., and Cohen, Bernard S. ENVIRONMENTAL RIGHTS AND REMEDIES. 2 vols. Rochester, N.Y.: Lawyers Cooperative Publishing Co., 1971. 1,359 p.

A handbook on environmental law which contains the law, science, strategy, and legal tools involved in environmental protection. A thorough examination of regulatory statutes, model statutes, prosecution and defense of environmental litigation, common law and constitutional legal theories, causes of action, procedure, practical aspects of preparation of documents and motions, use of expert witnesses, and excerpts from sample litigation. Organized by both legal and environmental categories.

Zurhorst, Charles. THE CONSERVATION FRAUD. New York: Cowles Book Co., 1970. 164 p.

Includes one chapter on environmental actions in the courts and sample environmental law complaints.

## ENVIRONMENTAL QUALITY LEGISLATION AND ADMINISTRATION

Anastaplo, G., et al. THE LEGAL AND ECONOMIC ASPECTS OF POLLUTION. Chicago: Center for Policy Study, University of Chicago, 1970. 37 p.

Anderson, Frederick R. NEPA IN THE COURTS: A LEGAL ANALYSIS OF THE NATIONAL ENVIRONMENTAL POLICY ACT. Baltimore, Md.: Johns Hopkins University Press for Resources for the Future, 1973. 324 p.

The study focuses on litigation surrounding NEPA's requirement that environmental impact statements be prepared for government projects affecting the environment. Recent court interpretation and probable future developments are emphasized.

Barbaro, Ronald, and Cross, Frank L. PRIMER OF ENVIRONMENTAL IMPACT STATEMENTS. Westport, Conn.: Technomic Publishing Co., 1973. 140 p. Pap., graphs, photos., tables, charts.

A technical guide to the preparation of the EIS with sections on recent legislation and air, water, solid waste, noise, and marine impacts.

Berry, Brian J.L., and Horton, Frank E. URBAN ENVIRONMENTAL MANAGEMENT; PLANNING FOR POLLUTION CONTROL. Englewood Cliffs, N.J.:

Prentice-Hall, 1974. 425 p. Tables, charts, graphs.


Bigham, D.A. THE LAW AND ADMINISTRATION RELATING TO PROTECTION OF THE ENVIRONMENT. London: Oyez Publications, 1973. 359 p. Pap.

A comprehensive, practical treatise on the law of Great Britain.

Boles, Donald E. ADMINISTRATIVE RULE MAKING IN WISCONSIN CONSERVATION. Publication no. 18, 377, University of Wisconsin Library, University Microfilms. Ann Arbor, Mich.: University Microfilms, 1956.


Center for Environmental Law. ENVIRONMENTAL LAW INDEX: JURISPRUDENCE, LEGISLATION AND DOCTRINE. Rev. ed. Montreal, Quebec: 1972.


Chanlett, Emil T. ENVIRONMENTAL PROTECTION. Water Resources and Environmental Engineering Series. New York: McGraw-Hill Book Co., 1973. 569 p. Illus.


Claremont, Calif. Environmental Resources Task Force. EXPANDING THE ENVIRONMENTAL RESPONSIBILITY OF LOCAL GOVERNMENT; CLAREMONT'S ENVIRONMENTAL TASK FORCE AND ITS RECOMMENDATIONS. Edited by Eleanor Cohen. Claremont: Center for California Public Affairs, 1972. 172 p.


Colley, Richard A., and Wandesforde-Smith, Geoffrey, eds. CONGRESS AND THE ENVIRONMENT. Seattle: University of Washington Press, 1970. 277 p. Maps.


Council of State Governments. ENVIRONMENTAL QUALITY AND STATE GOVERNMENT. Lexington, Ky.: 1970. 53 p.

Summaries of pollution problems and responsive federal and state programs in the areas of water, air, solid waste, pesticides. Also a section on the structures of new state environmental departments.


Davies, Clarence J. THE POLITICS OF POLLUTION. New York: Pegasus, 1970. 231 p.

A study of the total political process by which environmental legislation is made and enforced. Included are sections on existing federal legislation, Congress, the executive, state and local agencies, and enforcement of standards.


Ditton, Robert B. NATIONAL ENVIRONMENTAL POLICY ACT OF 1969 (P. L. 91-190): BIBLIOGRAPHY ON IMPACT ASSESSMENT METHODS AND LEGAL CONSIDERATIONS. Council of Planning Librarians Exchange Bibliography no. 415. Monticello, Ill.: Council of Planning Librarians, 1973. 22 p.


Dolgin, Erica L., and Guilbert, Thomas G., eds. FEDERAL ENVIRONMEN-

TAL LAW. St. Paul, Minn.: West Publishing Co. for the Environmental Law Institute, 1974. 1,600 p. Tables.

Eider, James R. LAW, POLLUTION, AND THE ENVIRONMENT: A VIEW OF POLLUTION CONTROL IN TEXAS. Prepared under the direction of the Committee on Laws Pertaining to Pollution of the State Bar of Texas. Austin: State Bar of Texas, 1970. 154 p.

Fadiman, Clifton, and White, Jean, eds. ECOCIDE--AND THOUGHTS TO-WARD SURVIVAL. Santa Barbara, Calif.: Center for the Study of Democratic Institutions, 1971. 202 p.

   The collection contains one paper relating to environmental law: M. Kitzmiller, "Environment and the Law," pp. 149-68.

Foss, Phillip O., ed. POLITICS AND ECOLOGY. Belmont, Calif.: Duxbury Press, 1972. 298 p.

   An anthology of essays and addresses by well known authors and politicians, many of which deal with regulatory legislation and its relation to the political background and to acute environmental demands.

Grad, Frank P., et al. ENVIRONMENTAL CONTROL: PRIORITIES, POLICIES AND THE LAW. Prepared by the Legislative Drafting Research Fund of Columbia University. New York: Columbia University Press, 1971. 311 p.

   Three substantial papers on issues of federal environmental policy and control mechanisms: G.W. Rathjens, "National Environmental Policy: Goals and Priorities"; F.P. Grad, "Intergovernmental Aspects of Environmental Controls"; and A.J. Rosenthal, "Federal Power to Preserve the Environment: Enforcement and Control Techniques."

Green, Harold P. THE NATIONAL ENVIRONMENTAL POLICY ACT IN THE COURTS. (January 1, 1970-April 1, 1972). Washington, D.C.: The Conservation Foundation, 1972. 31 p.

   An analysis of how the courts have construed NEPA as of the title date.

Hanks, Eva H., et al. CASES AND MATERIALS ON ENVIRONMENTAL LAW AND POLICY. St. Paul: West Publishing Co., 1974. 1,150 p.

Haskell, Elizabeth H., and Price, Victoria S. STATE ENVIRONMENTAL MAN-AGEMENT: CASE STUDIES OF NINE STATES. Praeger Special Studies in U.S. Economic, Social, and Political Issues. New York: Praeger, 1973. 283 p. Charts, tables.

   Part 1, "Environmental Departments Created through Reorganizations," includes studies of agencies in Illinois, Minnesota, Washington, Wisconsin, and New York. Part 2, "New State Strategies," discusses land-use management in Vermont and Maine, waste management in Maryland, and citizen lawsuits in Michigan.

Henkin, H., et al. THE ENVIRONMENT, THE ESTABLISHMENT AND THE LAW. Boston: Houghton Mifflin, 1971. 223 p.

Dramatic coverage of the hearings before the Wisconsin Department of Natural Resources on the banning of DDT. Excerpts of actual testimony present the inadequacies of federal pesticides regulation upon agriculture and industry. Appendices include "The Ruling" and a "Model Pesticide Law."

Hurley, William D. ENVIRONMENTAL LEGISLATION. Springfield, Ill.: Charles C. Thomas, 1971. 81 p.

Seeks to clarify and delineate the proper role of the federal government in environmental quality control. The general focus of the book is air and water pollution. Explanations and evaluations of the relevant legislation. Short section on solid waste.

Hutchison, Theodore M. METROPOLITAN AREA PROBLEMS: THE ROLE OF THE FEDERAL GOVERNMENT. Ann Arbor: Legislative Research Center, University of Michigan Law School, 1961. 65 p. Pap.

Among metropolitan problems affected by federal action discussed in the study are air pollution, water pollution, public works, and highways.

International Joint Conference of the American Division of the World Academy of Art and Science and the American Geographical Society, the Continuation Committee, and the New York Academy of Sciences, eds. PUBLIC POLICY TOWARD ENVIRONMENT 1973: A REVIEW AND APPRAISAL. Annals of the New York Academy of Sciences, vol. 216. New York: The New York Academy of Sciences, 1973. 202 p. Tables.

Twenty-one papers which contain some discussion of recent enforcement of national environmental legislation.

Kahl Associates. POLICY ANALYSIS OF THE CALIFORNIA POLLUTION INITIATIVE. Washington, D.C.: Kahl Associates, 1972. 420 p. Tables, graphs.

Includes legal analysis of the twenty-three specific sections of the initiative presented to the voters in June 1972.

Kerbec, Matthew J. YOUR GOVERNMENT AND THE ENVIRONMENT. Arlington, Va.: Output Systems Corp., 1971- . Annual, with 3 supplements per year.

Digest of federal environmental activities.

Levy, Elizabeth. THE PEOPLE LOBBY--THE SST STORY. New York: Delacorte Press, 1973. 160 p.

Juvenile literature. A story of opposing lobbying efforts aimed at recently proposed legislation concerning the supersonic transport plane.

Loth, David, and Ernst, Morris L. THE TAMING OF TECHNOLOGY. New York: Simon and Schuster, 1972. 256 p.

A primer on the legal restrictions available to curb the environmentally destructive aspects of technological growth. Deals with law in relation to such areas as medicine, computers, the ocean, outer space, communications, ecology, and weather control.

McClellan, Grant S., ed. PROTECTING OUR ENVIRONMENT. The Reference Shelf Series, vol. 42, no. 1. New York: H.W. Wilson, 1970. 218 p.

A compilation of articles on the pollution problem, some of which deal with legislation, regulatory agencies, and the courts.

MANAGEMENT APPROACHES TO POLLUTION CONTROL. Proceedings of a symposium, 25 June 1971, Winnipeg, Canada. Winnipeg: Agassiz Center for Water Studies, 1972. 74 p.

Marquis, Ralph W., ed. ENVIRONMENTAL IMPROVEMENT: AIR, WATER AND SOIL. Washington, D.C.: Graduate School, U.S. Department of Agriculture, 1966. 105 p. Ports.

Mitchell, John G., and Stallings, Constance L., eds. ECOTACTICS: THE SIERRA CLUB HANDBOOK FOR ENVIRONMENTAL ACTIVISTS. New York: Pocket Books, 1970. 288 p.

Three essays relevant to legal aspects: "A Challenge to the Law," "State Legislatures: the Next Target," and "Saving San Francisco Bay--In Sacramento."

Morrisey, Thomas J., ed. POLLUTION CONTROL PROBLEMS AND RELATED FEDERAL LEGISLATION. New York: MSS Information Corp., 1974. 289 p. Pap.

Murphy, Earl Finbar. MAN AND HIS ENVIRONMENT: LAW. New York: Harper and Row, 1971. 168 p.

For the general reader. Intended to convey a broad understanding of environmental problems, the bases for policy making, and the role of the law in regulating environmental quality.

Mylroie, Gerald R., et al. CALIFORNIA ENVIRONMENTAL LAW: A GUIDE.

Claremont: Center for California Public Affairs, 1972. 111 p. Bibliog.

An annual guide to California laws regulating the environment.
California code sections are summarized and arranged under topical
headings of general laws, air, water, land use, solid waste, noise
control, and pesticides and radiation. Includes new laws enacted
in 1971.

NATIONAL SYMPOSIUM ON STATE ENVIRONMENTAL LEGISLATION, SUM-
MARY REPORT. Report of a symposium held March 1972, Arlington, Va.
Washington, D.C.: Council of State Governments, 1972. 129 p.

Contains recommendations of ten workshops directed at the need
for strong protection programs at the state level and for strengthen-
ing the federal-state relationship. Deals with water, toxic waste,
soil erosion, feed lots, air, abandoned vehicles, noise, power
plant siting, land use, state policy, and historic preservation.

Oregon State University. Water Resources Research Institute. LAWS FOR A
BETTER ENVIRONMENT; SEMINAR CONDUCTED BY WATER RESOURCES RE-
SEARCH INSTITUTE, OREGON STATE UNIVERSITY, FALL QUARTER, 1971.
Corvallis: 1972. 97 p.

Practising Law Institute. POLLUTION AND INDUSTRIAL WASTE. Edited by
B. Handshu et al. New York: 1970. 514 p.

Based on the transcript of an Institute workshop. Includes chapters
on disposal, air and water quality, solid waste, financing, tort
liability and administrative controls, and federal executive and
legislative actions. Appendixes contain leading articles and the
Water Quality Improvement Act of 1969.

_____. POLLUTION AND INDUSTRIAL WASTE. 2d Criminal Law and Urban
Problems Course Handbook Series, no. 16. New York: 1970. 312 p.

Materials prepared for an Institute seminar include the Federal
Water Pollution Control Act, as amended, standards approved under the act, the Texas Water Quality Act of 1967, Proposed Air
Quality Improvement Act of 1969, and papers on solid waste, enforcement, financing, future legislation, damage awards, industrial
pollution, public relations, polluters' problems, and the pollution
control industry.

_____. POLLUTION AND INDUSTRIAL WASTE. Edited by Ira Cohen. Crim-
inal Law and Urban Problems Course Handbook Series, no. 9. New York:
1969. 216 p.

Materials distributed at an Institute workshop include the Federal
Water Pollution Control Act, as amended, standards approved under
the act, and papers on solid waste disposal, air pollution control,
the auto industry and air quality legislation, oil pollution control,

local solutions, financing, and a legal approach to industrial pollution.

Public Interest Research Group. LEGALIZED POLLUTION. St. Lucia, Australia: University of Queensland Press, 1973. 176 p. Illus.

Rohrer, David C., et al. THE ENVIRONMENT CRISIS: A BASIC OVERVIEW OF THE PROBLEM OF POLLUTION. Skokie, Ill.: National Textbook Co., 1970. 346 p.

> Policy determination, legislation, financing, and enforcement are discussed in chapters "States' Role," "Regional Approaches," "The Role of Local Governments," and "The Future." A substantial bibliography is appended.

Saltonstall, Richard, Jr. YOUR ENVIRONMENT AND WHAT YOU CAN DO ABOUT IT. New York: Walker and Co., 1970. 299 p.

> An informative work on pollution problems which includes discussion of control legislation in the various areas and a chapter entitled "Environmental Law" with emphasis on practical aspects of citizen-sponsored litigation.

Scheffey, Andrew J. CONSERVATION COMMISSIONS IN MASSACHUSETTS. Washington, D.C.: Conservation Foundation, 1969. 216 p. Illus.

Sloan, Irving J. ENVIRONMENT AND THE LAW. Dobbs Ferry, N.Y.: Oceana Publications, 1971. 120 p.

> Designed to give the general reader some background on the growing body of environmental law. In addition to discussing the law, each chapter defines the problem in its physical and social setting. Chapters on the federal programs, air pollution, water pollution, pesticides, land use, procedural aspects and the international outlook.

Stevens, Leonard A. HOW A LAW IS MADE: THE STORY OF A BILL AGAINST AIR POLLUTION. New York: Thomas Y. Crowell, 1970. 109 p.

> Designed as a citizen's guide. A simple narrative of citizen organization and lobbying for a fictional air pollution control bill and the process by which the bill was subsequently written and passed.

Tax Foundation. POLLUTION CONTROL: PERSPECTIVES ON THE GOVERNMENT ROLE. New York: 1971. 46 p.

Van Tassel, Alfred J. OUR ENVIRONMENT: OUTLOOK FOR THE 1980'S. Lexington, Mass.: Lexington Books, D.C. Heath & Co., 1973. 608 p.

A study and forecast of water, air, and solid waste pollution problems in fifteen major U.S. metropolitan areas. Not primarily legal, but includes some discussion of regulatory law.

# GOVERNMENT DOCUMENTS

Arkansas. Legislative Council. INCOME TAX DEPRECIATION ALLOWANCES AND OTHER TAX INCENTIVES PROVIDED INDUSTRIES COMPLYING WITH POLLUTION CONTROL LAWS AND REGULATIONS. Little Rock: 1970. 11 p.

California. Laws and Statutes. LAWS RELATING TO THE PROTECTION OF ENVIRONMENTAL QUALITY, 1970. Compiled by George H. Murphy, legislative counsel. Sacramento: State of California Department of General Services, Documents Section, 1971. 378 p.

California. Legislature. Assembly. Committee on Revenue and Taxation. TAXATION AS A MEANS OF ENVIRONMENTAL CONTROL. 2 vols. Sacramento: 1971.

California. Legislature. Assembly. Interim Committee on Judiciary. TRANSCRIPT OF HEARING ON ECOLOGY AND THE LAW. Sacramento: 1970. Var. pag.

California. Legislature. Assembly. Select Committee on Environmental Quality. ENVIRONMENTAL BILL OF RIGHTS. Sacramento: 1970. 48 p. Pap.

The committee's report and recommendations relative to the proposed Environmental Bill of Rights constitutional amendment, the California Environmental Quality Act of 1970, planning and policy development, implementation and oversight, environmental priorities, and financing.

Massachusetts. Legislative Research Council. REPORT RELATIVE TO THE PRESERVATION OF THE NATURAL ENVIRONMENT. Massachusetts House of Representatives Documents, no. 5301. Boston: 1971. 107 p.

Massachusetts. Office of Comprehensive Health Planning. COMPENDIUM OF ENVIRONMENTAL LEGISLATION, JUNE 1970. Boston: 1970. 105 p.

New Jersey. Legislature. General Assembly. Committee on Agriculture, Conservation and Natural Resources. PUBLIC HEARING ON ASSEMBLY BILL No. 1268 (PROTECTION OF AIR, WATER AND OTHER NATURAL RESOURCES) HELD FEBRUARY 11, 1971. Trenton: 1971. 97 p.

Texas. Legislature. Senate. Interim Committee on Pipeline Study. POLLU-

TION vs. THE PEOPLE: AN ANALYSIS OF THE PERFORMANCE OF TEXAS STATE AGENCIES IN PROTECTING THE ENVIRONMENT, WITH AN EXPLANATION OF PROPOSED LEGISLATION FOR AN ACTIVE ROLE FOR CONCERNED CITIZENS; JOINT REPORT OF THE INTERIM COMMITTEES ON PIPELINE STUDY AND BEACHES. Austin: 1971. Var. pag.

U.S. Congress. House. Committee on Education and Labor. Select Subcommittee on Education. ENVIRONMENTAL QUALITY EDUCATION ACT OF 1970: HEARINGS . . . ON H.R. 14753. 91st Cong., 2d sess. Washington, D.C.: Government Printing Office, 1970. 856 p.

_____. ENVIRONMENTAL QUALITY EDUCATION ACT OF 1970: HEARINGS ON OVERSIGHT INTO ADMINISTRATION OF THE ACT. 92d Cong., 1st sess. Washington, D.C.: Government Printing Office, 1972. 206 p. Illus.

U.S. Congress. House. Committee on Government Operations. Conservation and Natural Resources Subcommittee. TRANSFERRING ENVIRONMENTAL EVALUATION FUNCTIONS TO THE ENVIRONMENTAL QUALITY COUNCIL: HEARING . . . ON S. 11952. . . . 91st Cong., 1st sess. Washington, D.C.: Government Printing Office, 1969. 56 p.

U.S. Congress. House. Committee on Merchant Marine and Fisheries. Subcommittee on Fisheries and Wildlife Conservation. ADMINISTRATION OF THE NATIONAL ENVIRONMENTAL POLICY ACT: HEARING . . . 2 vols. 91st Cong., 2d sess. Washington, D.C.: Government Printing Office, 1971.

_____. ADMINISTRATION OF THE NATIONAL ENVIRONMENTAL POLICY ACT--1972: HEARINGS . . . ON NEPA OVERSIGHT . . . ; AMENDMENTS TO THE NATIONAL ENVIRONMENTAL POLICY ACT OF 1969 . . . ; FEDERAL AGENCY COMPLIANCE. . . . 92d Cong., 2d sess. Washington, D.C.: Government Printing Office, 1972. 562 p. Illus.

_____. ANNUAL REPORTS OF CEQ: HEARINGS. . . . 92d Cong., 1st and 2d sess. Washington, D.C.: Government Printing Office, 1972. 127 p.

_____. ENVIRONMENTAL DATA BANK: HEARINGS . . . ON H.R. 17436, H.R. 17779, H.R. 18141. . . . 91st Cong., 2d sess. Washington, D.C.: Government Printing Office, 1970. 395 p. Illus., maps.

_____. TEMPORARY EXEMPTION FROM SECTION 102 STATEMENTS: HEARINGS . . . ON H.R. 14103. . . . 92d Cong., 2d sess. Washington, D.C.: Government Printing Office, 1972. 253 p.

U.S. Congress. House. Committee on Science and Aeronautics. Subcommittee on Science, Research, and Development. ENVIRONMENTAL QUALITY; H.R. 7796 [and others]: HEARINGS. . . . 90th Cong., 2d sess. Washington, D.C.: Government Printing Office, 1968. 588 p. Illus.

U.S. Congress. Senate. Committee of Public Works. NATIONAL ENVIRON-
MENTAL LABORATORIES. Washington, D.C.: Government Printing Office,
1971. 459 p.

> A compilation of comments and materials related to a proposed en-
> vironmental laboratory. Includes the bill (SB3410) sponsored by
> Muskie and Baker.

U.S. Congress. Senate. Committee on Commerce. STATEMENT OF THE
COMMITTEE ON COMMERCE ON S. 1032, THE ENVIRONMENTAL PROTEC-
TION ACT OF 1972. . . . 92d Cong., 2d sess. Washington, D.C.: Gov-
ernment Printing Office, 1972. 5 p.

U.S. Congress. Senate. Committee on Commerce. Subcommittee on Energy,
Natural Resources, and the Environment. ENVIRONMENTAL PROTECTION
ACT OF 1970. HEARINGS . . . ON S. 3575. . . . 91st Cong., 2d
sess. Washington, D.C.: Government Printing Office, 1970. 169 p.

U.S. Congress. Senate. Committee on Commerce. Subcommittee on the Environment. ENVIRONMENTAL PROTECTION ACT OF 1971: HEARINGS. . .
ON S. 1032. 92d Cong., 1st sess. Part 2. Washington, D.C.: Government Printing Office, 1971. Pp. 201-94.

_____ . THE INNER CITY ENVIRONMENT AND THE ROLE OF THE ENVI-
RONMENTAL PROTECTION AGENCY: HEARINGS. . . . 92d Cong., 2d
sess. Washington, D.C.: Government Printing Office, 1972. 340 p. Illus.

U.S. Congress. Senate. Committee on Interior and Insular Affairs. NATION-
AL ENVIRONMENTAL POLICY: HEARINGS. . . . 91st Cong., 1st sess.
Washington, D.C.: Government Printing Office, 1969. 234 p.

U.S. Congress. Senate. Committee on Public Works. Subcommittee on Roads.
NATIONAL ENVIRONMENTAL POLICY ACT RELATIVE TO HIGHWAYS: HEAR-
ING . . . ON IMPLEMENTATION OF THE NATIONAL ENVIRONMENTAL
POLICY ACT AS IT RELATES TO THE PLANNING AND CONSTRUCTION OF
HIGHWAYS. . . . 91st Cong., 2d sess. Washington, D.C.: Government
Printing Office, 1970. 59 p. Illus.

U.S. Congress. Senate. Committee on the Judiciary. INTERSTATE ENVI-
RONMENT COMPACT: HEARINGS . . . ON S. 907. . . . 92d Cong.,
1st sess. Washington, D.C.: Government Printing Office, 1971. 144 p.

U.S. Department of State. Bureau of International and Technological Affairs.
U.S. NATIONAL REPORT ON THE HUMAN ENVIRONMENT. Conference on
Human Environment, Stockholm. Washington, D.C.: Government Printing
Office for United Nations, 1972. 53 p. Pap.

> Summarizes the environmental problems and existing and proposed

governmental actions in the areas of human settlements, natural
resources, and pollution and nuisances. Also a section on desir-
able international programs.

U.S. Department of the Interior. THE THIRD WAVE, AMERICA'S NEW CON-
SERVATION. Washington, D.C.: Government Printing Office, 1966. 128 p.
Photos.

> Highly pictorial. A simple agency-by-agency description of feder-
> al conservation programs.

U.S. Department of the Treasury. MATERIAL RELATING TO THE ADMINISTRA-
TION'S PROPOSALS FOR ENVIRONMENTAL PROTECTION, INCLUDING THE
MESSAGE OF THE PRESIDENT, LETTERS OF TRANSMITTAL OF DRAFT BILLS EN-
TITLED THE "PURE AIR TAX ACT OF 1972" AND THE "ENVIRONMENTAL
PROTECTION TAX ACT OF 1972," TEXT OF DRAFT BILLS (BOTH OF WHICH
HAVE BEEN REFERRED TO THE COMMITTEE ON WAYS AND MEANS), AND
OTHER EXPLANATORY MATERIAL PREPARED BY THE DEPARTMENT OF THE
TREASURY. Washington, D.C.: Government Printing Office, 1972. 54 p.

U.S. Environmental Protection Agency. THE CHALLENGE OF THE ENVIRON-
MENT; A PRIMER ON EPA'S STATUTORY AUTHORITY. Washington, D.C.:
1972. 34 p.

_____. CURRENT LAWS, STATUTES AND EXECUTIVE ORDERS. 3 vols.
Washington, D.C.: Government Printing Office, 1972. Loose-leaf.

> A working manual on the agency's current statutory authority with
> an updating loose-leaf service.

_____. INDEX OF EPA LEGAL AUTHORITY: STATUTES AND LEGISLATIVE
HISTORY, EXECUTIVE ORDERS, REGULATIONS. Washington, D.C.: Field
Operations Division, Environmental Protection Agency, 1973. 233 p. Pap.

_____. INDEX OF EPA LEGAL AUTHORITY: STATUTES AND LEGISLATIVE
HISTORY, EXECUTIVE ORDERS, REGULATIONS, GUIDELINES AND REPORTS.
Washington, D.C.: Government Printing Office, 1972. 218 p. Pap.

_____. LEGAL COMPILATION. 7 vols. Washington, D.C.: Government
Printing Office, 1973- . Supplements added irregularly.

> Seven compilations of the legal authority of the EPA to control
> air, water, noise, solid waste, and other forms of pollution. Vol-
> ume 5, NOISE, has two supplements published in 1974. Volume
> 1, AIR, has one supplement, also published in 1974.

U.S. Laws and Statutes. CURRENT LAWS: STATUTES AND EXECUTIVE OR-
DERS. Washington, D.C.: Environmental Protection Agency, for sale by the
Government Printing Office, 1972- . Annual. Loose-leaf.

U.S. Library of Congress. Congressional Research Service. Environmental Policy Division. CONGRESS AND THE NATION'S ENVIRONMENT; ENVIRONMENTAL AFFAIRS OF THE 91ST CONGRESS. Washington, D.C.: Government Printing Office, 1971. 288 p.

_____. CONGRESS AND THE NATION'S ENVIRONMENT; ENVIRONMENTAL AND NATURAL RESOURCES AFFAIRS OF THE 92D CONGRESS. 93d Cong., 1st sess. Washington, D.C.: Government Printing Office, 1973. 1,145 p.

_____. NATIONAL ENVIRONMENTAL POLICY ACT OF 1969; AN ANALYSIS OF PROPOSED LEGISLATIVE MODIFICATIONS. 93d Cong., 1st sess. Washington, D.C.: Government Printing Office, 1973. 78 p.

## INTERNATIONAL COOPERATION

### General Considerations

Barros, James, and Johnston, Douglas M. THE INTERNATIONAL LAW OF POLLUTION. New York: The Free Press, 1974. 476 p.

> A collection of international agreements and conventions in three parts: "The Pollution Problem in Science, Law, and Policy" with sections on municipal law doctrine and U.S. Supreme Court decisions; "The Emerging International Law of Pollution" with chapters on international inland waters, marine pollution, air pollution and international regulation; "Selected Issues in International Environmental Law" with chapters on internationally shared areas, weapons control, and radiation hazards.

Black, Cyril E., and Falk, Richard A., eds. THE FUTURE OF INTERNATIONAL LEGAL ORDER. Princeton, N.J.: Princeton University Press, 1972. 640 p. Pap.

Caldwell, Lynton K. IN DEFENSE OF EARTH: INTERNATIONAL PROTECTION OF THE BIOSPHERE. Bloomington: Indiana University Press, 1972. 304 p.

> Discusses international treaties and organizations for environmental protection in two of the eight chapters: "International Conservation Efforts" and "Inventing Transnational Structures."

Dinsmore, John, comp. INTERNATIONAL ENVIRONMENTAL POLICY; AN ANNOTATED BIBLIOGRAPHY OF SELECTED ARTICLES, REPORTS, BOOKS, DOCUMENTS, ETC., WHICH PRESENT DISCUSSIONS OF OR VIEWPOINTS ON THE FORMULATION OF INTERNATIONAL ENVIRONMENTAL POLICY, WITH SPECIAL EMPHASIS ON U.S. THOUGHT PRELIMINARY TO AND FO-

CUSED UPON THE UNITED NATIONS CONFERENCE ON THE HUMAN EN-
VIRONMENT, STOCKHOLM, JUNE 1972. UWGB Library Occasional Infocom-
pilation no. 2. Green Bay: University of Wisconsin-Green Bay, 1972. 20 p.

DRAFT CONVENTION ON ENVIRONMENT COOPERATION AMONG NA-
TIONS. Edited by Carl A. Fleischer. World Peace Through Law Center Pamphlet
Series, no. 16. Geneva: World Peace Through Law Center, 1970. 72 p. Pap.

> The convention was recommended at the 1969 Bangkok Conference
> on World Peace through Law. The editor is a professor of law at
> the University of Oslo.

DRAFT PROTOCOL ON WEATHER MODIFICATION. Edited by J.S. Samuels.
World Peace Through Law Center Pamphlet Series, no. 15. Geneva: World
Peace Through Law Center, 1971. 4 p. Pap.

> Draft of a treaty aimed at international control of national activity
> through the World Meteorological Organization.

Environmental Studies Board. Committee for International Environmental Programs. INSTITUTIONAL ARRANGEMENTS FOR INTERNATIONAL ENVIRON-
MENTAL COOPERATION, A REPORT TO THE DEPARTMENT OF STATE. Washington, D.C.: National Academy of Sciences, 1972. 74 p. Pap.

> Does not deal directly with legislation but studies institutional as-
> pects and possibilities for international agencies based upon exist-
> ing UN structure. Focused upon the issues on the agenda of the
> 1972 United Nations Conference on the Human Environment, but
> excludes the open seas and deep seabed.

Farvar, M. Taghi, and Soule, Theodore N. INTERNATIONAL DEVELOPMENT
AND THE HUMAN ENVIRONMENT: AN ANNOTATED BIBLIOGRAPHY.
Riverside, N.J.: CCM Information Co., 1972. 320 p.

FINAL ACT OF THE CONFERENCE WITH ATTACHMENTS INCLUDING THE
TEXT OF THE ADOPTED CONVENTION. Conference on the Establishment of
an International Compensation Fund for Oil Pollution Damage, Brussels, 1971.
London: Inter-Governmental Maritime Consultative Organization, 1972. 84 p.

Hargrove, John L., ed. LAW, INSTITUTIONS, AND THE GLOBAL ENVIRON-
MENT. Dobbs Ferry, N.Y.: Oceana Publications, 1972.

> Eight papers with accompanying editorial analysis: "International
> Institutions for the Environment," "Problems of Definition and
> Scope," "Development of an International Environmental Law--An
> Appraisal," "International Environmental Controls in the Scientific
> Age," "The IMCO Experience," "The Potential of Regional Or-
> ganizations in Managing Man's Environment," "Controlling Great
> Lakes Pollution: A Study in U.S.-Canada Environmental Co-
> operation."

Hull, E.W. Seabrook, and Koers, Albert W. INTRODUCTION TO A CON-

VENTION ON THE INTERNATIONAL ENVIRONMENT PROTECTION AGENCY. Kingston: Law of the Sea Institute, University of Rhode Island, 1971. 21 p. Pap.

> A proposal and twenty-nine-article draft convention for an international agency to protect the global environment.

Johnson, Brian. THE UNITED NATIONS SYSTEM AND THE HUMAN ENVIRONMENT: THE INSTITUTIONAL IMPLICATIONS OF INCREASED UNITED NATIONS ACTIVITIES TO PROTECT THE GLOBAL ENVIRONMENT. ISIO Monographs, 1st series, no. 5. Brighton, Engl.: Institute for the Study of International Organization, 1971. 51 p.

Kay, David A., and Skolnikoff, Eugene B., eds. WORLD ECO-CRISIS: INTERNATIONAL ORGANIZATIONS IN RESPONSE. Introduction by M.R. Strong. Madison: University of Wisconsin Press, 1972. 324 p.

Kneese, Allen V., et al., eds. MANAGING THE ENVIRONMENT: INTERNATIONAL ECONOMIC COOPERATION FOR POLLUTION CONTROL. New York: Praeger, 1971. 356 p.

> A work on economics, but appends "Legal Aspects of Environmental Management," a twenty-page overview by the Young Lawyers Section, ABA, of pollution regulation, legislation and litigation, recent Japanese laws, and NATO's cooperation.

Polunin, Nicholas, ed. THE ENVIRONMENTAL FUTURE: PROCEEDINGS OF THE FIRST INTERNATIONAL CONFERENCE ON ENVIRONMENTAL FUTURE, HELD IN FINLAND FROM 27 JUNE TO 3 JULY 1971. London: Macmillan, 1972. 660 p.

> Two of the papers presented at the conference explore the role of legal systems in an international effort to abate environmental hazards: H.G. Angelo, "The Need for Strengthening Legal Systems for Protection of the Environment;" E.S. Matthews, Jr., "Our Earth's Future: What International Law Could Do."

Ross, William M. OIL POLLUTION AS AN INTERNATIONAL PROBLEM: A STUDY OF PUGET SOUND AND THE STRAIT OF GEORGIA. Seattle: University of Washington Press, 1973. 224 p. Illus., bibliog.

Stein, Robert E. THE POTENTIAL OF REGIONAL ORGANIZATIONS IN MANAGING THE HUMAN ENVIRONMENT. Washington, D.C.: Woodrow Wilson International Center for Scholars, 1972. 16 p.

Teclaff, Ludwik A., and Utton, Albert E., eds. INTERNATIONAL ENVIRONMENTAL LAW. Praeger Special Studies in International Politics and Government. New York: Praeger, 1974. 270 p.

Utton, Albert E., ed. POLLUTION AND INTERNATIONAL BOUNDARIES: UNITED STATES-MEXICAN ENVIRONMENTAL PROBLEMS. Albuquerque: University of New Mexico Press, 1973. 144 p. Pap.

Utton, Albert E., and Henning, Daniel H., eds. ENVIRONMENTAL POLICY: CONCEPTS AND INTERNATIONAL IMPLICATIONS. New York: Praeger, 1973. 266 p.

A comprehensive collection of twenty-six papers which analyze current environmental policies and laws, both domestic and international. Among the topics are legislative and administrative policy making; the role of environmental litigation relative to power plant siting; public participation in policy making; international environmental regulation; changes in international policy making; pollution and the legal aspects of deep-sea mining; environmental law in Africa; problems of methodology, standard-setting, enforcement, international agreements, national sovereignty, individual rights; and legal education.

Winton, Harry N.M. MAN AND THE ENVIRONMENT: A BIBLIOGRAPHY OF THE UNITED NATIONS SYSTEM 1946-1971. New York: Unipub/R.R. Bowker, 1972. 305 p.

Includes references to works dealing with legal aspects of environmental problems in various nations.

## Government Documents

U.S. Congress. House. Committee on Foreign Affairs. Subcommittee on International Organizations and Movements. INTERNATIONAL COOPERATION IN THE HUMAN ENVIRONMENT THROUGH THE UNITED NATIONS. HEARINGS . . . ON H.R. 13116. . . . 92d Cong., 2d sess. Washington, D.C.: Government Printing Office, 1972. 101 p.

U.S. Congress. Senate. Committee on Commerce. THE NEED FOR A WORLD ENVIRONMENTAL INSTITUTE. 92d Cong., 2d sess. Washington, D.C.: Government Printing Office, 1972. 22 p.

_____. 1972 SURVEY OF ENVIRONMENTAL ACTIVITIES OF INTERNATIONAL ORGANIZATIONS. 92d Cong., 2d sess. Washington, D.C.: Government Printing Office, 1972. 187 p.

U.S. Department of State. WORLD ENVIRONMENTAL QUALITY: A CHALLENGE TO THE INTERNATIONAL COMMUNITY. Department of State Publication 8730. Washington, D.C.: Government Printing Office, 1973. 39 p. Pap., photos., table.

Contains a chapter on bilateral arrangements, regional activities and the UN's role, and brief discussion of various cooperative programs, such as wildlife preservation agreements.

# Section 2

# POLLUTION CONTROL

## GENERAL CONSIDERATIONS

Advisory Commission on Intergovernmental Relations. THE QUEST FOR ENVIRONMENTAL QUALITY: FEDERAL AND STATE ACTION, 1969-70, ANNOTATED BIBLIOGRAPHY. Washington, D.C.: Government Printing Office, 1971. 63 p.

American Society of International Law. THE QUESTION OF AN OCEAN DUMPING CONVENTION: CONCLUSIONS OF THE WORKING GROUP ON AN OCEAN DUMPING CONVENTION AND BACKGROUND PAPER BY LAWSON A.W. HUNT. Studies in Transnational Legal Policy, no. 2. Washington, D.C.: 1972. 53 p. Pap.

Includes a proposed convention.

Buggie, Frederick D., and Gurman, Richard. TOWARD EFFECTIVE AND EQUITABLE POLLUTION CONTROL REGULATION. An AMA Research Report. New York: American Management Association, 1972. 41 p. Illus.

Caldwell, Lynton K., ed., ENVIRONMENTAL STUDIES; PAPERS ON THE POLITICS AND PUBLIC ADMINISTRATION OF MAN-ENVIRONMENT RELATIONSHIPS. 4 vols. Bloomington: Institute of Public Administration, Indiana University, 1967.

Chicago. University of. Center for Policy Study. LEGAL AND ECONOMIC ASPECTS OF POLLUTION. Chicago: 1970. 37 p. Pap.

A panel discussion among selected faculty members.

Chinook Chemicals Corporation Limited, Information Services Division. ECO/LOG: CANADIAN POLLUTION LEGISLATION. Toronto: 1973- . Weekly. Loose-leaf.

A compilation of statutes and agency information and an updating loose-leaf service.

Cross, Frank L., Jr., and Ross, Roger W. CORPORATE COMMUNICATORS GUIDE FOR ENVIRONMENTAL CONTROL. Westport, Conn.: Technomic Publishing Co., 1973. 100 p. Pap.

A handbook for public relations departments. Offers guidelines for building a favorable corporate image. Includes sources of information and agencies involved in environmental control problems.


Currie, David P. POLLUTION: CASES AND MATERIALS. American Casebook Series. St. Paul, Minn.: West Publishing Co., 1975. 715 p.


Degler, Stanley E. FEDERAL POLLUTION CONTROL PROGRAMS: WATER, AIR AND SOLID WASTES. Washington, D.C.: Bureau of National Affairs, 1971. 176 p.

A summary of federal pollution control legislation and administration and the texts of NEPA, National Materials Policy Act of 1970, FWPCA Water Quality Standards, FWPCA Enforcement Program, Federal Water Pollution Control Act, Refuse Act, Executive Order 11574, Clean Air Act, and the Solid Waste Disposal Act.


Dworsky, Leonard B. POLLUTION. New York: Chelsea House Publishers, 1971. 911 p.

A documentary history of air and water pollution control in the United States. Includes a comprehensive study of all pre-1970 federal pollution control legislation. Although federal programs are emphasized, some treatment of local, state, and interstate programs is included, most of which focuses on the eastern states.


ENVIRONMENTAL PROTECTION DIRECTORY. 2d ed. Chicago: Marquis Publications, 1975.


Fontana, Joseph, and Wulf, Norman A., eds. POLLUTION AND THE LAW. Washington, D.C.: The Federal Bar Association, 1971. 28 p.

A pamphlet designed to introduce the high school student to how the law deals with various aspects of pollution.


Grad, Frank P. PUBLIC HEALTH LAW MANUAL: A HANDBOOK ON THE LEGAL ASPECTS OF PUBLIC HEALTH ADMINISTRATION AND ENFORCEMENT. Washington, D.C.: American Public Health Association, 1970. 243 p.

Aspects of public health law covered by separate chapters include the constitutional and legal bases for regulation, administrative law, the state and federal roles, legal tools for enforcement and their relation to individual rights, liability of officials, administrative techniques of information gathering, hearings and persuasion, and the public health officer and legislation.

Gunningham, Neil. POLLUTION, SOCIAL INTEREST AND THE LAW. London: Martin Robertson and Co., 1974. 120 p.

Handschu, Barbara, et al., eds. POLLUTION AND INDUSTRIAL WASTE. Criminal Law and Urban Problem Transcript Series, no. 4. New York: Practising Law Institute, 1970. 514 p.

Hodges, Laurent. ENVIRONMENTAL POLLUTION. New York: Holt, Rinehart and Winston, 1973. 384 p.

Includes sections on legal questions posed by pollution and on regulatory agencies.

Hyde, Margaret O. FOR POLLUTION FIGHTERS ONLY. New York: McGraw-Hill Book Co., 1971. 137 p. Illus.

Kiraldi, Louis, and Burk, Janet L. POLLUTION: A SELECTED BIBLIOGRAPHY OF U.S. GOVERNMENT PUBLICATIONS ON AIR, WATER, AND LAND POLLUTION. Kalamazoo: Western Michigan University Institute of Public Affairs, 1971. 78 p.

Lund, Herbert F., ed. INDUSTRIAL POLLUTION CONTROL HANDBOOK. New York: McGraw-Hill Book Co., 1971. Var. pag.

A lengthy study of engineering and management techniques available to the various industries for the control of air and water pollution. One chapter deals with history of federal pollution control legislation, another with state and local laws, and a third with air and water quality standards.

McKnight, Allan D., et al., eds. ENVIRONMENTAL POLLUTION CONTROL; TECHNICAL, ECONOMIC AND LEGAL ASPECTS. London: Allen & Unwin, 1974. 324 p. Tables, diagrs.

McLoughlin, James. THE LAW RELATING TO POLLUTION: AN INTRODUCTION. Manchester, Engl.: Manchester University Press, 1972. 133 p. Pap., illus.

An introductory explanation of the common and statutory law of Great Britain relating to fresh and ocean waters, air, noise, nuclear energy, and solid waste.

National Institute for Petroleum Landmen. PROCEEDINGS. New York: Matthew Bender, 1959- .

Papers presented by the International Oil and Gas Educational Center. Those relevant to environmental law are: 1972: "Pollution Control, Natural Gas Regulations and Other Recent Developments of Interest to Landmen"; 1971: "Recent Developments in the Law,

Including Court Decisions, Administrative Decisions, and Statutes of Interest to Landmen (as of March 15, 1971)," "Native Land Claims and Their Effects on Leasing in Alaska," "The Public Land Law Review Commission Recommendations and Beyond," "The Oil Industry and the Environment"; 1970: "Recent Developments in the Law . . ."; 1967: "Report on the Public Land Law Review Commission."

Price, Fred C., et al., eds. MCGRAW-HILL'S 1972 REPORT ON BUSINESS AND THE ENVIRONMENT. New York: McGraw-Hill Book Co., 1972. 473 p. Tables, photos., illus., charts, graphs.

Most chapters treat economic, planning, and technological aspects of environmental quality management by industry. Two chapters deal with policy making and laws and standards.

Rabin, Edward H., and Schwartz, Mortimer D., eds. THE POLLUTION CRISIS: OFFICIAL DOCUMENTS. Dobbs Ferry, N.Y.: Oceana Publications, 1972. 510 p.

Reports spanning 1965-70 by a number of federal agencies concerning the following topics: pollution of inland and ocean waters and estuaries; physical, health, and meteorological aspects of air pollution; land use control, management of federal lands, and highway policy; solid waste management; pollutants in relation to agriculture, forestry, and power generation.

Schroeder, Henry A. POLLUTION, PROFITS AND PROGRESS. Brattleboro, Vt.: S. Greene Press, 1971. 133 p.

Shuttlesworth, Dorothy E. CLEAN AIR, SPARKLING WATER: THE FIGHT AGAINST POLLUTION. Garden City, N.Y.: Doubleday and Co., 1968. 95 p. Illus.

Stepp, J.M., and Macaulay, H.H. THE POLLUTION PROBLEM. Washington, D.C.: American Enterprise Institute for Public Policy Research, 1968. 67 p.

A special analysis for the Institute which emphasizes economic analysis; although physical, political, and governmental aspects are touched upon.

Stewart, Alexander P., and Jenkins, Edward. THE MEDICAL AND LEGAL ASPECTS OF SANITARY REFORM. 1866. Reprint. Leicester, Engl.: Leicester University Press, 1969; dist. by Humanities Press, New York. 100 p.

A study of the need and possibilities for public health reform in Victorian England.

Tearle, Keith, ed. INDUSTRIAL POLLUTION CONTROL: THE PRACTICAL

IMPLICATIONS. London: Business Books, 1973. 230 p. Illus., photos., tables, charts, graphs.

Contains chapters on the English law relating to air pollution, water pollution, and disposal of solid and liquid wastes.

Wilson, Billy Ray, ed. ENVIRONMENTAL PROBLEMS; PESTICIDES, THERMAL POLLUTION, AND ENVIRONMENTAL SYNERGISMS. Philadelphia: Lippincott, 1968. 183 p. Illus.

## GOVERNMENT DOCUMENTS

Great Britain. Department of Local Government and Regional Planning. THE PROTECTION OF THE ENVIRONMENT: THE FIGHT AGAINST POLLUTION. London: Her Majesty's Stationery Office, 1970. 29 p. Pap.

Report on the problems and current abatement measures in the areas of air, fresh water, sea and beach, land, noise, and radiation pollution.

South Carolina. Pollution Control Authority. ANNUAL REPORTS. Columbia: 1948- . Pap.

Texas. Attorney General's Office. HANDBOOK ON POLLUTION. Prepared by J.B. Shepperd, Attorney General. Austin: 1953. 36 p.

Texas. Laws and Statutes. PRINCIPAL POLLUTION LAWS OF TEXAS FOR USE BY LOCAL GOVERNMENTS: TEXAS WATER QUALITY ACT, TEXAS CLEAN AIR ACT, SOLID WASTE DISPOSAL ACT, ARTICLE 698c, Vernon's Annotated Penal Code, ARTICLE 698d, Vernon's Annotated Penal Code, FORM PETITIONS, ETC. Austin: Distributed by the Attorney General's Office, Water Division, 1970. 188 p. Port.

U.S. Congress. House. Committee on Government Operations. Conservation and Natural Resources Subcommittee. THE ESTABLISHMENT OF A NATIONAL INDUSTRIAL WASTES INVENTORY: HEARING. . . . 91st Cong., 2d sess. Washington, D.C.: Government Printing Office, 1970. 229 p.

U.S. Congress. House. Committee on Public Works. Subcommittee on Conservation and Watershed Development. NON-POINT SOURCE POLLUTION FROM AGRICULTURAL, RURAL, AND DEVELOPING AREAS: HEARINGS . . . ON H.R. 15596 AND RELATED BILLS. 92d Cong., 2d sess. Washington, D.C.: Government Printing Office, 1972. 151 p. Illus.

U.S. Congress. House. Committee on Ways and Means. AMENDMENTS TO THE ANTI-DUMPING ACT OF 1921, AS AMENDED: HEARINGS . . . ON H.R. 6006, 6007, AND 5120, BILLS TO AMEND CERTAIN PROVISIONS OF

THE ANTIDUMPING ACT OF 1921. 85th Cong., 2d sess. Washington, D.C.: Government Printing Office, 1957. 430 p. Map, tables.

U.S. Congress. Senate. Committee on Commerce. Subcommittee on the Environment. THE TOXIC SUBSTANCES CONTROL ACT OF 1971 AND AMENDMENT: HEARINGS . . . ON S. 1478 . . . 3 vols. 92d Cong., 1st sess. Washington, D.C.: Government Printing Office, 1972. 1,251 p.

U.S. Department of Health, Education, and Welfare. ENVIRONMENTAL POLLUTION EFFECTS ON HEALTH. MESSAGE FROM THE PRESIDENT OF THE UNITED STATES, TRANSMITTING THE REPORT OF THE DEPARTMENT OF HEALTH, EDUCATION, AND WELFARE AND THE ENVIRONMENTAL PROTECTION AGENCY, ON THE HEALTH EFFECTS OF ENVIRONMENTAL POLLUTION, PURSUANT TO TITLE V OF PUBLIC LAW 91-515. 92d Cong., 2d sess. House Document no. 92-241. Washington, D.C.: Government Printing Office, 1972. 32 p.

U.S. Secretary of Commerce. THE EFFECTS OF POLLUTION ABATEMENT ON INTERNATIONAL TRADE; THE FIRST REPORT OF THE SECRETARY OF COMMERCE TO THE PRESIDENT AND CONGRESS IN COMPLIANCE WITH SECTION 6 OF THE FEDERAL WATER POLLUTION CONTROL ACT AMENDMENTS OF 1972 (PUBLIC LAW 92-500). 93d Cong., 1st sess. Washington, D.C.: Government Printing Office, 1973. 126 p.

# AIR POLLUTION

## Bibliographies

American Petroleum Institute. AIR POLLUTION, AN ANNOTATED BIBLIOGRAPHY. New York: 1960. 11 p.

California. State Library, Sacramento Law Library. LEGAL ASPECTS OF AIR POLLUTION, A SELECTIVE BIBLIOGRAPHY. Sacramento: 1967. 12 p.

Davenport, Sarah J., and Morgis, G.G. AIR POLLUTION: A BIBLIOGRAPHY. U.S. Bureau of Mines Bulletin no. 537. Washington, D.C.: Government Printing Office, 1952. 448 p.

Heere, W.P. INTERNATIONAL BIBLIOGRAPHY OF AIR LAW, 1900-1971. Leiden: A.W. Sijthoff, 1972; dist. by Oceana Publications. 850 p.

New York State Legislative Reference Library. AIR POLLUTION, A BIBLIOGRAPHY. Albany: 1961. 4 p.

U.S. National Air Pollution Control Administration. AIR POLLUTION PUBLI-

CATIONS: A SELECTED BIBLIOGRAPHY, 1955-1962. Washington, D.C.: 1962. 67 p.

van Nest, W.J. AIR POLLUTION AND URBAN PLANNING: A SELECTIVE ANNOTATED BIBLIOGRAPHY. Council of Planning Librarians Exchange Bibliography no. 257. Monticello, Ill.: Council of Planning Librarians, 1972. 64 p.

Contains literature published primarily after 1965.

## Authored Works and Conferences

American Health Association. Program Area Committee on Air Pollution. GUIDE TO THE APPRAISAL AND CONTROL OF AIR POLLUTION. 2d ed. New York: 1969. 80 p.

Written as a primer for individuals interested in local or regional air pollution control programs. Communicates information on basic physical, evaluation, and policy-making aspects of the problem. Chapters on the role of local government and initiating a program.

Bates, David V. A CITIZEN'S GUIDE TO AIR POLLUTION. Environmental Damage and Control in Canada, 2. Montreal: McGill-Queens University, 1972. 140 p. Illus.

Bell, William H. ORDINANCES AND LEGISLATION RELATED TO AIR POLLUTION. Austin: Texas State Department of Health, Division of Occupational Health, 1957. 27 p.

Bibbero, Robert J., and Young, Irving G. SYSTEMS APPROACH TO AIR POLLUTION CONTROL. New York: Wiley Interscience, 1974. 531 p.

Summarizes the planning and implementation of air pollution measurements. Analyzes the social and economic effects of air pollution and examines the evolution of legislative controls, giving special attention to current U.S. laws.

Bond, Richard G., and Staub, Conrad P., eds. AIR POLLUTION. CRC Handbook of Environmental Control, vol. 1. Cleveland: CRC Press, 1972. 576 p. Illus.

Brittin, Wesley E., et al., eds. AIR AND WATER POLLUTION. Boulder: Colorado Associated University Press, 1972. 615 p. Pap.

Proceedings of a summer workshop. Thirty-four lectures addressed to nonspecialist scientists.

The Conservation Foundation. A CITIZEN'S GUIDE TO CLEAN AIR. Washington, D.C.: 1972. 95 p.

Intended to familiarize citizens with the federal regulatory programs after the Clean Air amendments of 1970. Contains substantial summaries of the amendments, other existing legislation, and administrative standards and procedures.

_____. YOUR RIGHT TO CLEAN AIR: A MANUAL FOR CITIZEN ACTION. Washington, D.C.: 1970. 108 p. Pap.

Includes a short section summarizing the Air Quality Act of 1967.

Council of Europe, Committee of Experts on Air Pollution. LEGAL ASPECTS OF AIR POLLUTION CONTROL. Strasbourg, France: 1972. 67 p. Pap.

Consists of two papers: "Air Pollution Control: Study in Comparative Law," by C.A. Colliard; and "Efforts to Control Air Pollution at International Level," by A.C. Kiss.

Degler, Stanley E. STATE AIR POLLUTION CONTROL LAWS. Rev. ed. BNA's Environmental Management Series. Washington, D.C.: Bureau of National Affairs, 1970. 93 p.

A digest of summaries of state air pollution control laws. Intended to supplement the texts of the laws found in the ENVIRONMENT REPORTER. Excerpts from California Health and Safety Code as amended by the Pure Air Act of 1968 and by laws of 1969 and Model State Air Pollution Control Act are included.

Edelman, S[idney]. THE LAW OF AIR POLLUTION CONTROL. Wilton, Conn.: Environmental Science Serivce, 1970. 293 p.

Documents increasing government control rather than individual action and cooperation. Cases and rulings cited at end of each chapter.

Esposito, John C. VANISHING AIR: THE RALPH NADER STUDY GROUP ON AIR POLLUTION. New York: Grossman Publishers, 1970. 328 p. Pap.

Report on the causes of air pollution--automobiles, utilities, and manufacturers; its effects upon health; and the failure of the federal government to control it. The study traces federal abatement efforts from Senator Muskie's congressional activities to the practices of the National Air Pollution Control Administration.

Faith, W.L., and Atkisson, Arthur A., Jr. AIR POLLUTION. 2d ed. New York: Wiley Interscience, 1972. 393 p.

Although primarily a technical text, the legal and social aspects of air pollution control are discussed when important to an understanding of the subject. Two substantial chapters treat government regulation: "Air Quality Management" and "Organization and Operations of Air Pollution Agencies."

Garner, John F., and Crow, R.K. CLEAN AIR--LAW AND PRACTICE. 3d ed. London: Shaw & Sons, 1969. 506 p. Forms.

Analysis of Clean Air Act 1956 and Clean Air Act 1969 in England.

Hagevik, George H. DECISION-MAKING IN AIR POLLUTION CONTROL: A REVIEW OF THEORY AND PRACTICE, WITH EMPHASIS ON SELECTED LOS ANGELES AND NEW YORK CITY MANAGEMENT EXPERIENCES. New York: Praeger, 1970. 217 p. Bibliog.

Includes a review of the legal aspects of air quality control; development of management theories; decision-making processes and standards; detailed attention to ordinances and statutes relevant to the case studies; and discussions of the potential role of effluent fees, payments, and direct regulation in pollution abatement.

_____, ed. THE RELATIONSHIP OF LAND USE AND TRANSPORTATION PLANNING TO AIR QUALITY MANAGEMENT. New Brunswick, N.J.: Center for Urban Policies Research and Conferences Department, Rutgers University, 1972. 287 p. Pap., charts.

A number of the eighteen papers discuss statutory aspects of land-use planning, air pollution, and transportation planning.

Havighurst, Clark C. AIR POLLUTION CONTROL. Dobbs Ferry, N.Y.: Oceana Publications, 1969. 230 p.

Articles on health effects and their legal implications, control technology, economics of air pollution, Air Quality Act of 1967 and its deficiencies, California and federal control of auto emmissions, state control of interstate pollution, legal boundaries of pollution control, incentives, accommodation of theory to actual legislation, Federal Power Commission policy, and European cooperation.

Hertzendorf, Martin S. AIR POLLUTION CONTROL: GUIDEBOOK TO U.S. REGULATIONS. Westport, Conn.: Technomic Publishing Co., 1973. 266 p. Pap., charts, graphs, tables.

International Clean Air Congress, 1st, London, October 4-7, 1966. PROCEEDINGS: PART I. London: National Society for Clean Air for the International Union of Air Pollution Prevention Associations, 1966. 292 p.

Papers presented in French, German, and English. Session III includes papers presenting an international variety of approaches to town planning. Session VIII, "Standards, Regulations, Legislation, International Co-operation," consists of ten papers on air pollution law.

International Clean Air Congress, 2d, Washington, D.C., 1970. PROCEEDINGS. Edited by H.M. England and W.T. Berry. New York: Academic Press, 1971. xxv, 1,354 p.

Joyce, Joseph A., and Joyce, Howard C. TREATISE ON THE LAW GOVERN-
ING NUISANCES. Albany, N.Y.: Matthew Bender, 1906. 866 p.

> A study of nuisance theories. Two sections discuss their applica-
> tion to environmental problems through light and air easements and
> rights to pure and fresh air.

Krier, James E. ENVIRONMENTAL LAW AND POLICY: READINGS, MATE-
RIALS AND NOTES ON AIR POLLUTION AND RELATED PROBLEMS. Contemporary Legal Education Series. Indianapolis: Bobbs-Merrill, 1971. xxxii,
480 p.

> A coursebook which explores the conflicting demands upon environ-
> mental resources and the responses of the legal system. Examines
> numerous aspects of air pollution control at the local, state, and
> federal levels.

Kurtzweg, Jerry A. LAND USE PLANNING AND AIR POLLUTION CONTROL
IN THE CENTRAL PUGET SOUND REGION. Seattle: King County Planning
Department, 1967. 109 p. Illus.

Mackintosh, Douglas R. THE ECONOMICS OF AIRBORNE EMMISSIONS: THE
CASE FOR AN AIR RIGHTS MARKET. Praeger Special Studies in U.S. Economic, Social, and Political Issues. New York: Praeger, 1973. 121 p. Illus.

Magill, Paul L., et al., eds. AIR POLLUTION HANDBOOK. New York:
McGraw-Hill Book Co., 1956. 671 p.

> A source of useful information about facets of air pollution ranging
> from analytical methods to the effects of air pollution on farm ani-
> mals. The chapter "Air Pollution Legislation" has sections on the
> common law, the source of community legal authority, present
> (1956) legislation, existing state and municipal legislation, includ-
> ing tables organizing cities by types of ordinances, and recom-
> mended legislation.

Meetham, A.R. ATMOSPHERIC POLLUTION: ITS ORIGINS AND PREVEN-
TION. 3d ed. London: Pergamon Press, 1964. 301 p. Tables, maps, illus.

> Primarily technical, but contains chapters on British air pollution
> control legislation and legislation in seventeen other countries.

Mills, Clarence A. THIS AIR WE BREATHE. Boston: The Christopher Publishing House, 1962. 172 p.

> Emphasizes medical aspects of air pollution. One chapter on con-
> trol legislation prior to 1962.

Organization for Economic Co-operation and Development. AIR POLLUTION

IN THE IRON AND STEEL INDUSTRY. New York: McGraw-Hill Book Co., 1962. 135 p.

A highly technical study of pollutants, effects, and control equipment in Europe. One chapter summarizes air pollution control laws in Germany, Austria, France, Italy, the Netherlands, and the United Kingdom. Appended is bibliography of interested bodies and documentation centers in each country.

Pittsburgh. University of. Health Law Center. DIGEST OF MUNICIPAL AIR POLLUTION ORDINANCES. U.S. Public Health Service Publication no. 982. Washington, D.C.: Department of Health, Education and Welfare, Public Health Service, Division of Air Pollution, for sale by the Government Printing Office, 1962. 509 p.

Real Estate Research Corporation. AIR RIGHTS AND HIGHWAYS. Washington, D.C.: Urban Land Institute, 1969. 84 p. Illus.

One chapter explores the legal aspects of multiple uses of air space over highways in sections on enabling legislation and restrictions on acquisitions.

Rogers, Samuel M., and Edelman, Sidney. A DIGEST OF STATE AIR POLLUTION LAWS. U.S. Public Health Service Publication no. 711. Washington, D.C.: Department of Health, Education and Welfare, Public Health Service, Bureau of State Services, Division of Engineering Services, Air Pollution Engineering Program, 1959. 117 p.

Rossano, A.T., Jr., ed. AIR POLLUTION CONTROL: GUIDEBOOK FOR MANAGEMENT. Stamford, Conn.: ERA, 1969. 214 p.

Most of the individually authored chapters deal with scientific and technical aspects. Two chapters discuss the law: "Administrative and Regulatory Aspects of Air Pollution Control" and "Legal Aspects of Air Pollution." The latter chapter treats the development of standards, variances, enforcement and litigation, and summarizes federal, state, and local legislation.

Schachter, Ester R. ENFORCING AIR POLLUTION CONTROLS: CASE STUDY OF NEW YORK CITY. Praeger Special Studies in U.S. Economic, Social, and Political Issues. New York: Praeger Publishing Co., 1974. 104 p.

Scorer, R.S. POLLUTION IN THE AIR: PROBLEMS, POLICIES AND PRIORITIES. Boston and London: Routledge and Kegan Paul, 1973. 148 p.

Contains a long chapter entitled "A Theory of Anti-Pollution Law."

Selig, Edward I. EFFLUENT CHARGES ON AIR AND WATER POLLUTION: A CONFERENCE REPORT. ELI Monograph Series, no. 1. Washington, D.C.: Environmental Law Institute, 1973. 102 p.

Sproull, Wayne T. AIR POLLUTION AND ITS CONTROL. 2d ed. New York: Exposition Press, 1972. 131 p.

One section on legal and economic aspects.


Stern, Arthur C., ed. AIR POLLUTION, VOLUME III: SOURCES OF AIR POLLUTION AND THEIR CONTROL. 2d ed. New York: Academic Press, 1968. 866 p.

Part of a three-volume work which extensively covers the scientific and technical facets of air pollution and its control. Part IX, "Air Pollution Control," is comprised of substantial chapters on legislation, standards, administration, education, and literature resources. The chapter on legislation includes sections on existing national legislation, model legislation, and "guiding principles."


Strauss, Werner, ed. AIR POLLUTION CONTROL, PART 2. Environment Science and Technology Series of Monographs, Textbooks and Advances. New York: John Wiley, 1972. 300 p.


Tomany, J.P., ed. AIR POLLUTION: THE EMMISSIONS, THE REGULATIONS AND THE CONTROLS. New York: American Elsevier, 1974. 512 p.


U.S. Public Health Service. PROCEEDINGS. National Conference on Air Pollution, Washington, D.C. Washington, D.C.: Department of Health, Education and Welfare, Public Health Service, Division of Air Pollution, 1958. Illus., diagrs.


Weisburd, Melvin I. AIR POLLUTION CONTROL FIELD OPERATIONS MANUAL, A GUIDE FOR INSPECTION AND ENFORCEMENT. U.S. Public Health Service Publication no. 937. Washington, D.C.: Department of Health, Education and Welfare, Public Health Service, Division of Air Pollution, 1962. 285 p. Illus., diagrs., maps, forms, tables.

## Government Documents--Federal

U.S. Congress. House. Committee on Interstate and Foreign Commerce. AIR QUALITY ACT OF 1967: HEARINGS . . . ON H.R. 9509 [and] S. 780. 90th Cong., 1st sess. Washington, D.C.: Government Printing Office, 1967. 887 p. Illus., maps.


_____. AIR QUALITY ACT OF 1967; REPORT TOGETHER WITH ADDITIONAL VIEWS TO ACCOMPANY S. 780. . . . 90th Cong., 1st sess., House Report no. 728. Washington, D.C.: Government Printing Office, 1967. 97 p. Illus.


_____. CLEAN AIR ACT AMENDMENTS OF 1970; REPORT TO ACCOMPANY H.R. 17255. 91st Cong., 2d sess., House Report no. 91-1146. Washington, D.C.: Government Printing Office, 1970. 53 p.

_____. CLEAN AIR ACT, REPORT TO ACCOMPANY H.R. 6518. 88th Cong., 1st sess., House Report no. 508. Washington, D.C.: Government Printing Office, 1963. 32 p.

_____. CLEAN AIR AND SOLID WASTE DISPOSAL ACTS; REPORT TO AC-COMPANY S. 306. 89th Cong., 1st sess. House Report no. 899. Washington, D.C.: Government Printing Office, 1965. 66 p.

U.S. Congress. House. Committee on Interstate and Foreign Commerce. Subcommittee on Public Health and Environment. CLEAN AIR ACT OVERSIGHT: HEARINGS. . . . 92d Cong., 1st and 2d sess. Washington, D.C.: Government Printing Office, 1972. 555 p. Illus.

U.S. Congress. House. Committee on Interstate and Foreign Commerce. Subcommittee on Public Health and Welfare. AIR POLLUTION CONTROL AND SOLID WASTES RECYCLING. HEARINGS . . . ON H.R. 12934, H.R. 14960, H.R. 15137, AND H.R. 15192, H.R. 15848, H.R. 15847, AND RE-LATED BILLS. 2 vols. 91st Cong., 1st and 2d sess. Washington, D.C.: Government Printing Office, 1970.

_____. CLEAN AIR ACT AMENDMENTS. HEARINGS. . . . 89th Cong., 1st sess. Washington, D.C.: Government Printing Office, 1965. 427 p. Map.

_____. CLEAN AIR ACT AMENDMENTS OF 1966: HEARINGS . . . ON H.R. 13199 [and] S. 3112. 89th Cong., 2d sess. Washington, D.C.: Government Printing Office, 1966. 126 p. Illus.

U.S. Congress. Senate. Committee on Public Works. CLEAN AIR ACT; RE-PORT TO ACCOMPANY S. 432. 88th Cong., 1st sess. Senate Report no. 638. Washington, D.C.: Government Printing Office, 1963. 23 p.

_____. CLEAN AIR ACT AMENDMENTS; REPORT TO ACCOMPANY S. 3112. 89th Cong., 2d sess. Senate Report no. 1361. Washington, D.C.: Government Printing Office, 1966. 15 p.

_____. NATIONAL AIR QUALITY STANDARDS ACT OF 1970; REPORT TO-GETHER WITH INDIVIDUAL VIEWS TO ACCOMPANY S. 4358. 91st Cong., 2d sess., Senate Report no. 91-1196. Washington, D.C.: Government Printing Office, 1970. 129 p.

_____. RECOMMENDATIONS OF THE COMMITTEE ON PUBLIC WORKS TO THE COMMITTEE ON THE JUDICIARY REGARDING THE CONDITIONAL CONSENT OF THE CONGRESS TO VARIOUS INTERSTATE AIR POLLUTION CONTROL COMPACTS. 90th Cong., 2d sess. Washington, D.C.: Government Printing Office, 1968. 9 p.

U.S. Congress. Senate. Committee on Public Works. Subcommittee on Air and Water Pollution. AIR POLLUTION--1966: HEARINGS . . . ON S. 3112 [and] S. 3400. 89th Cong., 2d sess. Washington, D.C.: Government Printing Office, 1966. 453 p. Illus., maps.

_____. AIR POLLUTION--1968. HEARINGS ON AIR POLLUTION COMPACTS, S. 2350, S.J. RES. 95, S. 470. 90th Cong., 2d sess. Washington, D.C.: Government Printing Office, 1968. 1,132 p.

_____. AIR POLLUTION--1969. HEARINGS ON PROBLEMS AND PROGRAMS ASSOCIATED WITH CONTROL OF AIR POLLUTION. 91st Cong., 1st sess. Washington, D.C.: Government Printing Office, 1970. 244 p.

_____. AIR POLLUTION--1970. HEARINGS . . . ON S. 3229, S. 3466, [and] S. 3546. 91st Cong., 2d sess. Washington, D.C.: Government Printing Office, 1970. Pp. 1571-1691. Illus.

_____. AIR POLLUTION CONTROL: HEARINGS . . . ON S. 432 [and other] BILLS PERTAINING TO THE PREVENTION AND ABATEMENT OF AIR POLLUTION. 88th Cong., 1st sess. Washington, D.C.: Government Printing Office, 1963. 502 p. Illus., maps.

_____. FEDERAL INSTALLATIONS, FACILITIES, AND EQUIPMENT POLLUTION CONTROL ACT. HEARINGS . . . ON S. 560. 89th Cong., 1st sess. Washington, D.C.: Government Printing Office, 1965. 172 p. Maps.

_____. IMPLEMENTATION OF CLEAN AIR ACT AMENDMENTS OF 1970 (TITLE I): HEARINGS . . . 3 vols. 92d Cong., 2d sess. Washington, D.C.: Government Printing Office, 1972. 910 p. Illus.

_____. IMPLEMENTATION OF CLEAN AIR ACT AMENDMENTS OF 1970 (TITLE II): HEARINGS . . . 2 vols. 92d Cong., 2d sess. Washington, D.C.: Government Printing Office, 1972. Pp. 911-1622. Illus.

_____. STEPS TOWARD CLEAN AIR; REPORT FROM SPECIAL SUBCOMMITTEE ON AIR AND WATER POLLUTION. 89th Cong., 2d sess. Washington, D.C.: Government Printing Office, 1964. 40 p.

U.S. Congress. Senate. Committee on the Judiciary. INTERSTATE COMPACT ON AIR POLLUTION BETWEEN THE STATES OF OHIO AND WEST VIRGINIA; REPORT TO ACCOMPANY S. 2707. 91st Cong., 2d sess. Senate Report no. 645. Washington, D.C.: Government Printing Office, 1970. 12 p.

_____. MID-ATLANTIC STATES AIR POLLUTION CONTROL COMPACT: REPORT TO ACCOMPANY S.J. RES. 53. 91st Cong., 2d sess. Senate Report no. 91-975. Washington, D.C.: Government Printing Office, 1970. 18 p.

U.S. Department of Health, Education and Welfare. AUTOMOTIVE AIR POLLUTION: FOURTH REPORT. Washington, D.C.: Government Printing Office, 1966. 10 p. Pap.

Includes sections on implementation of the Motor Vehicle Air Pollution Control Act and current control measures.

_____. AUTOMOTIVE AIR POLLUTION: SIXTH REPORT. Washington, D.C.: Government Printing Office, 1967. 13 p.

Contains sections on federal vehicle certification and air quality standards.

_____. PROFILE OF AIR POLLUTION CONTROL ACTIVITIES IN FOREIGN COUNTRIES: FIRST YEAR REPORT. Springfield, Va.: National Technical Information Service, Department of Commerce, 1970. 828 p.

_____. PROGRESS IN THE PREVENTION AND CONTROL OF AIR POLLUTION. Washington, D.C.: Government Printing Office, 1968. 85 p.

_____. PROGRESS IN THE PREVENTION AND CONTROL OF AIR POLLUTION, SECOND REPORT. Washington, D.C.: Government Printing Office, 1969. 85 p.

U.S. Federal Power Commission. AIR POLLUTION AND THE REGULATED ELECTRIC POWER AND NATURAL GAS INDUSTRIES: A STAFF REPORT. Washington, D.C.: 1968. 366 p. Maps.

U.S. National Center for Air Pollution Control. A DIGEST OF STATE AIR POLLUTION LAWS. U.S. Public Health Service Publication, no. 711. Washington, D.C.: Public Health Service, 1959-66. Irregular.

U.S. National Center for Air Pollution Control. Abatement Program. A COMPILATION OF SELECTED AIR POLLUTION EMISSION CONTROL REGULATIONS AND ORDINANCES. Rev. ed. Environmental Health Series: Air Pollution. Washington, D.C.: Government Printing Office, 1968. 146 p. Illus.

U.S. President. Richard M. Nixon. MESSAGE ON ENVIRONMENT; MESSAGE FROM THE PRESIDENT OF THE UNITED STATES, OUTLINING LEGISLATIVE PROPOSALS AND ADMINISTRATIVE ACTIONS TAKEN TO IMPROVE ENVIRONMENTAL QUALITY. 91st Cong., 2d sess. House Document no. 91-225. Washington, D.C.: Government Printing Office, 1970. 14 p.

U.S. Public Health Service. Air Pollution Engineering Branch. DIGEST OF STATE AIR POLLUTION LAWS. Washington, D.C.: Government Printing Office, 1958? 167 p.

U.S. Robert A. Taft Sanitary Engineering Center, Cincinnati. A COMPILA-

TION OF SELECTED AIR POLLUTION EMISSION CONTROL REGULATIONS
AND ORDINANCES. Cincinnati: U.S. Department of Health, Education, and
Welfare, Public Health Service, Division of Air Pollution, 1965. 123 p.

## Government Documents--State and County

California. Legislature. Assembly. Interim Committee on Public Health.
MOTOR VEHICLE CREATED AIR POLLUTION, A CONTROL PROGRAM FOR
CALIFORNIA. Prepared by the Subcommittee on Air Pollution. Sacramento:
1967. 48 p. Illus.

California. Resources Agency. Air Resources Board. AIR POLLUTION IN
CALIFORNIA: ANNUAL REPORT 1972. Sacramento: 1972. 37 p. Pap.

Los Angeles County Air Pollution Control District. LEGAL OPINIONS CON-
CERNING AIR POLLUTION. Los Angeles: 1959. Var. pag.

_____. RULES AND REGULATIONS. Los Angeles: 1955? 341 p.

Missouri. Air Conservation Commission. AIR QUALITY STANDARDS AND
AIR POLLUTION CONTROL REGULATIONS FOR THE ST. LOUIS AREA, EF-
FECTIVE DATE, MARCH 24, 1967. Jefferson City: 1967? 32 p. Illus.

Nebraska. Environmental Control Council. RULES AND REGULATIONS IM-
PLEMENTING NEBRASKA AMBIENT AIR QUALITY STANDARDS, ADOPTED BY
NEBRASKA ENVIRONMENTAL CONTROL COUNCIL, EFFECTIVE JUNE 6,
1972. Lincoln: Department of Environmental Control, 1972. 25 p. Illus.

Nevada. Commission of Environmental Protection. AIR QUALITY REGULA-
TIONS; ADOPTED BY THE STATE COMMISSION OF ENVIRONMENTAL PRO-
TECTION JANUARY 18, 1972. Carson City: 1972. 27 p.

New Jersey. Air Pollution Commission. REPORT TO THE NEW JERSEY LEGIS-
LATURE ON AIR POLLUTION IN NEW JERSEY AND RECOMMENDATIONS
FOR ITS ABATEMENT. Trenton: 1952. 67 p.

New York-New Jersey Interstate Sanitation Commission. SMOKE AND AIR
POLLUTION: NEW YORK-NEW JERSEY. A REPORT ON PROPOSED SMOKE
AND AIR POLLUTION LEGISLATION FOR THE NEW YORK METROPOLITAN
AREA. New York: 1959. 41 p.

North Dakota. State Department of Health. AIR POLLUTION CONTROL
REGULATIONS ON THE STATE OF NORTH DAKOTA; REGULATIONS 23-25
(FORMERLY REGULATION 82). EFFECTIVE DATE: ORIGINAL--JULY 1, 1970;
REVISIONS--FEBRUARY 1, 1972. Bismark: 1972. 49 p.

Ohio. Legislative Service Commission. AIR AND WATER POLLUTION. Staff Research Report no. 84. Columbus: 1967. 86 p. Pap., maps, tables.

> Includes sections on Ohio's water quality and air quality control programs. Appendices include summaries of the Cleveland Air Pollution Control Ordinance and the Indiana-Illinois Interstate Compact.

Oregon. State Sanitary Authority. RULES AND REGULATIONS PERTAINING TO AIR POLLUTION CONTROL. Portland: 1960. 18 p.

Tennessee. General Assembly. Legislative Council Committee. STUDY ON NOISE AND AIR POLLUTION LAWS AND REFUSE DUMPING, 1970; FINAL REPORT. Nashville: 1970. 175 p.

Virginia. State Air Pollution Control Board. REGULATIONS FOR THE CONTROL AND ABATEMENT OF AIR POLLUTION. Richmond: 1972. 190 p. Illus.

Wisconsin. Legislative Reference Bureau. A PRICE OF AFFLUENCE: LEGISLATING AIR POLLUTION CONTROL. Madison: 1966. 18 p.

# WATER POLLUTION

## Bibliographies

Christol, Carl Q. OIL POLLUTION OF THE MARINE ENVIRONMENT--A LEGAL BIBLIOGRAPHY. Washington, D.C.: Government Printing Office for the Senate Committee on Public Works, 1971. 93 p. Pap.

> Divided into the following categories: articles; books; documents of international organizations; statutes, hearings and reports of the Congress, executive department, administrative agencies; treaties; statutes and documents of foreign states; statutes and governmental acts from selected states; and selected bibliographies.

Jacobstein, J. Myron, and Mersky, Roy M. WATER LAW BIBLIOGRAPHY 1847-1965 and SUPPLEMENT 1966-67. Silver Springs, Md.: Jefferson Law Book Co., 1966. 24 p.

> Includes titles and legislative histories of federal acts in the areas of pollution, flood control, weather modification, water conservation, and watershed protection.

Turney, Jack R., and Ellis, Harold H. STATE WATER-RIGHTS LAWS AND RELATED SUBJECTS: A BIBLIOGRAPHY. Washington, D.C.: Government Printing Office, 1962. 199 p. Pap.

> Annotated. Lists titles relevant to environmental law.

U.S. Department of the Interior. Water Resources Scientific Information Center. LEGAL ASPECTS OF WATER POLLUTION IN NEW JERSEY AND PENNSYLVANIA; A BIBLIOGRAPHY. Washington, D.C.: 1972. 233 p.

## Authored Works and Conferences

Beuscher, J.H. WATER RIGHTS. Madison, Wis.: College Printing and Typing Co., 1967. 343 p. Charts, maps, photos.

> One chapter on water pollution abatement.

Bollens, John C. THE PROBLEM OF GOVERNMENT IN THE SAN FRANCISCO BAY REGION. Berkeley: Bureau of Public Administration, University of California, 1948. 162 p. Bibliog.

> An early study of regional governmental problems which includes several sections on sewage and legislative and agency efforts to reduce pollution of the Bay.

California. University of. Berkeley. Committee on Research in Water Resources. CONFERENCE ON LEGAL PROBLEMS IN WATER RESOURCES. Edited by Leland O. Graham. Berkeley: Committee on Research in Water Resources, University of California, 1957. 262 p. Pap.

> Two presentations relevant to environmental problems: "Quality Control and Re-Use of Water in California" and "Federal, State and Local Cooperation in Conservation and Development of Water Resources."

California. University of. Davis. School of Law. LEGAL CONTROL OF WATER POLLUTION, U.C.D. LAW REVIEW, Vol. 1. Edited by F.B. Baldwin III. Davis: 1969. 273 p. Map.

Ciaccio, Leonard L., ed. WATER AND WATER POLLUTION HANDBOOK. 4 vols. New York: Marcel Dekker, 1972. 512 p.

> Compendium of lectures and papers focusing on the multidisciplinary aspects of environmental studies. The four volumes are divided into two parts: part 1, Environmental Systems; part 2, Chemical, Physical, Bacterial, Viral, Instrumental and Bioassay Techniques.

Clark, Chapin D. SURVEY OF OREGON'S WATER LAWS. Corvallis: Water Resources Research Institute, Oregon State University, 1974. 217 p.

Clark, Robert Emmet, ed. WATERS AND WATER RIGHTS: A TREATISE ON THE LAW OF WATERS AND ALLIED PROBLEMS. 6 vols. Indianapolis:

The Allen Smith Co., 1967. 3,468 p.

All six volumes are concerned with water pollution regulation. Of special interest is volume 3, WATER POLLUTION AND QUALITY CONTROLS, by Burton J. Gindler. This volume is comprised of the following chapters: "Water Quality Controls--the Problems and the Solutions," "Water Quality Controls Enforceable in Courts Under State Law," "State Administrative Regulation of Water Quality," and "Water-Quality Control in the Federal Jurisdiction."

Cleary, Edward J. THE ORSANCO STORY: WATER QUALITY MANAGEMENT IN THE OHIO VALLEY UNDER AN INTERSTATE COMPACT. Baltimore, Md.: The Johns Hopkins Press for Resources for the Future, 1967. 335 p. Charts.

Chapters on the planning, structure, administration, and legal scope of the Ohio River Valley Water Sanitation Commission.

Colorado. Water Pollution Control Commission. STREAM CLASSIFICATION FOR SURFACE WATERS OF COLORADO, INCLUDING: STREAM QUALITY STANDARDS, PLAN OF IMPLEMENTATION [AND] ENFORCEMENT PROCEDURES. Denver: 1967. Var. pag.

Connor, Larry J., et al. A SUMMARY OF STATE REGULATIONS PERTAINING TO ANIMAL WASTE MANAGEMENT IN THE NORTH CENTRAL REGION OF THE UNITED STATES. Agricultural Economics Report no. 193. East Lansing: Department of Agricultural Economics, Michigan State University, 1971. 25 p. Forms.

Cooke, Norman E., et al. WATER POLLUTION CONTROL: A DIGEST OF LEGISLATION AND REGULATIONS IN FORCE IN CANADA; REPORT PREPARED FOR CANADIAN INDUSTRIES LIMITED. 3d ed. Montreal: Canadian Council of Resource Ministers, 1967. Var. pag.

Craine, Lyle E. MARYLAND'S ROLE IN WATER RESOURCES DEVELOPMENT. College Park: Water Resources Study Committee, University of Maryland, 1966. 85 p.

Several sections on the state's regulation of waste discharge and water quality.

Danzig, Aaron L. MARINE POLLUTION--A FRAMEWORK FOR INTERNATIONAL CONTROL. Washington, D.C.: 1972. 65 p.

David Davies Memorial Institute of International Studies. WATER POLLUTION AS A WORLD PROBLEM: THE LEGAL, SCIENTIFIC AND POLITICAL ASPECTS. Conference on Law, Science and Politics: Water Pollution and its Effects Considered as a World Problem, Aberystwyth, Wales, 1970. London: Europa Publications, 1971. 240 p.

Includes three papers on law: "Nuclear and Thermal Waste Pollution: Some Legal Considerations," pp. 22-27; "Oil Pollution: The Law," pp. 77-83; and "Chemical and Pesticide Pollution: The Law," pp. 115-21. Also includes President Nixon's Message on Ocean Dumping, 1970; Arctic Waters Pollution Bill; and Convention on Wetlands of International Importance Especially as Waterfowl Habitat.

Degler, Stanley E., ed. OIL POLLUTION: PROBLEMS AND POLICIES. Washington, D.C.: Bureau of National Affairs, 1969. 142 p.

Largely concerned with national and international regulatory mechanisms. Chapters on the law generally, a report to the president, a multiagency oil and hazardous materials pollution contingency plan, and oil pollution acts of 1924 and 1961.

Deutsch, Morris. GROUND-WATER CONTAMINATION AND LEGAL CONTROLS IN MICHIGAN. U.S. Geological Survey Water Supply Paper no. 1691. Washington, D.C.: Government Printing Office, 1963. 79 p. Maps, diagrs.

Dewsnup, Richard L., and Jensen, Dallin W., eds. A SUMMARY DIGEST OF STATE WATER LAWS. Arlington, Va.: Government Printing Office, 1973. 826 p. Pap.

Part 1, pp. 1-73, traces the development of state water laws, the organization of state water agencies, and discusses laws relating to surface and ground waters. Part 2, pp. 75-809, describes in detail the water laws of each of the fifty states.

Ellis, Harold H., et al. WATER-USE LAW AND ADMINISTRATION IN WISCONSIN. Madison: Department of Law, University Extension, University of Wisconsin, 1970. xxv, 694 p. Illus., maps, port.

Includes one chapter on administration of pollution control laws.

Elmore, George Roy, Jr. GEORGIA LAWS, POLICIES AND PROGRAMS PERTAINING TO WATER AND RELATED LAND RESOURCES. Atlanta: Water Resources Center, Georgia Institute of Technology, 1967. 112 p. Illus.

Includes sections on water quality control, fish and game, forestry, soil conservation and parks, and summaries of court opinions.

Fallows, James M. THE WATER LORDS: RALPH NADER'S STUDY GROUP REPORT ON INDUSTRY AND ENVIRONMENTAL CRISIS IN SAVANNAH, GEORGIA. New York: Grossman, 1971. 294 p.

One chapter, "Bringing Down the Law," on the legal aspects of the Savannah situation.

Farnham, Henry P. THE LAW OF WATERS AND WATER RIGHTS. 3 vols. Rochester, N.Y.: The Lawyers Co-operative Publishing Co., 1904. 2,956 p.

Includes sections on the pollution of streams and springs in the chapters on fisheries, nuisances, rights in watercourses and sub-terranean waters.

Flaherty, Paul, and Thornett, Geoffrey M. LAWS AND REGULATIONS RE-LATING TO WATER POLLUTION CONTROL AFFECTING THE DISTRICT OF COLUMBIA. Washington, D.C.: Department of Public Health, Government of the District of Columbia, 1967.

Chapters on federal statutes, federal regulations, local statutes, District of Columbia regulations, and interstate compacts and re-gional agreements.

Fox, Irving K., ed. WATER RESOURCES LAW AND POLICY IN THE SOVIET UNION. Madison: The University of Wisconsin Press, 1971. 254 p.

Chapters on conservation of water resources and water pollution control.

Galbreath, Paul M. MARYLAND WATER LAW: WATER LAWS AND LEGAL PRINCIPLES AFFECTING THE USE OF WATER IN MARYLAND. College Park: Water Resources Study Committee, University of Maryland, 1965. 87 p.

Includes sections on legislation pertaining to pollution control, dams, and erosion control.

Garner, John F. THE LAW OF SEWERS AND DRAINS UNDER THE PUBLIC HEALTH ACT. London: Shaw, 1960. 186 p.

Garretson, A.H., et al., eds. THE LAW OF INTERNATIONAL DRAINAGE BASINS. Dobbs Ferry, N.Y.: Oceana Publications, 1967. 916 p.

A substantial chapter on pollution problems, which also arise in subsequent case studies.

Gilliam, Harold. BETWEEN THE DEVIL AND THE DEEP BLUE BAY: THE STRUGGLE TO SAVE SAN FRANCISCO BAY. San Francisco: Chronicle Books, 1969. 151 p. Photos.

Chronicles the Bay conservation movement and some of its legal battles and includes a section on the San Francisco Bay Plan.

Gold, Edgar. OIL POLLUTION: A SURVEY OF WORLDWIDE LEGISLATION. Arendal, Norway: Assuranceforeningen GARD (gjensidig), 1972?- . Irregular, loose-leaf.

Goldman, Charles R.; McEvoy, James III; and Richerson, Peter J. ENVIRON-MENTAL QUALITY AND WATER DEVELOPMENT. San Francisco: W.H. Free-man and Co., 1973. 510 p.

A variety of experts attempts to formulate basic principles of water resources planning through an exploration of technical, political, psychological, legislative, and administrative aspects of an historical conflict between environmental quality and water resources development. Numerous case studies of individual projects and protection plans are employed.

Grava, Sigurd. URBAN PLANNING ASPECTS OF WATER POLLUTION CONTROL. New York: Columbia University Press, 1969. 223 p.

Includes one chapter on administrative and regulatory aspects of water pollution control.

Grimes, Marcene D. GOVERNMENT AND NATURAL RESOURCES IN KANSAS: WATER. Lawrence: Governmental Research Center, University of Kansas, 1957. 87 p. Illus.

Harris, Richard W., et al. INTERSTATE ENVIRONMENTAL PROBLEMS; A GUIDE TO WATER POLLUTION AND WATER SCARCITY. Stanford, Calif.: Stanford Environmental Law Society, Stanford Law School, 1974. 161 p. Bib., fold. map, tables.

Heath, Milton S., Jr. A COMPARATIVE STUDY OF STATE WATER POLLUTION CONTROL LAWS AND PROGRAMS. Chapel Hill: University of North Carolina, Water Resources Research Institute, 1972. 265 p.

Detailed studies of programs in Maine, Michigan, New York, North Carolina, Pennsylvania, and Virginia. More general treatment of common law influences, interstate measures, federal programs, federal-state interaction. Appends a summary of relevant literature, North Carolina laws, and an example of a citizen suit.

Hines, N. William. NOR ANY DROP TO DRINK: PUBLIC REGULATION OF WATER QUALITY.

Three parts: "State Pollution Control Programs," "Interstate Arrangements for Pollution Control," and "The Federal Effort." Originally published in the IOWA LAW REVIEW 52 (October 1966): 186-235.

Hoeh, Roger Smith. WATER RESOURCES ADMINISTRATION IN DELAWARE. Newark: University of Delaware Water Resources Center, 1966. 175 p.

Includes sections on conservation and regulatory agencies and interstate pollution control.

Kates, Robert Clark. GEORGIA WATER LAW. Athens: Institute of Government, University of Georgia, 1969. 385 p.

A substantial chapter on water pollution in Georgia.

Kneese, Allen V. APPROACHES TO REGIONAL WATER QUALITY MANAGE-

MENT. Washington, D.C.: Resources for the Future, 1967. 47 p. Pap.

A presentation of information about and assessment of legal and institutional approaches to water quality management in various parts of the world.

Kneese, Allen V., and Bower, Blair T. MANAGING WATER QUALITY: ECONOMICS, TECHNOLOGY, INSTITUTIONS. Baltimore, Md.: The Johns Hopkins Press for Resources for the Future, 1968. 328 p.

Includes sections on regional agencies in the Ruhr area, England and Wales, France and the Delaware Basin.

Leonard, Robert L. AN ECONOMIC EVALUATION OF CONNECTICUT WATER LAW: WATER RIGHTS, PUBLIC WATER SUPPLY AND POLLUTION CONTROL. Storrs: University of Connecticut, 1970. 67 p.

The section on pollution control includes discussion of standard-setting under federal legislation, cost-sharing, regulatory powers and procedures, and economic incentives.

MacDonald, James B., and Beuscher, J.H. WATER RIGHTS. 2d ed. Madison, Wis.: American Printing and Publishing, 1973. 662 p. Pap., charts, photos.

Mack, Leslie E. WATER LAW IN ARKANSAS. Little Rock: Industrial Research and Extension Center, University of Arkansas, 1963. 74 p.

Includes a short section on pollution control laws.

McNickle, Roma K., ed. WATER: DEVELOPMENT, UTILIZATION, CONSERVATION. Western Resources Papers 1963. Boulder: University of Colorado Press, 1964. 244 p.

Papers presented at the fifth annual Western Resources Conference, 1963. Chapter on pollution control includes papers on Federal Water Pollution Control Act impact on the West, pesticides and water quality, and compatibility of recreation and water supply.

Maloney, Frank E., et al. WATER LAW AND ADMINISTRATION: THE FLORIDA EXPERIENCE. Gainesville: University of Florida Press, 1968. 488 p. Illus.

A comprehensive study of Florida's water law which includes the chapter "The Law and Administration of Pollution Control in Florida."

Martin, Roscoe C. WATER FOR NEW YORK: A STUDY IN STATE ADMINISTRATION OF WATER RESOURCES. Syracuse, N.Y.: Syracuse University Press, 1960. 264 p. Maps, tables.

Chapters on agency organization and programs, including water quality control, the law, and a case study of the pollution abatement program for the Buffalo River.

Maryland. University of. School of Law. LEGAL PROBLEMS OF COAL MINE RECLAMATION: A STUDY IN MARYLAND, OHIO, PENNSYLVANIA AND WEST VIRGINIA. Water Pollution Control Research Series. Washington, D.C.: Government Printing Office for the Environmental Protection Agency, 1972. 236 p.

Missouri. University of. Air and Water Pollution Control Conference. PROCEEDINGS. Columbia, Mo.: 1955- . Annual. Illus., maps, diagrs.

Murphy, Earl Finbar. WATER PURITY: A STUDY IN LEGAL CONTROL OF NATURAL RESOURCES. Madison: University of Wisconsin Press, 1961. 212 p.

> A study of the legal control of purity of water supply in Wisconsin, including water pollution control.

Nash, A.E. Keir, et al. OIL POLLUTION AND THE PUBLIC INTEREST: A STUDY OF THE SANTA BARBARA OIL SPILL. Berkeley: Institute of Government Studies, University of California, 1972. 157 p. Pap.

> A study of the institutional responses to the spill and the roles of the various actors. Chapters directly involving legal aspects on administering offshore oil, executive and legislative remedies, legal remedies, and the future.

National Association of Counties Research Foundation. COMMUNITY ACTION PROGRAM FOR WATER POLLUTION CONTROL. Washington, D.C.: 1967. 182 p. Photos., tables, charts.

> Includes the association's action guides on enabling legislation, the legal basis for federal, state, and local pollution control programs, and on organizing pollution control programs.

New York. State University of. Buffalo. Water Symposium, 1966. THE FRESH WATER OF NEW YORK STATE: ITS CONSERVATION AND USE. Dubuque, Iowa: William C. Brown Co., 1967. 255 p. Charts, photos.

> Includes the papers "Pollution of New York State Waters--What is Being Done, What Lies Ahead," "International Joint Commission Activities Related to New York State Water Resources," "Legal Aspects for Control of Intrastate, Interstate and International Waters," and "Legal Aspects of Control of Pollution of International Waters."

Newsom, George Harold, and Sherratt, J.G. WATER POLLUTION. Altrincham, Engl.: Sherratt, 1972. xii, 322 p.

> On law and legislation of Great Britain.

Nickolaieff, George A., ed. THE WATER CRISIS. The Reference Shelf, vol. 38, no. 6. New York: H.W. Wilson Co., 1967. 192 p.

A collection of articles, essays, and addresses, some of which deal with federal pollution control legislation, agencies, and standards.

Odell, Rice. THE SAVING OF SAN FRANCISCO BAY; A REPORT ON CITIZEN ACTION AND REGIONAL PLANNING. Washington, D.C.: The Conservation Foundation, 1972. 115 p. Photos.

The report is in part a history of recent legislation and agency actions relating to conservation of the Bay. Includes the McAteer-Petris Act, as amended through 1970, which created the San Francisco Bay Conservation and Development Commission.

Oregon State University. Water Resources Research Institute. WATER QUALITY CONTROL: SEMINAR PROCEEDINGS. Corvallis: 1965. 120 p.

One session entitled "Legal and Administrative Aspects."

Potomac Planning Force. THE POTOMAC: A REPORT ON ITS IMPERILED FUTURE AND A GUIDE FOR ITS ORDERLY DEVELOPMENT. Washington, D.C.: Government Printing Office for the Department of the Interior, 1967. 103 p. Photos.

Includes recommendations for regional cooperation through state, local and federal agencies and for the establishment of a Potomac Development Foundation.

Reis, Robert I. CONNECTICUT WATER LAW: JUDICIAL ALLOCATION OF WATER RESOURCES. Storrs: University of Connecticut, 1967. 215 p.

A study of court cases and decisions which includes sections on recreational uses, municipal liability for pollution, and reclamation.

Ross, Ernest F. STATE SUPERVISION OF MICHIGAN LOCAL GOVERNMENTS: THE WATER POLLUTION PROBLEM. Ann Arbor: Institute of Public Administration, University of Michigan, 1960. 64 p.

Ross, William M. OIL POLLUTION AS AN INTERNATIONAL PROBLEM: A STUDY OF PUGET SOUND AND THE STRAIT OF GEORGIA. Seattle: University of Washington Press, 1973. 279 p. Tables, maps, photos.

Deals extensively with legal remedies, jurisdiction, legal history, legislation and international organizations pertaining to oil pollution and its prevention, with emphasis on the regions noted in the title. Selected bibliography included.

Sax, Joseph L. WATER LAW: CASES AND COMMENTARY. Preliminary ed. Boulder, Colo.: Pruett Press, 1965. 442 p.

A study of the legal doctrines of water law designed for use in courses on the subject. Includes a chapter on water pollution and the law.

Schachter, Oscar, and Serwer, Daniel. MARINE POLLUTION PROBLEMS AND REMEDIES. UNITAR Research Reports, no. 4. New York: United Nations Institute for Training and Research, 1970. 41 p.

Schramm, Gunter, and Burt, Robert E., Jr. AN ANALYSIS OF FEDERAL WATER RESOURCE PLANNING AND EVALUATION PROCEDURES. Ann Arbor: University of Michigan School of Natural Resources, 1972. 106 p.

> The analysis focuses on the benefit-cost determination under current legislation and administrative procedure.

Scott, Stanley, and Bollens, John C. GOVERNMENT: REGIONAL ORGANI-ZATION FOR BAY CONSERVATION AND DEVELOPMENT. San Francisco: San Francisco Bay Conservation and Development Commission, 1967. 235 p.

> A background report on possible structures of regional government for the BCDC and their relative merits.

Sibthorp, M.M. OCEANIC POLLUTION: A SURVEY AND SOME SUGGES-TIONS FOR CONTROL. London: David Davies Memorial Institute of Inter-national Studies, 1969. 53 p.

Smith, Frank E., ed. LAND AND WATER: 1492-1900, CONSERVATION IN THE UNITED STATES: A DOCUMENTARY HISTORY. 2 vols. New York: Chelsea House, 1971. 1,561 p.

> A comprehensive documentation by congressional acts, documents and hearings, presidential orders, speeches and vetoes, reports of commissions, letters, articles, and other literature.

Stevens, R. Michael. GREEN LAND--CLEAN STREAMS: A REPORT OF THE CENTER FOR THE STUDY OF FEDERALISM ON THE BENEFICIAL USE OF WASTE WATER THROUGH LAND TREATMENT. Philadelphia: Center for the Study of Federalism, Temple University, 1972. 330 p.

Teclaff, Ludwick A. THE RIVER BASIN IN HISTORY AND LAW. The Hague, Netherlands: Martinus Nijoff, 1967. 228 p.

> An international appraisal which is most relevant to environmental law in sections on authorities involved in dam building.

Texas. University of. School of Law. PROCEEDINGS, WATER LAW CON-FERENCE. Austin, 1952- . Annual.

> Beginning with 1955, the proceedings of the conferences include papers on the legal aspects of water quality control.

Todd, David Keith, ed. THE WATER ENCYCLOPEDIA: A COMPENDIUM OF
USEFUL INFORMATION ON WATER RESOURCES. Port Washington, N.Y.:
Water Information Center, 1970. 559 p. Maps, charts, tables.

> Largely technical, but one chapter on federal, state, and inter-
> state agencies.

United Nations. Food and Agriculture Organization. POLLUTION: AN IN-
TERNATIONAL PROBLEM FOR FISHERIES. Rome: 1971. 85 p. (Originally
printed as pages 121-70 of THE STATE OF FOOD AND AGRICULTURE. World
Food Problems Series, no. 14. Rome: 1971.)

> Primarily deals with chemical, biological, and monitoring aspects
> of fresh water and ocean fisheries. One chapter, "Administration
> and Legal Aspects of Aquatic Pollution," treats national adminis-
> tration and legislation and international cooperation.

United Nations Secretariat. POLLUTION OF THE SEAS BY OIL. New York:
1956. 235 p. Tables.

> The study emphasizes physical aspects, but includes one part which
> summarizes legislation and regulations in a number of countries.

U.S. Department of Health, Education, and Welfare. CLEAN WATER, A
CHALLENGE TO THE NATION; SUMMARY REPORT: HIGHLIGHTS AND REC-
OMMENDATIONS OF THE NATIONAL CONFERENCE ON WATER POLLU-
TION, WASHINGTON, D.C., DECEMBER 1960. U.S.P.H.S. Publication
no. 816. Washington, D.C.: Government Printing Office, 1960. 41 p. Il-
lus.

_____. PROCEEDINGS. Washington, D.C.: Government Printing Office,
1961. 607 p. Maps, tables.

> Includes papers on the activities of federal, state, interstate and
> local agencies, and the legal aspects of water pollution.

U.S. Department of State and Department of the Interior. WATER FOR PEACE.
8 vols. International Conference on Water for Peace, Washington, D.C.,
1967. Washington, D.C.: Government Printing Office, 1968. 7,666 p.

> Includes 600 technical papers submitted at the conference sponsored
> by the Departments of State and the Interior. Papers relevant to ad-
> ministrative and legislative aspects in sections on pollution control,
> organization, international agencies, governmental agencies, plan-
> ning water programs, concepts and procedures, and water quality
> control.

U.S. Department of the Interior. Water Resources Scientific Information Center. LEGAL ASPECTS OF WATER POLLUTION IN NEW ENGLAND: A BIB-
LIOGRAPHY. Washington, D.C.: 1971. Unpaged.

Willrich, Ted L., and Hines, William N., eds. WATER POLLUTION CON-
TROL AND ABATEMENT. Ames: Iowa State University Press, 1967. 194 p.
Photos., charts.

> Papers, several of which deal with legal aspects of water pollu-
> tion control in Iowa, presented at an Iowa Water Resources Pollu-
> tion Control and Abatement Seminar held at Iowa State University,
> November 9-11, 1965.

Wisdom, A.S. THE LAW ON THE POLLUTION OF WATERS. 2d ed. London: Shaw and Sons, 1966. 409 p.

> Covers the laws of England and Wales as of March 1966.

_____. WATER RIGHTS, INCLUDING FISHING RIGHTS. Longson: Oyez
Publications, 1969. 138 p.

> Includes sections on rights to water quality and of fishery.

Wright, Gordon P. DESIGNING WATER POLLUTION DETECTION SYSTEMS;
ENVIRONMENTAL LAW ENFORCEMENT ON THE U.S. COASTAL WATERS
AND THE GREAT LAKES. Cambridge, Mass.: Ballinger Publishing Co., 1974.
225 p.

# Government Documents--Federal

Federal Water Pollution Control Administration. REPORT OF THE COMMITTEE
ON WATER QUALITY CRITERIA. Washington, D.C.: Department of the Interior, 1968. 234 p.

U.S. Ad Hoc Advisory Committee for State Legislation on Planning of Urban
Water Supply and Sewerage Systems. RECOMMENDED STATE LEGISLATION
AND REGULATIONS. Washington, D.C.: Department of Health, Education,
and Welfare, Public Health Service, Division of Environmental Engineering, for
sale by the Government Printing Office, 1965. 109 p. (FS 2.6/2:WW 29/5.)

U.S. Advisory Commission on Intergovernmental Relations. INTERGOVERN-
MENTAL RESPONSIBILITIES FOR WATER SUPPLY AND SEWAGE DISPOSAL IN
METROPOLITAN AREAS. Washington, D.C.: Government Printing Office,
1962. 135 p.

U.S. Congress. Conference Committees, 1965. WATER QUALITY ACT OF
1965; CONFERENCE REPORT TO ACCOMPANY S. 4. 89th Cong., 1st sess.,
House Report no. 1022. Washington, D.C.: Government Printing Office,
1965. 14 p.

U.S. Congress. Conference Committees, 1966. CLEAN WATERS RESTORATION
ACT OF 1966; CONFERENCE REPORT TO ACCOMPANY S. 2947. 89th Cong.,

2d sess., House Report no. 2289. Washington, D.C.: Government Printing Office, 1966. 23 p.

U.S. Congress. Conference Committees, 1970. WATER QUALITY IMPROVE-MENT ACT OF 1970; CONFERENCE REPORT TO ACCOMPANY H.R. 4148. 91st Cong., 2d sess., House Report no. 91-940. Washington, D.C.: Government Printing Office, 1970. 109 p.

U.S. Congress. House. Committee on Foreign Affairs. GREAT LAKES BASIN COMPACT. HEARINGS . . . ON H.R. 4314 [and others] GRANTING THE CONSENT AND APPROVAL OF CONGRESS TO A GREAT LAKES BASIN COM-PACT. 85th Cong., 1st and 2d sess. Washington, D.C.: Government Print-ing Office, 1958. 121 p.

U.S. Congress. House. Committee on Government Operations. Conservation and Natural Resources Subcommittee. MERCURY POLLUTION AND ENFORCE-MENT OF THE REFUSE ACT OF 1899. HEARING. . . . 92d Cong., 1st sess. Washington, D.C.: Government Printing Office, 1971. 1,089 p. Il-lus.

_____. PHOSPHATES AND PHOSPHATE SUBSTITUTES IN DETERGENTS. HEARINGS . . . 2 vols. 92d Cong., 1st sess. Washington, D.C.: Gov-ernment Printing Office, 1972. 844 p. Illus.

_____. QUI TAM ACTIONS AND THE 1899 REFUSE ACT: CITIZEN LAW-SUITS AGAINST POLLUTERS OF THE NATION'S WATERWAYS. 91st Cong., 2d sess. Washington, D.C.: Government Printing Office, 1970. 26 p.

U.S. Congress. House. Committee on Government Operations. Executive and Legislative Reorganization Subcommittee. REORGANIZATION PLAN No. 2 OF 1966 (WATER POLLUTION CONTROL). HEARINGS. . . . 89th Cong., 2d sess. Washington, D.C.: Government Printing Office, 1966. 111 p.

U.S. Congress. House. Committee on Merchant Marine and Fisheries. Sub-committee on Coast Guard, Coast and Geodetic Survey, and Navigation. COAST GUARD LEGISLATION, 1966. HEARINGS. . . . 89th Cong., 2d sess. Washington, D.C.: Government Printing Office, 1966. 56 p.

U.S. Congress. House. Committee on Public Works. EXTENSION OF WATER POLLUTION CONTROL ACT. HEARINGS BEFORE THE SUBCOMMITTEE ON RIVERS AND HARBORS OF THE COMMITTEE ON PUBLIC WORKS ON H.R. 6856, A BILL TO EXTEND THE DURATION OF THE WATER POLLUTION CON-TROL ACT. 82d Cong., 2d sess. Washington, D.C.: Government Printing Office, 1952. 82 p. Maps, diagrs.

_____. FEDERAL WATER POLLUTION CONTROL. HEARINGS . . . ON H.R. 4036, TO AMEND THE FEDERAL WATER POLLUTION CONTROL ACT; TO PRO-

VIDE FOR A MORE EFFECTIVE PROGRAM OF WATER POLLUTION CONTROL. . . . 87th Cong., 1st sess. Washington, D.C.: Government Printing Office, 1961. 349 p. Diagrs., tables.

_____. FEDERAL WATER POLLUTION CONTROL ACT. AMENDMENTS OF 1961; REPORT TO ACCOMPANY H.R. 6441, A BILL TO AMEND THE FEDERAL WATER POLLUTION CONTROL ACT TO PROVIDE FOR A MORE EFFECTIVE PROGRAM OF WATER POLLUTION CONTROL, TOGETHER WITH MINORITY VIEWS. 87th Cong., 1st sess. House Report no. 306. Washington, D.C.: Government Printing Office, 1961. 44 p. Table.

_____. FEDERAL WATER POLLUTION CONTROL ACT AMENDMENTS; REPORT TO ACCOMPANY S. 649. 88th Cong., 2d sess., House Report no. 1885. Washington, D.C.: Government Printing Office, 1964. 29 p.

_____. FEDERAL WATER POLLUTION CONTROL ACT AMENDMENTS, 1968. HEARINGS . . . ON H.R. 15906 AND RELATED BILLS. . . . 90th Cong., 2d sess. Washington, D.C.: Government Printing Office, 1968. 718 p. Illus.

_____. FEDERAL WATER POLLUTION CONTROL ACT AMENDMENTS, 1969. HEARINGS . . . ON H.R. 4148 AND RELATED BILLS. 91st Cong., 1st sess. Washington, D.C.: Government Printing Office, 1969. 677 p. Illus.

_____. FEDERAL WATER POLLUTION CONTROL ACT AMENDMENTS OF 1961. COMPARATIVE PRINT SHOWING CHANGES IN THE FEDERAL WATER POLLUTION CONTROL ACT AS AGREED TO IN COMMITTEE OF CONFERENCE ON H.R. 6441. 87th Cong., 1st sess. Washington, D.C.: Government Printing Office, 1961. 6 p.

_____. FEDERAL WATER POLLUTION CONTROL ACT AMENDMENTS OF 1972; REPORT, WITH ADDITIONAL AND SUPPLEMENTAL VIEWS [on] H.R. 11896. . . . 92d Cong., 2d sess., House Report no. 92-911. Washington, D.C.: Government Printing Office, 1972. 424 p.

_____. FEDERAL WATER POLLUTION CONTROL ACT, 1966. HEARINGS . . . H.R. 13104 AND H.R. 16076, AND RELATED BILLS. 89th Cong., 2d sess. Washington, D.C.: Government Printing Office, 1966. 333 p. Illus., maps.

_____. LAWS OF THE UNITED STATES RELATING TO WATER POLLUTION CONTROL AND ENVIRONMENTAL QUALITY. 93d Cong., 1st sess. Washington, D.C.: Government Printing Office, 1970. 265 p.

_____. LAWS OF THE UNITED STATES RELATING TO WATER POLLUTION

CONTROL AND ENVIRONMENTAL QUALITY. 2d ed. 92d Cong., 2d sess. Washington, D.C.: Government Printing Office, 1973. 522 p.

_____. REDUCTION OF POLLUTION IN THE POTOMAC RIVER. HEARING BEFORE THE SUBCOMMITTEE ON RIVERS AND HARBORS . . . ON H.R. 7196 [and others] TO AUTHORIZE THE CONSTRUCTION OF WASTE DISPOSAL FACILITIES TO REDUCE THE POLLUTION OF THE POTOMAC RIVER FROM STORM WATER OVERFLOWS, AND FOR OTHER PURPOSES. 86th Cong., 2d sess. Washington, D.C.: Government Printing Office, 1960. 41 p. Map.

_____. SECTION-BY-SECTION ANALYSIS OF H.R. 13104: CLEAN RIVERS RESTORATION ACT OF 1966, AS SUBMITTED IN DRAFT TO THE COMMITTEE ON PUBLIC WORKS. 89th Cong., 2d sess. Washington, D.C.: Government Printing Office, 1966. 11 p.

_____. WATER POLLUTION CONTROL. 89th Cong., 2d sess. Washington, D.C.: Government Printing Office, 1966. 97 p. Pap.

Report of Committee on Public Works with supplementary and additional views on H.R. 16076.

_____. WATER POLLUTION CONTROL: REPORT WITH SUPPLEMENTARY AND ADDITIONAL VIEWS, ON H.R. 16076, TO AMEND THE FEDERAL WATER POLLUTION CONTROL ACT. 89th Cong., 2d sess., House Report no. 2021. Washington, D.C.: Government Printing Office, 1966. 97 p.

_____. WATER POLLUTION CONTROL ACT AMENDMENTS. HEARINGS . . . ON S. 649 [and Others]. 88th Cong., 1st and 2d sess. Washington, D.C.: Government Printing Office, 1964. 949 p. Illus., maps.

_____. WATER POLLUTION CONTROL HEARINGS ON WATER QUALITY ACT OF 1965. HEARINGS . . . ON H.R. 3988, S. 4, AND RELATED BILLS. 89th Cong., 1st sess. Washington, D.C.: Government Printing Office, 1965. 399 p.

_____. WATER POLLUTION CONTROL LEGISLATION--1971 (H.R. 11896, H.R. 11895). HEARINGS. . . . 92d Cong., 1st sess. Washington, D.C.: Government Printing Office, 1972. 972 p.

_____. WATER POLLUTION CONTROL LEGISLATION--1971 (OVERSIGHT OF EXISTING PROGRAM). HEARINGS. . . . 92d Cong., 1st sess. Washington, D.C.: Government Printing Office, 1971. 715 p. Illus.

_____. WATER POLLUTION CONTROL LEGISLATION--1971 (PROPOSED AMENDMENTS TO EXISTING LEGISLATION). HEARINGS. . . . 92d Cong., 1st sess. Washington, D.C.: Government Printing Office, 1971. 2,435 p. Illus.

_____. WATER QUALITY ACT OF 1965; REPORT TO ACCOMPANY S. 4. 88th Cong., 1st sess., House Report no. 215. Washington, D.C.: Government Printing Office, 1965. 29 p.

U.S. Congress. House. Committee on the Judiciary. U.S. DISTRICT COURT JURISDICTION AND VENUE IN INTERSTATE RIVER POLLUTION COMPACT CASES. HEARINGS BEFORE SUBCOMMITTEE NO. 3 . . . ON H.R. 6717, A BILL PROVIDING THAT THE UNITED STATES DISTRICT COURTS SHALL HAVE JURISDICTION OF CERTAIN CASES INVOLVING POLLUTION OF INTERSTATE RIVER SYSTEMS, AND PROVIDING FOR VENUE THEREOF. 87th Cong., 1st sess. Washington, D.C.: Government Printing Office, 1962. 19 p.

U.S. Congress. Senate. Committee on Commerce. Subcommittee on Oceans and Atmosphere. HEARINGS . . . [on S. 1067, S. 1070, and S. 1351 ocean pollution]. 93d Cong., 1st sess. Washington, D.C.: Government Printing Office, 1974. 393 p.

U.S. Congress. Senate. Committee on Government Operations. Subcommittee on Executive Reorganization. REORGANIZATION PLAN NO. 2 OF 1966 (WATER POLLUTION CONTROL). HEARINGS. . . . 89 Cong., 2d sess. Washington, D.C.: Government Printing Office, 1966. 99 p.

U.S. Congress. Senate. Committee on Public Works. FEDERAL WATER POLLUTION CONTROL ACT AMENDMENTS AND CLEAN RIVERS RES-TORATION ACT OF 1966; REPORT TO ACCOMPANY S. 2947. 89th Cong., 2d sess., Senate Report no. 1367. Washington, D.C.: Government Printing Office, 1966. 49 p.

_____. FEDERAL WATER POLLUTION CONTROL ACT AMENDMENTS OF 1971; REPORT, TOGETHER WITH SUPPLEMENTAL VIEWS TO ACCOMPANY S. 2770. 92d Cong., 1st sess., Senate Report no. 92-414. Washington, D.C.: Government Printing Office, 1971. 120 p.

_____. WATER POLLUTION CONTROL. HEARINGS BEFORE A SPECIAL SUBCOMMITTEE ON AIR AND WATER POLLUTION . . . ON S. 649 [and others]. . . . 88th Cong., 1st sess. Washington, D.C.: Government Printing Office, 1963. 716 p. Illus.

_____. WATER POLLUTION CONTROL. HEARINGS BEFORE A SUBCOM-MITTEE . . . ON S. 45 [and others] AMENDING THE FEDERAL WATER POL-LUTION CONTROL ACT TO PROVIDE FOR A MORE EFFECTIVE PROGRAM OF WATER POLLUTION CONTROL. 87th Cong., 1st sess. Washington, D.C.: Government Printing Office, 1961. 288 p. Maps, diagrs., tables.

U.S. Congress. Senate. Committee on Public Works. Special Subcommittee on Air and Water Pollution. FEDERAL INSTALLATIONS, FACILITIES, AND EQUIPMENT POLLUTION CONTROL ACT. HEARINGS . . . ON S. 560.

89th Cong., 1st sess. Washington, D.C.: Government Printing Office, 1965. 172 p. Maps.

_____. STEPS TOWARD CLEAN WATER; REPORT. Washington, D.C.: Government Printing Office, 1966. 22 p.

_____. WATER POLLUTION CONTROL LEGISLATION. HEARINGS. . . . 7 vols. 92d Cong., 1st sess. Washington, D.C.: Government Printing Office, 1971. 3,616 p. Illus.

_____. WATER POLLUTION, 1966. HEARINGS . . . ON S. 2947 [and others]. 89th Cong., 2d sess. Washington, D.C.: Government Printing Office, 1966. 666 p. Illus., map.

_____. WATER POLLUTION, 1969. HEARINGS . . . ON S. 7 AND S. 544. 91st Cong., 1st sess. Washington, D.C.: Government Printing Office, 1969. Pp. 919-1584. Map.

_____. WATER POLLUTION--1970. HEARINGS, ON S. 3687. S. 3468, S. 3470, S. 3471, S. 3472, S. 3181, S. 3484, S. 3500, S. 3507, S. 3614, S. 3688, AND S. 3697. . . . 91st Cong., 2d sess. Washington, D.C.: Government Printing Office, 1970. Pp. 903-1379.

_____. WATER QUALITY ACT OF 1965. HEARINGS. . . . 89th Cong., 1st sess. Washington, D.C.: Government Printing Office, 1965. 139 p. Map.

U.S. Congress. Senate. Committee on the Judiciary. GREAT LAKES BASIN COMPACT. HEARINGS BEFORE A SUBCOMMITTEE . . . ON S. 1416, GRANTING THE CONSENT AND APPROVAL OF CONGRESS TO A GREAT LAKES BASIN COMPACT, AND FOR RELATED PURPOSES. 85th Cong., 2d sess. Washington, D.C.: Government Printing Office, 1958. 133 p.

U.S. Council on Environmental Quality. OCEAN DUMPING: A NATIONAL POLICY; A REPORT TO THE PRESIDENT. Washington, D.C.: Government Printing Office, 1970. 45 p.

U.S. Department of the Interior. THE NATIONAL ESTUARINE POLLUTION STUDY, A REPORT TO THE CONGRESS. Washington, D.C.: Government Printing Office, 1970. 633 p.

> A broad study of estuarine zones in the United States, including chapters on the responsibilities, laws, and programs of local, state and federal governments and proposed amendments to the Federal Water Pollution Control Act.

U.S. Department of the Interior. Sport Fisheries and Wildlife Bureau. NA-

TIONAL ESTUARY STUDY. 7 vols. Washington, D.C.: Government Printing Office, 1970. Approx. 1,111 p. Pap.

> Volume 6 of the study includes "Federal, State and Local Laws and Tax Policies Affecting the Use of Estuarine Resources" with sections on land controls, transportation, fish and wildlife, pollution control, resources, recreation and shoreline protection.

U.S. Environmental Protection Agency. ACTION FOR ENVIRONMENTAL QUALITY: STANDARDS AND ENFORCEMENT FOR AIR AND WATER POLLUTION CONTROL. Washington, D.C.: Government Printing Office, 1973. 21 p. Pap., photos.

U.S. General Accounting Office. CONTROLLING INDUSTRIAL WATER POLLUTION--PROGRESS AND PROBLEMS; REPORT TO THE CONGRESS [on the] FEDERAL WATER QUALITY ADMINISTRATION, DEPARTMENT OF INTERIOR, BY THE COMPTROLLER GENERAL OF THE UNITED STATES. Washington, D.C.: Government Printing Office, 1970. 72 p.

_____. NEED FOR IMPROVING PROCEDURES TO ENSURE COMPLIANCE WITH LAW REGARDING DEPOSITION OF INDUSTRIAL WASTE SOLIDS INTO NAVIGABLE WATERS, CORPS OF ENGINEERS (CIVIL FUNCTIONS) DEPARTMENT OF THE ARMY; REPORT TO THE CONGRESS OF THE UNITED STATES BY THE COMPTROLLER GENERAL OF THE UNITED STATES. Washington, D.C.: Government Printing Office, 1966. 25 p.

_____. WATER POLLUTION ABATEMENT PROGRAM: ASSESSMENT OF FEDERAL AND STATE ENFORCEMENT EFFORTS; REPORT TO THE CONGRESS [on the] ENVIRONMENTAL PROTECTION AGENCY BY THE COMPTROLLER GENERAL OF THE UNITED STATES. Washington, D.C.: Government Printing Office, 1972. 55 p.

U.S. Laws and Statutes. COMPILATION OF SELECTED PUBLIC HEALTH LAWS, INCLUDING PARTICULARLY THE PUBLIC HEALTH SERVICE ACT, THE FEDERAL WATER POLLUTION CONTROL ACT, AND ACTS RELATING TO AIR POLLUTION. Washington, D.C.: Government Printing Office, 1963. 157 p.

_____. LAWS OF THE UNITED STATES RELATING TO WATER POLLUTION CONTROL AND ENVIRONMENTAL QUALITY. Compiled by the Committee on Public Works, House of Representatives. Washington, D.C.: Government Printing Office, 1970. 265 p.

U.S. Library of Congress. Congressional Research Service. Environmental Policy Division. A LEGISLATIVE HISTORY OF THE WATER POLLUTION CONTROL ACT AMENDMENTS OF 1972. 2 vols. Washington, D.C.: Government Printing Office, 1973. 1,766 p. Pap.

U.S. National Water Commission. A SUMMARY-DIGEST OF STATE WATER LAWS. Edited by R.L. Dewsnup and D.W. Jensen. Washington, D.C.: Government Printing Office, 1973. 826 p. Pap.

_____. A SUMMARY-DIGEST OF THE FEDERAL WATER LAWS AND PROGRAMS. Edited by J.L. De Weerdt and P.M. Glick. Washington, D.C.: Government Printing Office, 1973. 205 p. Pap.

U.S. President's Water Resources Council. POLICIES, STANDARDS, AND PROCEDURES IN THE FORMULATION, EVALUATION, AND REVIEW OF PLANS FOR USE AND DEVELOPMENT OF WATER AND RELATED LAND RESOURCES. Washington, D.C.: Government Printing Office, 1962. 13 p. Pap.

U.S. President's Water Resources Policy Commission. REPORT. 3 vols. Washington, D.C.: Government Printing Office, 1960. 2,023 p. Maps, photos., charts, tables.

> Volume 1, A WATER POLICY FOR THE AMERICAN PEOPLE, contains a chapter on pollution control including the section "Federal Authority under the 1948 Statute," and volume 3, WATER RESOURCES LAW, deals at length with reclamation and power and briefly with water quality control.

U.S. Public Health Service. WATER POLLUTION SERIES. Washington, D.C.: Government Printing Office, 1951- . Illus.

_____. WATER QUALITY MANAGEMENT. 86th Cong., 2d sess., Publication no. 24. Washington, D.C.: Government Printing Office, 1960. 14 p.

U.S. Public Health Service. Division of Water Pollution Control. GUIDE TO SOURCE MATERIAL ON WATER POLLUTION CONTROL. Washington, D.C.: Government Printing Office, 1950. 14 p. Illus.

U.S. Public Health Service. Division of Water Supply and Pollution Control. PROTECTING OUR WATER RESOURCES, THE FEDERAL WATER POLLUTION CONTROL PROGRAM. Public Health Service Publication no. 950. Washington, D.C.: Government Printing Office, 1962. 27 p. Illus., maps.

_____. SUGGESTED STATE WATER POLLUTION CONTROL ACT AND EXPLANATORY STATEMENT. Public Health Service Publication no. 49. Washington, D.C.: Government Printing Office, 1950. 23 p.

_____. SYMPOSIUM ON STREAMFLOW REGULATION FOR QUALITY CONTROL. Washington, D.C.: Government Printing Office, 1965. 400 p. Photos., graphs.

Largely technical, but sections on the water quality responsibilities, especially relating to streamflow, of the Public Health Service, Corps of Engineers, Bureau of Reclamation, and Federal Power Commission.

U.S. Treaties, 1963-1969. Lyndon B. Johnson. SEWAGE DISPOSAL SYSTEM. AGREEMENT BETWEEN THE UNITED STATES OF AMERICA AND CANADA, EFFECTED BY EXCHANGE OF NOTES DATED AT OTTAWA JANUARY 13, APRIL 22, AND JUNE 9, 1966. Treaties and Other International Acts Series no. 6037. Washington, D.C.: Government Printing Office, 1966. 3 p.

## Government Documents--State

California. Legislature. Assembly. Interim Committee on Water. THE LEGISLATIVE ACTION PROGRAM FOR LAKE TAHOE POLLUTION CONTROL. Sacramento: July 1966. 24 p. Pap.

Illinois. Pollution Control Board. WATER POLLUTION REGULATIONS OF ILLINOIS. Springfield: State of Illinois Environmental Protection Agency, 1972. 36 p.

Interstate Commission on the Potomac River Basin. THE POTOMAC: WATER QUALITY PLANNING. New Carrolton, Md.: 1973. 32 p. Pap., graphs, charts.

> The proceedings of the Water Quality Planning Seminar which includes presentations on legislative policy and planning and on the proposed Potomac River Basin Compact.

Kentucky. Laws and Statutes. THE LAWS GOVERNING THE MINING OF COAL AND CLAY, THE DRILLING OF OIL, GAS AND SALT WATER WELLS THROUGH SEAMS OF COAL IN THE STATE OF KENTUCKY, KENTUCKY REVISED STATUTES, CHAPTERS 351, 352, 353, and 354. New York: Bobbs-Merrill Co., 1973. Pp. 561-639.

Maryland. Laws and Statutes. WATER POLLUTION CONTROL LAW, 1959. Baltimore, Md.: Water Pollution Control Commission, 1959. 22 p. Map.

Maryland. Water Resources Commission. WATER RESOURCES REGULATIONS AND RULES OF PROCEDURE. Annapolis: 1966. 93 p.

> One section on pollution abatement regulations.

Massachusetts. Division of Water Pollution Control. RULES AND REGULATIONS FOR ADJUDICATORY PROCEEDINGS. Boston: 1967. 18 p.

Massachusetts. General Court. Senate. Select Committee Established to Investigate and Study Water Pollution in Rivers and River Networks in Massachusetts. REPORT. Boston: 1966. 77 p. Pap.

Includes acts providing for a water pollution control agency, an accelerated water pollution control program, and tax incentives for the construction and improvement of industrial waste treatment facilities.

Michigan. Laws and Statutes. LAWS RELATING TO WATER. Lansing: 1966. 415 p. Pap.

Includes statutes relating to conservation, water pollution, and soil conservation.

New York. Water Resources Commission. THE COORDINATED PROGRAM FOR THE WATER RESOURCES OF NEW YORK STATE. Albany: 1966. 79 p. Charts, maps.

Explanation of agency functions, structures and interactions, and summaries of relevant legislation.

Texas. Water Quality Board. RULES OF THE TEXAS WATER QUALITY BOARD. Austin: 1968. 75 p.

Virginia. Laws and Statutes. STATE WATER CONTROL LAW, CHAPTER 2, TITLE 62, CODE OF VIRGINIA, 1950, WITH ALL AMENDMENTS MADE BY SUBSEQUENT GENERAL ASSEMBLIES. Richmond: Virginia Division of Purchasor and Print, 1964. 13 p.

Washington. Laws and Statutes. WATER POLLUTION CONTROL LAWS. Olympia: Water Pollution Control Commission, 1968. 33 p.

_____. WATER POLLUTION CONTROL LAWS. Olympia: Department of Ecology, 1970. 28 p.

Washington. Water Pollution Control Commission. IMPLEMENTATION AND ENFORCEMENT PLAN FOR INTERSTATE AND COASTAL WATERS, STATE OF WASHINGTON. Olympia: 1967. 146 p. Illus., maps.

_____. A REGULATION RELATING TO WATER QUALITY STANDARDS FOR INTERSTATE AND COASTAL WATERS OF THE STATE OF WASHINGTON AND A PLAN FOR IMPLEMENTATION AND ENFORCEMENT OF SUCH STANDARDS. Olympia: 1967. 23 p. Pap.

## Government Documents--Foreign

Great Britain. CONVENTION FOR THE PREVENTION OF MARINE POLLUTION BY DUMPING FROM SHIPS AND AIRCRAFT, OSLO, FEB. 15, 1972.

London: H.M. Stationery Office, 1972. 12 p. Pap.

> Signatories are Federal Republic of Germany, Belgium, Denmark, Spain, Finland, France, United Kingdom, Iceland, Norway, Netherlands, Portugal, and Sweden.

## NOISE POLLUTION

Baron, Robert Alex. THE TYRANNY OF NOISE. New York: St. Martins Press, 1970. 294 p.

> The chapter "No Legal Recourse" deals with the structure and historical development of local noise control legislation.

Berland, Theodore. THE FIGHT FOR QUIET. Englewood Cliffs, N.J.: Prentice-Hall, 1970. 370 p.

> Not primarily legal, but includes one short chapter entitled "Legal Anti-Aircraft Weapons."

_____. NOISE--THE THIRD POLLUTION. Public Affairs Pamphlet no. 449. New York: The Public Affairs Committee, 1970. 20 p. Pap.

> A pamphlet on the general problem with a short section on relevant laws.

Bragdon, Clifford R. NOISE POLLUTION: THE UNQUIET CRISIS. Philadelphia: University of Pennsylvania Press, 1971. xxii, 280 p. Illus.

Chalupnik, James D., ed. TRANSPORTATION NOISES: A SYMPOSIUM ON ACCEPTABILITY CRITERIA. Seattle: University of Washington Press, 1970. 358 p.

> One address deals with legislative aspects of noise control: "Criteria for Legislation" by Theodore R. Kupferman, State Supreme Court Justice, State of New York.

Dickerson, David O. TRANSPORTATION NOISE POLLUTION: CONTROL AND ABATEMENT. Springfield, Va.: National Technical Information Service, 1970. 190 p.

> A report resulting from a systems design research program at NASA Langley Research Center. One short chapter concerns responsibility for noise abatement, common law remedies, federal, state and local powers, airport noise ordinances, zoning and land-use planning, sonic boom, and recommended legislation.

Duerdon, C. NOISE ABATEMENT. London: Butterworths, 1970. 280 p.

> A textbook which largely deals with technical and investigatory

aspects of noise abatement. The chapter "Legislation" discusses local acts, the Noise Abatement Act of 1960 and several court cases. Appended are local and national statutes of England and summaries of foreign legislation.

Harris, Cyril M., ed. HANDBOOK OF NOISE CONTROL. New York: Mc Graw-Hill Book Co., 1957. Var. pag.

Contributions by experts in the many fields concerned with noise control. Noise regulation and liability are treated in "Legal Liability for Loss of Hearing," "Legal Aspects of the Aircraft Noise Problem," "Anti-Noise Ordinances," and "Noise Control Requirements in Building Codes."

Hildebrand, James L., ed. NOISE POLLUTION AND THE LAW. Buffalo, N.Y.: W.S. Hein, 1970. 354 p. Illus.

A series of articles which define the problem, discuss the development of noise law, and emphasize the law related to aircraft noise, specifically noise as a taking of property, noise litigation, legal theories for recovery for ground damage due to sonic boom, tort liability for sonic booms, noise from supersonic jet transports, and the Federal Aircraft Noise Abatement Act.

King, Richard L. AIRPORT NOISE POLLUTION: A BIBLIOGRAPHY OF ITS EFFECTS ON PEOPLE AND PROPERTY. Metuchen, N.J.: The Scarecrow Press, 1973. 380 p.

Includes sections on legal aspects and government agencies concerned with the problem.

McNairn, Colin H. AIRPORT NOISE POLLUTION: THE PROBLEM AND THE REGULATORY RESPONSE. University of Toronto-York University Joint Program in Transportation. Transportation Reprint no. 6. Toronto: Toronto-York University, 1972. 655 p.

Reprinted from the CANADIAN BAR REVIEW 50 (May 1972): 249-94.

NOISE REGULATION REPORTER. Washington, D.C.: Bureau of National Affairs, 1974- . Biweekly. Loose-leaf.

A reference service covering noise abatement and control regulations, legislation, and corrective methods.

Stephen, John E., and Tondell, Lyman M., Jr. LEGAL AND RELATED ASPECTS OF AIRCRAFT NOISE REGULATION: PAPERS PRESENTED AT THE INTERNATIONAL CONFERENCE ON THE REDUCTION OF NOISE AND DISTURBANCE CAUSED BY CIVIL AIRCRAFT, LONDON, ENGLAND, NOVEM-

BER 22-30, 1966. Washington, D.C.: Government Printing Office, 1967. 206 p. Illus.

## Government Documents

Tennessee. General Assembly. Legislative Council Committee. STUDY ON NOISE AND AIR POLLUTION LAWS AND REFUSE DUMPING, 1970; FINAL REPORT. Nashville: 1970. 175 p.

U.S. Congress. House. Committee on Interstate and Foreign Commerce. LEG-ISLATIVE HISTORY OF NOISE CONTROL ACT OF 1972 (H.R. 92-842 and H.R. 11021, AS REPORTED). Washington, D.C.: Government Printing Office, 1972. 73 p.

U.S. Congress. House. Committee on Interstate and Foreign Commerce. Sub-committee on Public Health and Environment. NOISE CONTROL. HEARINGS. . . . 92 Cong., 1st sess. Washington, D.C.: Government Printing Of-fice, 1971. 504 p. Illus.

U.S. Congress. Senate. Committee on Commerce. Subcommittee on the En-vironment. NOISE CONTROL ACT OF 1971 AND AMENDMENTS. HEARINGS . . . ON S. 1016 . . . AND S. 1566 . . . . 2 vols. 92d Cong., 1st sess. Washington, D.C.: Government Printing Office, 1971-72. 984 p. Il-lus.

U.S. Congress. Senate. Committee on Public Works. Subcommittee on Air and Water Pollution. NOISE POLLUTION. HEARINGS . . . ON S. 1016 . . . S. 3342 . . . [and] H.R. 11021. . . . 92d Cong., 2d sess. Wash-ington, D.C.: Government Printing Office, 1972. 604 p. Illus.

U.S. Environmental Protection Agency. AN ASSESSMENT OF NOISE CON-CERN IN OTHER NATIONS. 2 vols. Washington, D.C.: Government Print-ing Office, 1971. 528 p. Charts, pap.

> A multidisciplinary study. Includes the sections "Significant Noise-Related Organizations and Conferences" and "The Laws on Noise."

_____. LAWS AND REGULATORY SCHEMES FOR NOISE ABATEMENT. Washington, D.C.: Government Printing Office, 1971. 616 p. Pap., charts.

> The study contains four sections: "Current Governmental Noise Reg-ulatory Schemes," "Analysis of Existing Legal Regulatory Structure for Noise Abatement and Control," "The Effectiveness of Existing Noise Control Regulation," "Proposals and Problems in the Regula-tion and Abatement of Noise." Includes tables of noise regula-tions by locality, state, and jurisdictional level.

_____. LEGAL COMPILATION, VOL. 1: NOISE. Washington, D.C.: Government Printing Office, 1973. 496 p. Illus.

A compilation of the EPA's legal authority as it relates to noise pollution control. Seven other volumes on types of pollution are forthcoming.

_____. NOISE SOURCE REGULATION IN STATE AND LOCAL ORDINANCES. Washington, D.C.: Government Printing Office, 1973. 10 p. Pap., tables.

U.S. Environmental Protection Agency. Office of Noise Abatement and Control. STATE AND MUNICIPAL NON-OCCUPATIONAL NOISE PROGRAMS. Washington, D.C.: Government Printing Office, 1971. 24 p.

_____. SUMMARY OF NOISE PROGRAMS IN THE FEDERAL GOVERNMENT, DECEMBER 31, 1971. Washington, D.C.: Government Printing Office, 1972. 137 p. Charts, illus.

Details programs in seventeen agencies.

U.S. Federal Council for Science and Technology. Committee on Environmental Quality. NOISE: SOUND WITHOUT VALUE. Washington, D.C.: Government Printing Office, 1968. 56 p.

An evaluation of the noise problem with summaries of current federal programs and recommendations for federal actions in the areas of aircraft, surface transportation, outdoor, indoor, and occupational noises.

U.S. Office of Science and Technology. Jet Aircraft Noise Panel. ALLEVIATION OF JET AIRCRAFT NOISE NEAR AIRPORTS. Washington, D.C.: Government Printing Office, 1966. 167 p.

The section "General Economic Considerations, Land Utilization, and Legal Problems in Noise Abatement" includes papers on noise litigation, property rights in air space, and zoning.

## ENERGY

American Bar Association. Section on Natural Resources Law. THE ENERGY CRISIS AND THE LAWYER; NATIONAL INSTITUTE PROCEEDINGS. Chicago: 1974. 206 p. Bibliog.

Association of the Bar of the City of New York. Special Committee on Electric Power and the Environment. ELECTRICITY AND THE ENVIRONMENT: THE REFORM OF LEGAL INSTITUTIONS; REPORT. St. Paul, Minn.: West Publishing Co., 1972. 332 p.

Beard, Daniel. CONSIDERATIONS IN THE FORMULATION OF NATIONAL ENERGY POLICY. PREPARED AT THE REQUEST OF HENRY M. JACKSON, CHAIRMAN, COMMITTEE ON INTERIOR AND INSULAR AFFAIRS, UNITED STATES SENATE, PURSUANT TO S. RES. 45. . . . Washington, D.C.: Government Printing Office, 1971. 115 p. Illus.

Brannon, Gerard M. ENERGY TAXES AND SUBSIDIES. A report to the Energy Policy Project of the Ford Foundation. Cambridge, Mass.: Ballinger Publishing Co., 1974. 177 p.

Commerce Clearing House. ENERGY MOVEMENT. Topical Law Reports. Chicago: 1973- . Loose-leaf.

   Pooling of all government energy resources information.

Ellingen, Dana C., and Towsey, William E., Jr. A BIBLIOGRAPHY OF CONGRESSIONAL PUBLICATIONS ON ENERGY FROM THE 89TH CONGRESS TO JULY 1, 1971. Washington, D.C.: Government Printing Office for the Senate Committee on Interior and Insular Affairs, 1971. 45 p. Pap.

   Topically organized.

ENERGY USERS REPORT. Washington, D.C.: Bureau of National Affairs, 1974- . Weekly. Loose-leaf.

   A notification and reference service covering energy-related legislation, regulations, court decisions, and technological advances.

Kavass, Igor I., and Bieber, Doris M. ENERGY AND CONGRESS: AN ANNOTATED BIBLIOGRAPHY OF CONGRESSIONAL HEARINGS AND REPORTS; 1971-1973. Buffalo: Hein & Co., 1974. 87 p. Tables.

Merrill, Maurice H. THE PUBLIC'S CONCERN WITH THE FUEL MINERALS. St. Louis, Mo.: Thomas Law Book, 1960. 129 p.

   Lectures on the law and the fuel mineral industry: "Legal Foundation for Mineral Development," "Policing Matured Industries," and "Modern Problems."

U.S. Congress. Senate. Committee on Government Operations. HEARINGS . . . ON S. 2135 TO ESTABLISH A DEPARTMENT OF ENERGY AND NATURAL RESOURCES, BY REORGANIZING AND CONSOLIDATING OTHERS IN A NEW ENERGY RESEARCH AND DEVELOPMENT ADMINISTRATION. 93d Cong., 1st sess. Washington, D.C.: Government Printing Office, 1974. 233 p.

U.S. Congress. Senate. Committee on Interior and Insular Affairs. CALVERT CLIFFS COURT DECISION. HEARING, PURSUANT TO S. RES. 45, A NATIONAL FUELS AND ENERGY POLICY STUDY. . . . 2 vols. 92d Cong.,

1st sess. Washington, D.C.: Government Printing Office, 1971. 833 p.
Illus.

_____. LEGISLATIVE HISTORY OF S. RES. 45: A NATIONAL FUELS AND
ENERGY POLICY STUDY. Washington, D.C.: Government Printing Office,
1971. 51 p.

_____. NATIONAL FUELS AND ENERGY POLICY. HEARING . . . ON
S. RES. 45. . . . 92 Cong., 1st sess. Washington, D.C.: Government
Printing Office, 1971. 129 p.

U.S. Library of Congress. Environmental Policy Division. A REVIEW OF
ENERGY ISSUES AND THE 91ST CONGRESS. Washington, D.C.: Government Printing Office, 1971. 38 p.

## Atomic Energy and Radioactive Pollution

Atomic Industrial Forum. THE IMPACT OF THE PEACEFUL USES OF ATOMIC
ENERGY ON STATE AND LOCAL GOVERNMENT; A SUMMARY OF PAPERS
AND DISCUSSIONS FROM A CONFERENCE SPONSORED BY THE ATOMIC
INDUSTRIAL FORUM. Prepared and edited by Saul J. Harris. New York:
1959. 92 p. Diagrs.

_____. THE NEW ATOMIC ENERGY LAW; WHAT IT MEANS TO INDUSTRY:
PROCEEDINGS OF A MEETING FOR MEMBERS AND GUESTS, SEPTEMBER
27-28, 1954. New York: 1954. 181 p.

_____. STATE ACTIVITIES IN ATOMIC ENERGY: A CUMULATIVE SUM-
MARY, AUGUST 1954-JULY 1958. Compiled and edited by Saul J. Harris.
New York: 1958. 51 p.

Berman, William H., and Hydeman, Lee M. A STUDY: FEDERAL AND STATE
RESPONSIBILITIES FOR RADIATION PROTECTION; THE NEED FOR FEDERAL
LEGISLATION. Ann Arbor: University of Michigan Law School, 1959. 120
p.

Bryerton, Gene. NUCLEAR DILEMMA. Foreword by D.R. Inglis. New York:
Ballantine Books, 1970. 138 p. Illus., map.

Bureau of National Affairs. ATOMIC INDUSTRY REPORTER. 3 sections.
Washington: 1955- . Section 1, weekly. Sections 2 and 3, irregular.
Loose-leaf.

Chicago. University of. School of Law. CONFERENCE ON ATOMIC RADIA-
TION AND THE LAW, NOVEMBER 1961; PAPERS. Chicago: 1961. 58 p.

Licensing and regulatory process; tort liability, government indemni-
fication and insurance; safety standards; nuclear patents; treaties
and agreements.

Commerce Clearing House. ATOMIC ENERGY LAW REPORTER. Chicago:
1958- . Irregular. Loose-leaf.

Statutes, regulations, decisions, industrial check lists, reference
sources, and glossary of terms.

Conference on Atomic Radiation and the Law, University of Chicago.

See Chicago. University of. School of Law, above.

Council of State Governments. Committee on State Officials on Suggested
State Legislation. ATOMIC ENERGY AND RADIATION PROPOSALS. Chicago: 1958. 28 p.

Donnelly, Warren H. EFFECT OF CALVERT CLIFFS AND OTHER COURT DECI-
SIONS UPON NUCLEAR POWER IN THE UNITED STATES. Washington, D.C.:
Government Printing Office for the Senate Committee on Interior and Insular
Affairs, 1972. 57 p. Pap.

Sections on the Calvert Cliffs decision on "environmental impact,"
subsequent judicial interpretations of NEPA, the AEC response,
implications for electricity supply, environmental jurisdictions, and
new perspectives on agency procedure.

Ellet, William C. ATOMIC CITIES: THE ATOMIC ENERGY ACT AND THE
STATES. Ann Arbor, Mich.: University Microfilms, 1956. Microfilm.

ENVIRONMENTAL ASPECTS OF NUCLEAR POWER STATIONS. PROCEEDINGS
OF A SYMPOSIUM . . . HELD BY THE INTERNATIONAL ATOMIC ENERGY
AGENCY IN CO-OPERATION WITH THE UNITED STATES ATOMIC ENERGY
COMMISSION IN NEW YORK, 10-14 AUG. 1970. Vienna: International
Atomic Energy Agency, 1971. 970 p. Illus.

Foreman, Harry, ed. NUCLEAR POWER AND THE PUBLIC. Garden City,
N.Y.: Doubleday and Co., 1970. 273 p.

Green, Harold P. NUCLEAR TECHNOLOGY AND THE FABRIC OF GOVERN-
MENT. Program on Policy Studies in Science and Technology, Paper no. 7.
Washington, D.C.: George Washington University, 1965. 41 p.

Hutton, Gerald L. LEGAL CONSIDERATIONS ON IONIZING RADIATION:
RADIONUCLIDES AND RADIATION EMITTING DEVICES. Springfield, Ill.:
Thomas, 1966. 93 p.

Hydeman, Lee M., and Berman, William H. INTERNATIONAL CONTROL OF NUCLEAR MARITIME ACTIVITIES. Ann Arbor: University of Michigan Law School, 1960. 384 p.

International Atomic Energy Agency. AGREEMENTS REGISTERED WITH THE INTERNATIONAL ATOMIC ENERGY AGENCY. 3d ed. Vienna: 1969. 91 p. (Sold in the U.S. by Unipub, New York).

List of all agreements made with the International Atomic Energy Agency during the period of its activities from 1957 to December 31, 1968.

_____. NUCLEAR POWER AND THE ENVIRONMENT. New York: Unipub, 1973. 85 p. Illus.

_____. REGULATIONS FOR THE SAFE TRANSPORT OF RADIOACTIVE MATERIALS, 1964. Rev. ed. Vienna: 1965. 104 p. Illus.

_____. REGULATIONS FOR THE SAFE TRANSPORT OF RADIOACTIVE MATERIALS, 1967. Vienna: 1967. 117 p. Figures, tables.

_____. SAFE OPERATION OF NUCLEAR POWER PLANTS. CODE OF PRACTICE SPONSORED BY THE INTERNATIONAL ATOMIC ENERGY AGENCY AND THE WORLD HEALTH ORGANIZATION, AND TECHNICAL APPENDICES. Vienna: 1969. 125 p. Illus.

International Atomic Energy Agency. Training Course on the Legal Aspects of Peaceful Uses of Atomic Energy, Vienna, 1968. NUCLEAR LAW OF A DEVELOPING WORLD. LECTURES GIVEN AT THE TRAINING COURSE . . . HELD BY THE INTERNATIONAL ATOMIC ENERGY AGENCY IN VIENNA, 16-26 APRIL 1968. Legal Series, no. 5. Vienna: 1969. 329 p. Illus.

Iowa. University of. Institute of Public Affairs. STATE CONTROL AND ADMINISTRATION OF ATOMIC RADIATION. By. W.C. Ellet. Iowa City: 1957. 48 p.

Leachman, Robert B., and Athoff, Phillip, eds. PREVENTING NUCLEAR THEFT; GUIDELINES FOR INDUSTRY AND GOVERNMENT. Praeger Special Studies in International Politics and Public Affairs. New York: Praeger Publishing Co., 1972. xxxi, 377 p. Illus.

Lewis, Richard S. THE NUCLEAR-POWER REBELLION: CITIZENS VS. THE ATOMIC INDUSTRIAL ESTABLISHMENT. New York: Viking Press, 1972. 313 p.

Marks, Herbert S., and Trowbridge, George F. FRAMEWORK FOR ATOMIC INDUSTRY: A COMMENTARY ON THE ATOMIC ENERGY ACT OF 1954.

Washington, D.C.: Bureau of National Affairs, 1955. Var. pag.

Stason, E[dwin]. Blythe, et al. ATOMS AND THE LAW. Ann Arbor: University of Michigan Law School, 1959. 1,512 p. Diagrs.

> Parts relevant to environmental law are "State Regulation of Atomic Energy," comprised of six chapters, and "Federal Regulatory and Administrative Limitations Upon Atomic Activities," comprised of three chapters.

_____. STATE REGULATION OF ATOMIC ENERGY. Ann Arbor: University of Michigan Press, 1956. 186 p. Tables.

SYMPOSIUM ON ATOMIC ENERGY AND THE LAW. Held at the University of California, Berkeley, 1957. Berkeley: 1958. 125 p.

Szasz, Paul C. THE LAW AND PRACTICES OF THE INTERNATIONAL ATOMIC ENERGY AGENCY. Vienna: International Atomic Energy Agency, 1970. 1,176 p.

> An explanation of the statutes and internal procedures, rules and regulations by which the agency functions. Chapters are "Foundation," "Structure," "Relationships," "Activities," "Administration," "Legal Matters," and "Procedures."

Tsivoglou, E.C. RADIOACTIVE POLLUTION CONTROL IN MINNESOTA; FINAL REPORT. Minneapolis: Minnesota Pollution Control Agency, 1969. 192 p. Illus.

Wilrich, Mason, ed. INTERNATIONAL SAFEGUARDS AND NUCLEAR INDUSTRY. Baltimore, Md.: Johns Hopkins University Press, 1973. 307 p.

WORKSHOPS ON LEGAL PROBLEMS OF ATOMIC ENERGY, HELD AT UNIVERSITY OF MICHIGAN LAW SCHOOL, SEPTEMBER 13-SEPTEMBER 15, 1956. Foreword by E[dwin]. Blythe Stason. Ann Arbor: University of Michigan Law School, 1956. 220 p.

## GOVERNMENT DOCUMENTS--FEDERAL

U.S. Atomic Energy Commission. ATOMIC ENERGY LEGISLATION, 84th CONGRESS. CHRONOLOGY. Washington, D.C.: Government Printing Office, 1956. 20 p.

_____. LEGISLATIVE HISTORY OF THE ATOMIC ENERGY ACT OF 1954, PUBLIC LAW 703, 83d CONGRESS. 3 vols. Compiled by M.W. Losee. Washington, D.C.: Government Printing Office, 1955. 4,094 p. Illus.

_____. NUCLEAR POWER AND THE ENVIRONMENT. Oak Ridge, Tenn.: U.S. Atomic Energy Commission, Division of Technical Information, for sale by the Government Printing Office, 1969. 30 p. Illus.

_____. RULES AND REGULATIONS (TITLE 10, CODE OF FEDERAL REGULA-TIONS, CHAPTER 1). Washington, D.C.: Law Library, U.S. Atomic Energy Commission, 1958. Var. pag.

_____. RULES AND REGULATIONS (TITLE 10, CODE OF FEDERAL REGULA-TIONS, CHAPTER 1). Washington, D.C.: Law Library, Office of the General Counsel, U.S. Atomic Energy Commission, 1962. Var. pag.

_____. RULES AND REGULATIONS (TITLE 10, CHAPTER 1, CODE OF FED-ERAL REGULATIONS). Washington, D.C., Division of State and Licensee Relations, U.S. Atomic Energy Commission; for sale by the Government Printing Office, 1965. 397 p. Loose-leaf.

U.S. Congress. House. Committee on Merchant Marine and Fisheries. Sub-committee on Fisheries and Wildlife Conservation. INTERIM NUCLEAR LICEN-SING. HEARINGS . . . ON H.R. 13752. . . . 92d Cong., 2d sess. Washington, D.C.: Government Printing Office, 1972. 360 p. Illus.

U.S. Congress. Joint Committee on Atomic Energy. AEC OMNIBUS BILLS FOR 1963 AND 1964. HEARINGS BEFORE THE SUBCOMMITTEE ON LEGIS-LATION. . . . 88th Cong., 1st and 2d sess. Washington, D.C.: Govern-ment Printing Office, 1964. 263 p. Illus., map.

_____. FEDERAL-STATE RELATIONSHIPS IN THE ATOMIC ENERGY FIELD. HEARINGS. 86th Cong., 1st sess. Washington, D.C.: Government Printing Office, 1959. 504 p. Maps, tables.

_____. H.R. 13731 AND H.R. 13732, TO AMEND THE ATOMIC ENERGY ACT OF 1954 REGARDING THE LICENSING OF NUCLEAR FACILITIES. HEAR-INGS. . . . 2 vols. 92d Cong., 2d sess. Washington, D.C.: Government Printing Office, 1972. 1,028 p. Illus.

_____. PARTICIPATION BY SMALL ELECTRICAL UTILITIES IN NUCLEAR POWER. HEARINGS. . . . 2 vols. 90th Cong., 2d sess. Washington, D.C.: Government Printing Office, 1968. 1,382 p.

_____. SELECTED MATERIALS ON ENVIRONMENTAL EFFECTS OF PRODUC-ING ELECTRIC POWER. Washington, D.C.: Government Printing Office, 1969. 533 p. Illus., maps.

_____. SELECTED MATERIALS ON FEDERAL-STATE COOPERATION IN THE ATOMIC ENERGY FIELD. Washington, D.C.: Government Printing Office, 1959. 520 p. Illus.

_____. SELECTED MATERIALS ON THE CALVERT CLIFFS DECISION, ITS ORIGIN AND AFTERMATH. 92d Cong., 1st sess. Washington, D.C.: Government Printing Office, 1972. 676 p.

U.S. Congress. Joint Committee on Atomic Energy. Subcommittee on Legislation. AEC LICENSING PROCEDURE AND RELATED LEGISLATION. HEARINGS. . . . 4 vols. 92d Cong., 1st sess. Washington, D.C.: Government Printing Office, 1971. 2,090 p. Illus.

U.S. Congress. Senate. Committee on Interior and Insular Affairs. THE PRESIDENT'S ENERGY MESSAGE. HEARING . . . PURSUANT TO S. RES. 45. . . . 92d Cong., 1st sess. Washington, D.C.: Government Printing Office, 1971. 271 p. Illus.

U.S. Laws and Statutes. ATOMIC ENERGY ACT OF 1954. Chicago: Commerce Clearing House, 1954. 63 p.

_____. ATOMIC ENERGY LEGISLATION THROUGH 84th CONGRESS. Washington, D.C.: Government Printing Office, 1957. 166 p.

U.S. National Committee on Radiation Protection and Measurements. Subcommittee on Radiation Exposure. REGULATION OF RADIATION EXPOSURE BY LEGISLATIVE MEANS: RECOMMENDATIONS OF THE NATIONAL COMMITTEE ON RADIATION PROTECTION. U.S. National Bureau of Standards Handbook no. 61. Washington, D.C.: Government Printing Office, 1955. 60 p. Illus.

U.S. Treaties. ATOMIC ENERGY: APPLICATION OF AGENCY SAFEGUARDS TO CERTAIN UNITED STATES REACTOR FACILITIES; AGREEMENT BETWEEN THE UNITED STATES OF AMERICA AND THE INTERNATIONAL ATOMIC ENERGY AGENCY EXTENDING THE AGREEMENT OF JUNE 15, 1964, AS EXTENDED, EFFECTED BY EXCHANGE OF LETTERS SIGNED AT VIENNA, FEBRUARY 3 AND 9, 1970. Treaties and Other International Acts Series, no. 6826. Washington, D.C.: Government Printing Office, 1970. 2 p.

_____. ATOMIC ENERGY: APPLICATION OF AGENCY SAFEGUARDS TO CERTAIN UNITED STATES REACTOR FACILITIES. AGREEMENT BETWEEN THE UNITED STATES OF AMERICA AND THE INTERNATIONAL ATOMIC ENERGY AGENCY EXTENDING THE AGREEMENT OF JUNE 15, 1964, EFFECTED BY EXCHANGE OF LETTERS SIGNED AT VIENNA, JULY 28 AND 31, 1969. Treaties and Other International Acts Series, no. 6769. Washington, D.C.: Government Printing Office, 1969. 3 p.

_____. ATOMIC ENERGY: APPLICATION OF AGENCY SAFEGUARDS TO CERTAIN UNITED STATES REACTOR FACILITIES. AGREEMENT BETWEEN THE UNITED STATES OF AMERICA AND THE INTERNATIONAL ATOMIC ENERGY

AGENCY, SIGNED AT VIENNA, JUNE 15, 1964. Treaties and Other International Acts Series, no. 5621. Washington, D.C.: Government Printing Office, 1964. 7 p.

_____. ATOMIC ENERGY: APPLICATION OF SAFEGUARDS BY THE IAEA TO THE UNITED STATES-BRAZIL COOPERATION AGREEMENT. AGREEMENT BETWEEN THE UNITED STATES OF AMERICA, BRAZIL, AND THE INTERNATIONAL ATOMIC ENERGY AGENCY, AMENDING THE AGREEMENT OF MARCH 10, 1967, SIGNED AT VIENNA, JULY 27, 1972. Treaties and Other International Acts Series, no. 7440. Washington, D.C.: Government Printing Office, 1972. 3 p.

_____. ATOMIC ENERGY: APPLICATION OF SAFEGUARDS BY THE IAEA TO THE UNITED STATES-JAPAN COOPERATIVE AGREEMENT. AGREEMENT BETWEEN THE UNITED STATES OF AMERICA, JAPAN, AND THE INTERNATIONAL ATOMIC ENERGY AGENCY, SIGNED AT VIENNA, SEPTEMBER 23, 1963. Treaties and Other International Acts Series, no. 5429. Washington, D.C.: Government Printing Office, 1963. 10 p.

_____. ATOMIC ENERGY: COOPERATION FOR CIVIL USES. AGREEMENT BETWEEN THE UNITED STATES OF AMERICA AND BRAZIL, SIGNED AT WASHINGTON, JULY 17, 1972. Treaties and Other International Acts Series, no. 7439. Washington, D.C.: Government Printing Office, 1972. 49 p.

_____. ATOMIC ENERGY: COOPERATION FOR CIVIL USES. AGREEMENT BETWEEN THE UNITED STATES OF AMERICA AND THE REPUBLIC OF CHINA SIGNED AT WASHINGTON, APRIL 4, 1972. Treaties and Other International Acts Series, no. 7354. Washington, D.C.: Government Printing Office, 1972. 21 p.

## GOVERNMENT DOCUMENTS--STATE

Illinois. Laws and Statutes. "Radiation Installation Registration Law." SMITH-HURD ILLINOIS ANNOTATED STATUTES, Chapter 111 1/2, sections 194-200, pp. 330-36. St. Paul, Minn.: West Publishing Co., 1966.

Louisiana. Board of Nuclear Energy. Division of Radiation Control. LOUISIANA RADIATION REGULATIONS. Baton Rouge: 1971? 19 p.

Virginia. Advisory Legislative Council. STATE REGULATION OF THE USES OF ATOMIC ENERGY. A REPORT TO THE GOVERNOR AND THE GENERAL ASSEMBLY OF VIRGINIA. Richmond: Commonwealth of Virginia Division of Purchasor and Print, 1958. 8 p.

## Power Plants

Bette, A., et al. COMPENSATION OF NUCLEAR DAMAGE IN EUROPE,

SYSTEM CREATED BY THE BRUSSELS CONVENTION OF 31ST JANUARY 1963, SUPPLEMENTARY TO THE PARIS CONVENTION OF JULY 1960 ON THIRD PARTY LIABILITY IN THE FIELD OF NUCLEAR ENERGY. Brussels: 1965. 95 p.

Ducsik, Dennis W., ed. POWER, POLLUTION, AND PUBLIC POLICY: ISSUES IN ELECTRIC POWER PRODUCTION, SHORELINE RECREATION, AND AIR AND WATER POLLUTION FACING NEW ENGLAND AND THE NATION. Massachusetts Institute of Technology. Sea Grant Project Office, Report no. MITSG 71-8. Cambridge, Mass.: M.I.T. Press, 1971. 322 p. Illus.

Jimison, John. A REVIEW OF ENERGY POLICY ACTIVITIES OF THE 92D CONGRESS. PREPARED AT THE REQUEST OF HENRY M. JACKSON, CHAIRMAN, COMMITTEE ON INTERIOR AND INSULAR AFFAIRS, U.S. SENATE, PURSUANT TO S. RES. 45, A NATIONAL FUELS AND ENERGY POLICY STUDY. Washington, D.C.: Government Printing Office, 1973. 118 p.

Pennsylvania Society of Professional Engineers. PROCEEDINGS. Power Plant Siting Symposium, Pittsburgh, 1971. Edited by E.B. Stuart. Baltimore, Md.: Mono Book Corp., 1971. 46 p.

Public Affairs Research Council of Louisiana, Inc. THE POWER USE TAX AND ELECTRIC GENERATION TAX; A PAR STUDY. Baton Rouge: 1955. 19 p.

Scott, David L. POLLUTION IN THE ELECTRIC POWER INDUSTRY: ITS CONTROL AND COSTS. Lexington, Mass.: D.C. Heath and Co., 1973. 104 p.

Talbot, Allan R. POWER ALONG THE HUDSON: THE STORM KING CASE AND THE BIRTH OF ENVIRONMENTALISM. New York: Dutton, 1972. 244 p.

## GOVERNMENT DOCUMENTS--FEDERAL

U.S. Commission on Organization of the Executive Branch of the Government (1953-1955). WATER RESOURCES AND POWER. 2 vols. Washington, D.C.: Government Printing Office, 1955. 218 p. Pap.

> Study and recommendations in large part concerned with the relationships between water uses and reclamation projects. Discussion of relevant agencies and legislation included.

U.S. Congress. House. BILLS RELATING TO POWERPLANT SITING AND ENVIRONMENTAL PROTECTION, ACCOMPANIED BY EXPLANATORY MATERIALS. 92d Cong., 1st sess. Washington, D.C.: Government Printing Office, 1971. 219 p.

U.S. Congress. House. Committee on Interstate and Foreign Commerce. Sub-

committee on Communications and Power. POWERPLANT SITING AND EN-
VIRONMENTAL PROTECTION. HEARINGS. . . . 3 vols. 92d Cong., 1st.
sess. Washington, D.C.: Government Printing Office, 1971. 1,194 p.

_____. SUMMARY AND SECTION-BY-SECTION ANALYSIS OF H.R. 11066,
ELECTRIC POWER SUPPLY AND ENVIRONMENTAL PROTECTION ACT, TO-
GETHER WITH TEXT OF H.R. 11066. Washington, D.C.: Government Print-
ing Office, 1971. 50 p.

U.S. Congress. Senate. Committee on Commerce. POWERPLANT SITING.
HEARINGS . . . ON S. 1684 . . . S. 1915 . . . S. 3631. . . . 92d
Cong., 2d sess. Washington, D.C.: Government Printing Office, 1972.
1,026 p.

U.S. Congress. Senate. Committee on Government Operations. Subcommittee
on Intergovernmental Relations. INTERGOVERNMENTAL COORDINATION OF
POWER DEVELOPMENT AND ENVIRONMENTAL PROTECTION ACT. HEAR-
INGS . . . ON S. 2752. . . . Part 1. 91st Cong., 2d sess. Washington, D.C.: Government Printing Office, 1970. 446 p.

U.S. Federal Power Commission. National Power Survey Task Force on Environment. MANAGING THE POWER SUPPLY AND THE ENVIRONMENT; RE-
PORT. Washington, D.C.: 1971. 41 p. Illus.

U.S. Library of Congress. Environmental Policy Division. A REVIEW OF
ENERGY ISSUES AND THE 91ST CONGRESS. Washington, D.C.: Government Printing Office for the Senate Committee on Interior and Insular Affairs,
1971. 38 p. Pap.

> A report on legislation enacted and on the major energy policy is-
> sues of oil, gas supply, energy shortages, electric power genera-
> tion and transmission, and nuclear energy.

# PESTICIDES

## Authored Works

Benvene, A., and Kawaro, Y. "Pesticides, Pesticide Residues, Tolerances,
and the Law (U.S.A.)." RESIDUE REVIEWS 35 (1971): 103-49.

> Legislation, agency formations, and actions influencing pesticide
> regulations.

Bloom, Sandra C., and Degler, Stanley E. PESTICIDES AND POLLUTION.
Washington, D.C.: Bureau of National Affairs, 1969. 99 p.

> Discusses federal regulations, state laws and legal considerations
> and includes Federal Insecticide, Fungicide, and Rodenticide Act;
> Uniform State Insecticide, Fungicide, and Rodenticide Act; Offi-

cial Regulations Under the Model State Insecticide, Fungicide and
Rodenticide Act; and An Act Relating to Custom Application of
Pesticides.

Chemical Specialties Manufacturers Association. COMPILATION OF FEDERAL
AND STATE ECONOMIC POISONS (PESTICIDES) LAWS, REGULATIONS, RUL-
INGS, AND OTHER EXPLANATORY MATTER. Edited by J.D. Conner and
R.L. Ackerly. New York: 1961- . Irregular. Loose-leaf.

The Conservation Foundation. POLLUTION BY PESTICIDES: SOME NOT VERY
WELL CALCULATED RISKS AND SOME ALTERNATIVES FOR BETTER REGULA-
TION. Washington, D.C.: 1969. 32 p. Pap., illus.

   A reprint of two issues of CF LETTER, a publication of the Conservation Foundation. Part 1 covers the widespread use of pesticides, their effects on fish, wildlife, and natural systems, their
   possible effects on man, and some international ramifications. Part
   2 deals with government attempts to limit the dangers, the politics
   of pesticides, and alternative approaches to pest control problems.

Day, James W. POISON ON THE LAND: THE WAR ON WILD LIFE, AND
SOME REMEDIES. New York: Philosophical Library, 1957. 246 p.

   Describes the revolution in British farming and the resulting men-
   ace to wildlife.

Deck, G. "Federal and State Pesticide Regulations and Legislation." AN-
NUAL REVIEW OF ENTOMOLOGY 20 (1975): 119-31.

Dunning, H.C. "Pests, Poisons, and the Living Law: The Control of Pesticides in California's Imperial Valley." ECOLOGY LAW QUARTERLY 2 (1972):
633-93.

   Regulatory, legal, and biological information.

Edwards, C.A., ed. ENVIRONMENTAL POLLUTION BY PESTICIDES. New
York: Plenum, 1973. 440 p.

   Brings together available data on pesticide residues in plants, animals, air, water, and soil. Each chapter written by a recognized
   authority in a specific field.

Epstein, S.S., and Grundy, R.D., eds. THE LEGISLATION OF PRODUCT
SAFETY: CONSUMER HEALTH AND PRODUCT HAZARDS. Vol. 2. Cambridge, Mass.: The M.I.T. Press, 1974. 342 p.

Hazeltine, W. THE LEGISLATIVE HISTORY AND MEANING OF THE FEDER-
AL INSECTICIDE, FUNGICIDE AND RODENTICIDE ACT AS AMENDED, 1972.
Oroville, Calif.: Privately printed, 1975. Var. pag.

   Comments by author on laws and congressional hearings and the shortcomings of the Environmental Protection Agency.

Headley, J.C., and Lewis, J.N. THE PESTICIDE PROBLEMS: AN ECONOMIC APPROACH TO PUBLIC POLICY. Washington, D.C.: Resources for the Future, 1967. 141 p. Pap.

Henkin, Harmon, et al. THE ENVIRONMENT, THE ESTABLISHMENT AND THE LAW. New York: Houghton Mifflin, 1971. 223 p. Photos.

The story of the 1968-69 Department of Natural Resources hearing to determine whether DDT was a pollutant of the waters of Wisconsin. Much text is hearing transcript. Included are the petition to the Department of Natural Resources seeking a ruling on the use of DDT and a model pesticide law.

McNeil, Richard J. PESTICIDES. Current Topics in Conservation, series II, no. 8. Ithaca: Department of Conservation, New York State College of Agriculture, State University of New York, Cornell University, 1966. 28 p. Illus.

Mellanby, Kenneth. PESTICIDES AND POLLUTION. 2d rev. ed. London: Collins, 1970. 221 p. Maps, diagrs., illus.

Environmental pollution in Britain.

National Agricultural Chemicals Association. FEDERAL ENVIRONMENTAL PESTICIDE CONTROL ACT OF 1972, AMENDING THE FEDERAL INSECTICIDE, FUNGICIDE AND RODENTICIDE ACT; A COMPILATION OF THE STATUTE AND LEGISLATIVE HISTORY. Washington, D.C.: 1973. 271 p.

Rudd, Robert L. PESTICIDES AND THE LIVING LANDSCAPE. Madison: University of Wisconsin Press, 1964. 320 p. Bibliog.

Analyzes the conflict between man and other living things and the methods used to reduce this conflict.

Van Tiel, N. "Principles and Problems of Pesticides Registration." PESTICIDES SCIENCE 6 (1975): 189-97.

Von Rumker, Rosmarie, et al. THE USE OF PESTICIDES IN SUBURBAN HOMES AND GARDENS AND THEIR IMPACT ON THE AQUATIC ENVIRONMENT. Washington, D.C.: Environmental Protection Agency, Office of Water Programs, for sale by Government Printing Office, 1972. Var. pag. Illus.

World Health Organization. CONTROL OF PESTICIDES: A SURVEY OF EXISTING LEGISLATION, 1970. Geneva: 1970. 150 p.

## Government Documents--Federal

U.S. Agricultural Research Service. INTERPRETATIONS OF THE REGULATIONS FOR THE ENFORCEMENT OF THE FEDERAL INSECTICIDE, FUNGICIDE, AND RODENTICIDE ACT. Department of Agriculture Service and Regulatory Announcements, no. 167. Washington, D.C.: Government Printing Office, 1948. 52 p.

_____. INTERPRETATIONS OF THE REGULATIONS FOR THE ENFORCEMENT OF THE FEDERAL INSECTICIDE, FUNGICIDE, AND RODENTICIDE ACT. REISSUED WITH AMENDMENTS. Washington, D.C.: Government Printing Office, 1955. 37 p.

U.S. Congress. House. Committee on Agriculture. ADMINISTRATION OF PESTICIDE LAWS AND REGULATIONS. HEARINGS. . . . 88th Cong., 2d sess. Washington, D.C.: Government Printing Office, 1964. 39 p.

_____. AMENDMENT TO THE FEDERAL INSECTICIDE, FUNGICIDE, AND RODENTICIDE ACT. HEARING . . . ON H.R. 6436. Washington, D.C.: Government Printing Office, 1959. 24 p.

_____. FEDERAL ENVIRONMENTAL PESTICIDE CONTROL ACT OF 1971; REPORT, TOGETHER WITH ADDITIONAL VIEWS TO ACCOMPANY H.R. 10729. 92d Cong., 1st sess., House Report no. 92-511. Washington, D.C.: Government Printing Office, 1971. 82 p.

_____. FEDERAL PESTICIDE CONTROL ACT OF 1971. HEARINGS. . . . 92d Cong., 1st sess. Washington, D.C.: Government Printing Office, 1971. 906 p.

_____. PLANT PESTS, CONTROL AND ERADICATION. HEARING BEFORE THE SUBCOMMITTEE ON RESEARCH AND EXTENSION . . . ON H.R. 3476 [and others]. . . . 85th Cong., 1st sess. Washington, D.C.: Government Printing Office, 1957. 51 p. Tables.

_____. REGISTRATION OF ECONOMIC POISONS. HEARINGS BEFORE THE SUBCOMMITTEE ON DEPARTMENTAL OVERSIGHT AND CONSUMER RELATIONS . . . ON H.R. 6828, H.R. 6913, AND H.R. 7336. 88th Cong., 1st sess. Washington, D.C.: Government Printing Office, 1963. 69 p.

U.S. Congress. House. Committee on Agriculture. Subcommittee on Departmental Operations. PROHIBIT IMPORTATION OF CERTAIN AGRICULTURAL COMMODITIES TO WHICH ECONOMIC POISONS HAVE BEEN APPLIED. HEARING . . . ON H.R. 15560 AND H.R. 16576. . . . 91st Cong., 2d sess. Washington, D.C.: Government Printing Office, 1970. 21 p.

U.S. Congress. House. Committee on Banking and Currency. RAT EXTER-
MINATION ACT OF 1967; REPORT, TOGETHER WITH SUPPLEMENTAL AND
MINORITY VIEWS, TO ACCOMPANY H.R. 11000. 90th Cong., 1st sess.
House Report no. 474. Washington, D.C.: Government Printing Office, 1967.
13 p.

U.S. Congress. House. Committee on Government Operations. DEFICIEN-
CIES IN ADMINISTRATION OF FEDERAL INSECTICIDE, FUNGICIDE, AND
RODENTICIDE ACT; ELEVENTH REPORT. 91st Cong., 1st sess., House Report
no. 91-637. Washington, D.C.: Government Printing Office, 1969. 71 p.

U.S. Congress. House. Committee on Interstate and Foreign Commerce.
AMENDING THE FEDERAL FOOD, DRUG AND COSMETIC ACT WITH RESPECT
TO RESIDUES OF PESTICIDE CHEMICALS IN OR ON RAW AGRICULTURAL
COMMODITIES; REPORT TO ACCOMPANY H.R. 7125. 83d Cong., 2d sess.
Washington, D.C.: Government Printing Office, 1954. 22 p.

U.S. Congress. House. Committee on Merchant Marine and Fisheries. PESTI-
CIDE CONTROLS. HEARINGS BEFORE THE SUBCOMMITTEE ON FISHERIES
AND WILDLIFE CONSERVATION . . . ON H.R. 2857 [and others]. . . .
88th Cong., 1st sess. Washington, D.C.: Government Printing Office, 1963.
155 p. Illus.

U.S. Congress. Senate. Committee on Agriculture and Forestry. REGISTRA-
TION OF PESTICIDE CHEMICALS; REPORT TO ACCOMPANY S. 1605. 88th
Cong., 1st sess. Senate Report no. 573. Washington, D.C.: Government
Printing Office, 1963. 29 p.

U.S. Congress. Senate. Committee on Agriculture and Forestry. Subcommittee on Agricultural Research and General Legislation. FEDERAL ENVIRON-
MENTAL PESTICIDE CONTROL ACT. HEARINGS. . . . 92d Cong., 1st
sess. Washington, D.C.: Government Printing Office, 1971. 792 p.

U.S. Congress. Senate. Committee on Commerce. PESTICIDE RESEARCH AND
CONTROLS. HEARING. . . . 88th Cong., 1st sess. Washington, D.C.:
Government Printing Office, 1965. 66 p. Illus.

_____. PESTICIDES HAZARDOUS TO FISH AND WILDLIFE. HEARING. . .
ON S. 3328 AND H.R. 15979. . . . 90th Cong., 2d sess. Washington,
D.C.: Government Printing Office, 1968. 52 p.

_____. PROTECTION OF FISH AND WILDLIFE FROM PESTICIDES; REPORT
TO ACCOMPANY S. 1251. 88th Cong., 2d sess., Senate Report no. 1053.
Washington, D.C.: Government Printing Office, 1964. 28 p.

_____. PROTECTION OF FISH AND WILDLIFE FROM PESTICIDES; REPORT

TO ACCOMPANY S. 1623. 89th Cong., 1st sess., Senate Report no. 169. Washington, D.C.: Government Printing Office, 1965. 11 p.

U.S. Congress. Senate. Committee on Commerce. Subcommittee on Energy, Natural Resources, and the Environment. PESTICIDE AMENDMENTS TO HAZ-ARDOUS SUBSTANCES ACT. HEARINGS . . . ON S. 3866. . . . 91st Cong., 2d sess. Washington, D.C.: Government Printing Office, 1970. 88 p.

U.S. Congress. Senate. Committee on Commerce. Subcommittee on the En-vironment. FEDERAL ENVIRONMENTAL PESTICIDE CONTROL ACT OF 1971. HEARINGS . . . ON H.R. 10729. . . . 92d Cong., 2d sess. Washington, D.C.: Government Printing Office, 1972. 275 p.

U.S. Congress. Senate. Committee on Government Operations. INTERAGENCY COORDINATION IN ENVIRONMENTAL HAZARDS (PESTICIDES). HEARINGS BEFORE THE SUBCOMMITTEE ON REORGANIZATION AND INTERNATIONAL ORGANIZATIONS . . . AGENCY COORDINATING STUDY, PURSUANT TO S. RES. 27, 88TH CONGRESS, AS AMENDED. COORDINATION OF ACTIVI-TIES RELATING TO THE USE OF PESTICIDES. . . . 4 Parts. Washington, D.C.: Government Printing Office, 1964. 1,044 p. Illus.

_____. INTERAGENCY ENVIRONMENTAL HAZARDS COORDINATION: PES-TICIDES AND PUBLIC POLICY. REPORT. . . . 89th Cong., 2d sess., Senate Report no. 1379. Washington, D.C.: Government Printing Office, 1966. 86 p.

U.S. Department of the Interior. Water Resources Scientific Information Cen-ter. DDT IN WATER: A BIBLIOGRAPHY. Washington, D.C.: 1971. Un-paged.

U.S. Environmental Protection Agency. LAWS AND INSTITUTIONAL MECH-ANISMS CONTROLLING THE RELEASE OF PESTICIDES INTO THE ENVIRON-MENT. Washington, D.C.: Government Printing Office, 1972. 140 p. Pap., charts.

> A report on federal, state, and international laws and mechanisms and on interagency and intra-agency pesticide control mechanisms.

## Government Documents--State

California. Governor's Conference on Pesticide Review. REPORT ON PESTI-CIDES IN CALIFORNIA. Sacramento: 1965. 121 p.

> Subtitled: "A Description of Current Programs in the Control of Pesticides, an Identification of Shortcomings in the Present Programs,

and Recommendations for New Programs Needed to Meet the State's Total Obligation to Its Citizens." One section on legal tools.

California. Laws and Statutes. STRUCTURAL PEST CONTROL ACT, WITH RULES AND REGULATIONS. LAW INCLUDES AMENDMENTS THROUGH 1968. RULES AND REGULATIONS INCLUDE AMENDMENTS THROUGH JANUARY 2, 1968. Sacramento: Structural Pest Control Board, 1968. 55 p.

California. Legislature. Joint Committee on Agriculture and Livestock Problems. SPECIAL REPORT ON ENFORCEMENT OF STATE LAWS RELATING TO AGRICULTURAL PEST CONTROL OPERATORS AND THEIR USE OF INJURIOUS MATERIALS. Sacramento: Senate of the State of California, 1953. 37 p. Illus.

Florida. Laws and Statutes. FLORIDA PESTICIDE LAW, RULES AND REGULATIONS. CHAPTER 487, FLORIDA STATUTES. Tallahassee: State Department of Agriculture, 1968. 16 p.

## SOLID WASTE

American Society of International Law. THE QUESTION OF AN OCEAN DUMPING CONVENTION. Studies in Transnational Legal Policy, no. 2. Washington, D.C.: 1972. 53 p.

Autocomp Incorporated. SOLID WASTE LAWS IN THE U.S. TERRITORIES AND STATES. Solid Waste Management Series, SW-40c. Washington, D.C.: U.S. Environmental Protection Agency, 1972. 502 p.

Center for Political Research. Research Services Division. THE FEDERAL ROLE IN SOLID WASTE MANAGEMENT. Washington, D.C.: Center for Political Research, 1970. 47 p.

Illinois Solid Waste Management Task Force. BEVERAGE CONTAINERS; RECOMMENDATIONS. IIEQ Document no. TF-1. Springfield: Illinois Institute for Environmental Quality, 1971. 180 p.

National Center For Resource Recovery. MUNICIPAL SOLID WASTE COLLECTION: A STATE-OF-THE-ART STUDY. Lexington, Mass.: Lexington Books, 1973. xv, 110 p.

Includes one chapter on the regulatory role of the federal government.

Powell, Mel B., et al. DIGEST OF SELECTED LOCAL SOLID WASTE MANAGEMENT ORDINANCES. Washington, D.C.: Environmental Protection Agency, 1972. 376 p.

Sherman, Anthony C. LAND AND TRASH: OUR WOUNDED LAND. Now Age Books, Ecology Series. West Haven, Conn.: Pendulum Press, 1972. 64 p. Illus.

Smith, David S., and Brown, Robert P. OCEAN DISPOSAL OF BARGE-DELIVERED LIQUID AND SOLID WASTES FROM U.S. COASTAL CITIES. For U.S. EPA, Solid Waste Management Office. Washington, D.C.: Government Printing Office, 1973. 119 p.

Short sections on regulatory monitoring, legal aspects, and recommendations for federal action.

Spooner, Charles S. SOLID WASTE MANAGEMENT IN RECREATIONAL FOREST AREAS. Washington, D.C.: U.S. Solid Waste Management Office, for sale by the Government Printing Office, 1971. 96 p. Illus., forms, maps.

Toftner, Richard O., and Clark, Robert M. INTERGOVERNMENTAL APPROACHES TO SOLID WASTE MANAGEMENT. Washington, D.C.: Government Printing Office, 1972. 17 p.

Study of possible regional and intergovernmental management systems which includes planning, organization, operation, and controls.

U.S. Congress. House. Committee on Government Operations. Conservation and Natural Resources Subcommittee. THE ESTABLISHMENT OF A NATIONAL INDUSTRIAL WASTES INVENTORY. HEARING. . . . 91st Cong., 2d sess. Washington, D.C.: Government Printing Office, 1970. 229 p.

U.S. Congress. House. Committee on Interstate and Foreign Commerce. RESOURCE RECOVERY ACT OF 1970; REPORT TO ACCOMPANY H.R. 11833. 91st Cong., 2d sess., House Report no. 91-1155. Washington, D.C.: Government Printing Office, 1970. 15 p.

U.S. Congress. House. Committee on Interstate and Foreign Commerce. Subcommittee on Public Health and Welfare. AIR POLLUTION CONTROL AND SOLID WASTES RECYCLING. HEARINGS . . . ON H.R. 12934, H.R. 14960, H.R. 15137, AND H.R. 15192, H.R. 15848, H.R. 15847, AND RELATED BILLS. 2 vols. 91st Cong., 1st and 2d sess. Washington, D.C.: Government Printing Office, 1970. 891 p.

_____. PROHIBIT CERTAIN NO-DEPOSIT, NO-RETURN CONTAINERS. HEARING. . . . 91st Cong., 2d sess. Washington, D.C.: Government Printing Office, 1971. 61 p.

U.S. Congress. Senate. Committee on Commerce. Subcommittee on Oceans and Atmosphere. OCEAN WASTE DISPOSAL. HEARINGS. . . . 92d Cong., 1st sess. Washington, D.C.: Government Printing Office, 1971. 340 p. Maps.

U.S. Congress. Senate. Committee on Public Works. RESOURCES RECOVERY ACT OF 1970; REPORT TO ACCOMPANY S. 2005, TOGETHER WITH AN INDIVIDUAL VIEW. 91st Cong., 2d sess., Senate Report no. 91-1034. Washington, D.C.: Government Printing Office, 1970. 41 p.

U.S. Congress. Senate. Committee on Public Works. Subcommittee on Air and Water Pollution. IMPLEMENTATION OF THE RESOURCE RECOVERY ACT OF 1970. HEARING. . . . 92d Cong., 2d sess. Washington, D.C.: Government Printing Office, 1972. 48 p.

_____. RESOURCE RECOVERY ACT OF 1969. HEARINGS. . . . Part 1. 91st Cong., 1st sess. Washington, D.C.: Government Printing Office, 1969. 495 p.

_____. RESOURCE RECOVERY ACT OF 1969. HEARINGS. . . . Part 2. 91st Cong., 2d sess. Washington, D.C.: Government Printing Office, 1969. Pp. 497-1418. Illus.

U.S. Department of Health, Education, and Welfare. Solid Waste Management Bureau. National Research Council. POLICIES FOR SOLID WASTES MANAGEMENT. Washington, D.C.: Government Printing Office, 1970. 64 p.

Definition of solid waste management problems and resultant recommendations, principally involving research, standard-setting, and funding.

U.S. Solid Waste Management Office. STATE SOLID WASTE PLANNING GRANTS, AGENCIES, AND PROGRESS--1970; REPORT OF ACTIVITIES THROUGH JUNE 30, 1970. Public Health Service Publication no. 2109. Compiled by R.O. Toftner et al. Washington, D.C.: Government Printing Office, 1971. 26 p.

## Section 3

## CONSERVATION OF RESOURCES

### FISH AND WILDLIFE

### Authored Works and Conferences

Bayitch, S.A. INTERAMERICAN LAW OF FISHERIES: AN INTRODUCTION WITH DOCUMENTS. Published for the Interamerican Law Program, School of Law, University of Miami. New York: Oceana Publications, 1957. 117 p.

Bayliff, William H., and Morton, Ruvelle S. SUMMARY OF MARYLAND LAWS RELATING TO PLANTS AND ANIMALS. Annapolis, Md.: Board of Natural Resources, 1953. 32 p. Illus., map.

Beak, Thomas W. SALMON AND TROUT FISHING LAW OF SCOTLAND. Edinburgh: Gloster Publishers, 1954? 35 p.

Bumgarner, Willis C. GUIDEBOOK FOR WILDLIFE PROTECTORS. Chapel Hill: Institute of Government, University of North Carolina for North Carolina Wildlife Resources Commission, 1955. 196 p.

_____. GUIDEBOOK FOR WILDLIFE PROTECTORS. Rev. and enl. by L.P. Watts. Chapel Hill: Institute of Government, University of North Carolina for the North Carolina Wildlife Resources Commission, 1962. 387 p. Illus.

Burke, William T. SOME THOUGHTS ON FISHERIES AND A NEW CONFERENCE ON THE LAW OF THE SEA. Kingston: Law of the Sea Institute, University of Rhode Island, 1971. 17 p. Pap.

A paper delivered at the Natural Resources Public Policy Seminar, University of Washington, 1970.

Connery, Robert H. GOVERNMENT PROBLEMS IN WILD LIFE CONSERVATION. Studies in History, Economics, and Public Law, no. 411. New York: AMS Press, 1968. 250 p.

Crutchfield, James Arthur. THE PACIFIC SALMON FISHERIES; A STUDY OF IRRATIONAL CONSERVATION. Baltimore, Md.: Published for Resources for the Future by Johns Hopkins Press, 1969. 220 p. Maps, illus.

_____, ed. THE FISHERIES: PROBLEMS IN RESOURCE MANAGEMENT. Seattle: University of Washington Press, 1965. 136 p. Illus.

Garcia Amador y Rodriguez, F. THE EXPLOITATION AND CONSERVATION OF THE RESOURCES OF THE SEA: A STUDY OF CONTEMPORARY INTERNATIONAL LAW. 2d rev. and enl. ed. Leyden, Netherlands: A.W. Sythoff, 1963. 212 p.

Hayden, Sherman S. THE INTERNATIONAL PROTECTION OF WILD LIFE: AN EXAMINATION OF TREATIES AND OTHER AGREEMENTS FOR THE PRESERVATION OF BIRDS AND MAMMALS. Studies in History, Economics, and Public Law, 491. New York: AMS Press, 1970. 246 p. Illus.

Hornaday, William T. THIRTY YEARS WAR FOR WILDLIFE: ITS EXTERMINATION AND PRESERVATION. American Environmental Studies. 1913. Reprint. New York: Arno, 1970. 411 p. Illus., maps, ports.

Hunt, Robert L., et al. EFFECTS OF ANGLING REGULATIONS ON A WILD BROOK TROUT FISHERY. Wisconsin Conservation Department Technical Bulletin no. 26. Madison: Wisconsin Conservation Department, 1962. 58 p. Illus.

International Wildfowl Research Bureau. LEGISLATIVE AND ADMINISTRATIVE MEASURES FOR WILDFOWL CONSERVATION IN EUROPE AND NORTH AFRICA. LeSambuc, France: 1966? Loose-leaf, maps.

Johnston, Douglas M. THE INTERNATIONAL LAW OF FISHERIES; A FRAMEWORK FOR POLICY-ORIENTED INQUIRIES. New Haven, Conn.: Yale University Press, 1965. xxiv, 554 p.

> Begins with a value analysis of competing fishery interests and proceeds to "Patterns of Exploitation Authority," "Patterns of Conservation Authority" and conclusions. Major conventions, reports and actions of the UN are appended.

McPhee, John A. ENCOUNTERS WITH THE ARCHDRUID. New York: Farrar, Straus and Giroux, 1971. 245 p.

Myren, Richard A. INDIANA CONSERVATION OFFICERS' MANUAL OF LAW AND PRACTICE. Bloomington: Bureau of Government Research, Indiana University, 1961. 205 p. Map, diagr., table.

North Carolina. University of. Institute of Government. LOCAL GAME AND

INLAND FISHING LAWS (OTHER THAN FOX LAWS) ENACTED PRIOR TO 1965: A STUDY CONDUCTED BY THE INSTITUTE OF GOVERNMENT FOR THE 1965 GENERAL ASSEMBLY. Chapel Hill: 1965. 41 p.

Oda, Shigeru. INTERNATIONAL CONTROL OF SEA RESOURCES. Leyden, Netherlands: A.W. Sythoff, 1962. 215 p.

> The three parts of this study are: "Fundamental Problems of International Fisheries," "The Inadequacies of Present Concepts of the Continental Shelf," and "Misapplications in the Treatment of the Sedentary Fishery."

Pan American Union. General Legal Division. CONVENTION ON NATURE PROTECTION AND WILD LIFE PRESERVATION IN THE WESTERN HEMISPHERE, OPENED FOR SIGNATURE AT THE PAN AMERICAN UNION, OCTOBER 1940. Serie Sobre Tratados, no. 31. Washington, D.C.: Union Panamericana, 1964. 25 p.

Riesenfeld, Stefan A. PROTECTION OF COASTAL FISHERIES UNDER INTERNATIONAL LAW. Washington, D.C.: Carnegie Endowment for International Peace, 1942. Reprint. New York: Johnson Reprint Corp., 1971. 296 p.

> Sections on international legal theory and associations, congresses and conferences, the practices of various countries grouped by region, and international arbitration.

Sigler, William F. WILDLIFE LAW ENFORCEMENT. Dubuque, Iowa: William C. Brown Co., 1956. 318 p. Illus.

_____. WILDLIFE LAW ENFORCEMENT. 2d ed. Dubuque, Iowa: William C. Brown Co., 1972. xxviii, 360 p. Illus.

Street, Philip. WILDLIFE PRESERVATION. Chicago: H. Regnery Co., 1970. 141 p. Illus.

Tomasevich, Jozo. INTERNATIONAL AGREEMENTS ON CONSERVATION OF MARINE RESOURCES WITH SPECIAL REFERENCE TO THE NORTH PACIFIC. Stanford, Calif.: Food Research Institute, Stanford University, 1943. Reprint. New York: Kraus Reprint Co., 1971. 297 p.

> One section on international law and fisheries and special attention to international regulation of fur seals, halibut, and sockeye salmon.

United Nations. First Conference on the Law of the Sea, Geneva, 29 April-31 October 1958. CONVENTION ON FISHING AND CONSERVATION OF THE LIVING RESOURCES OF THE HIGH SEAS. Great Britain Foreign Office, Treaty series, 1966, no. 39. London: H.M. Stationery Office, 1966. 72 p.

_____. THE LAW OF THE SEA. London: Eastern Press, 1958. 42 p.

The final act and annexes. Resolutions on conservation, international and coastal fisheries, nuclear tests, radioactive pollution, and the killing of marine life.

United Nations. International Technical Conference on the Conservation of the Living Resources of the Sea. PAPERS. New York: 1956. 371 p. Charts.

Includes a number of papers on international conventions and commissions relating to the conservation of fish, whales, and other endangered marine animals.

Weeden, Robert B. WILDLIFE MANAGEMENT AND ALASKA LAND USE DECISIONS. ISEGR Occasional Papers, no. 8. Fairbanks: Institute of Social, Economic and Government Research, University of Alaska, 1973. 51 p.

Worcester, Joann. GOVERNMENT AND NATURAL RESOURCES IN KANSAS: WILDLIFE AND RECREATION. Lawrence: Governmental Research Center, University of Kansas, 1958. 48 p. Illus.

## Government Documents--Federal

U.S. Congress. House. Committee on Merchant Marine and Fisheries. ENDANGERED SPECIES. REPORT TO ACCOMPANY H.R. 11618. 90th Cong., 2d sess., House Report no. 1102. Washington, D.C.: Government Printing Office, 1968. 25 p.

_____. ENDANGERED SPECIES. REPORT TO ACCOMPANY H.R. 11363. 91st Cong., 1st sess., House Report no. 91-382. Washington, D.C.: Government Printing Office, 1969. 34 p.

_____. FEDERAL AID TO WILDLIFE RESTORATION IN HAWAII. HEARING BEFORE THE SUBCOMMITTEE ON FISHERIES AND WILDLIFE CONSERVATION . . . ON H.R. 5790, A BILL TO AMEND THE FEDERAL AID TO WILDLIFE RESTORATION ACT, AS AMENDED, AND H.R. 9426, A BILL TO PROVIDE THAT THE UNITED STATES SHALL AID THE STATES IN WILDLIFE RESTORATION PROJECTS, AND FOR OTHER PURPOSES. 84th Cong., 2d sess. Washington, D.C.: Government Printing Office, 1956. 16 p.

_____. MISCELLANEOUS FISH AND WILDLIFE BILLS. HEARINGS . . . ON H.R. 783 [and others]. 85th Cong., 2d sess. Washington, D.C.: Government Printing Office, 1958. 83 p.

_____. PROTECTION OF ENDANGERED SPECIES OF FISH AND WILDLIFE; REPORT TO ACCOMPANY H.R. 9424. 89th Cong., 1st sess. House Report no. 1168. Washington, D.C.: Government Printing Office, 1965. 25 p.

_____. PROTECTION OF FISH AND WILDLIFE FROM PESTICIDES; REPORT TO ACCOMPANY S. 1623. 89th Cong., 1st sess., House Report no. 1002. Washington, D.C.: Government Printing Office, 1965. 7 p.

_____. WILDLIFE REFUGE DISPOSAL POLICY. HEARINGS . . . ON H.R. 5306, H.R. 6723, AND H.R. 8839, BILLS TO PROTECT AND PRESERVE THE NATIONAL WILDLIFE REFUGES, AND FOR OTHER PURPOSES. 84th Cong., 2d sess. Washington, D.C.: Government Printing Office, 1956. 283 p. Tables.

U.S. Congress. House. Committee on Merchant Marine and Fisheries. Sub-committee on Conservation of Wildlife Resources. AMENDMENTS TO THE MIGRATORY BIRD TREATY ACT FOR REGULATION BY FLYWAYS AND TO ESTABLISH A MIGRATORY GAME BIRD ADVISORY COMMITTEE. HEARINGS. . . . Washington, D.C.: Government Printing Office, 1949. 531 p. Maps.

_____. PROMOTING THE CONSERVATION OF WILDLIFE. HEARINGS . . . ON H.R. 2472, A BILL TO PROVIDE EXPERT ASSISTANCE AND TO COOPER-ATE WITH FEDERAL, STATE AND OTHER SUITABLE AGENCIES, IN PROMOT-ING SOUND LAND-USE PRACTICES, AND FOR OTHER PURPOSES. JULY 2, 1947. 80th Cong., 1st sess. Washington, D.C.: Government Printing Office, 1947.

U.S. Congress. House. Committee on Merchant Marine and Fisheries. Sub-committee on Fisheries and Wildlife Conservation. ENDANGERED SPECIES. HEARINGS. . . . 91st Cong., 1st sess. Washington, D.C.: Government Printing Office, 1969. 201 p.

_____. ESTUARINE AND WETLANDS LEGISLATION. HEARINGS. . . . 89th Cong., 2d sess. Washington, D.C.: Government Printing Office, 1966. 297 p. Illus., maps.

_____. FISH AND WILDLIFE LEGISLATION. HEARINGS. . . . 90th Cong., 1st and 2d sess. Washington, D.C.: Government Printing Office, 1967.

_____. FISH AND WILDLIFE LEGISLATION. HEARINGS. . . . 3 vols. 91st Cong., 1st and 2d sess. Washington, D.C.: Government Printing Office, 1969-71. Illus., maps.

Hearings on bills concerning disposal of poisonous gases, fisheries protection, estuaries, pesticides, water pollution, fish disease, hu-man health, and fish and wildlife protection.

_____. FISH AND WILDLIFE LEGISLATION. HEARINGS. . . . 3 vols. 92d Cong., 1st sess. Washington, D.C.: Government Printing Office, 1971-72.

Hearings on bills concerning game management, hawks, owls, eagles, recreational development, San Francisco Bay National Wildlife Ref-uge, Tinicum Environmental Center, and fish farming.

_____. MISCELLANEOUS FISH AND WILDLIFE BILLS. HEARINGS . . . ON H.R. 579, MAY 12, 13, AND 24, 1949. 81st Cong., 1st sess. Washington, D.C.: Government Printing Office, 1949. 116 p.

_____. MISCELLANEOUS FISH AND WILDLIFE BILLS. HEARINGS . . . ON H.R. 230 AND OTHERS. 81st Cong., 2d sess. Washington, D.C.: Government Printing Office, 1950. 144 p.

_____. MISCELLANEOUS FISH AND WILDLIFE BILLS. HEARINGS . . . ON H.R. 783 [and others[. 85th Cong., 2d sess. Washington, D.C.: Government Printing Office, 1958. iii, 83 p.

_____. MISCELLANEOUS FISHERIES AND WILDLIFE LEGISLATION, 1965. HEARINGS. . . . 89th Cong., 1st sess. Washington, D.C.: Government Printing Office, 1965. 224 p.

_____. MISCELLANEOUS FISHERIES LEGISLATION. HEARINGS . . . ON H.R. 11967 [and others]. Part 1. 89th Cong., 1st and 2d sess. Washington, D.C.: Government Printing Office, 1966. 355 p.

_____. 1962 MISCELLANEOUS FISH AND WILDLIFE LEGISLATION. HEARINGS. . . . 87th Cong., 2d sess. Washington, D.C.: Government Printing Office, 1962-63. Illus.

_____. PREDATORY MAMMALS AND ENDANGERED SPECIES. HEARINGS. . . . 92d Cong., 2d sess. Washington, D.C.: Government Printing Office, 1972. 594 p. Illus.

U.S. Congress. Senate. Committee on Commerce. COMPILATION OF FEDERAL LAWS RELATING TO THE CONSERVATION AND DEVELOPMENT OF OUR NATION'S FISH AND WILDLIFE RESOURCES. Washington, D.C.: Government Printing Office, 1965. 472 p. Pap.

_____. COMPILATION OF FEDERAL LAWS RELATING TO THE CONSERVATION AND DEVELOPMENT OF OUR NATION'S FISH AND WILDLIFE RESOURCES, ENVIRONMENTAL QUALITY, AND OCEANOGRAPHY. Washington, D.C.: Government Printing Office, 1972. 618 p.

_____. CONSERVATION OF ENDANGERED SPECIES OF FISH AND WILDLIFE; REPORT TO ACCOMPANY H.R. 9424. 89th Cong., 2d sess., Senate Report no. 1463. Washington, D.C.: Government Printing Office, 1966. 30 p.

_____. CONTROL, REGULATION, AND MANAGEMENT OF FISH AND WILDLIFE. HEARINGS . . . ON S. 1232 AND S. 1401. . . . 91st Cong., 1st sess. Washington, D.C.: Government Printing Office, 1969. 52 p.

_____. ENDANGERED SPECIES; REPORT TO ACCOMPANY H.R. 11363. 91st Cong., 1st sess., Senate Report No. 91-526. Washington, D.C.: Government Printing Office, 1969. 41 p.

_____. MANAGEMENT OF FISH AND RESIDENT WILDLIFE ON FEDERAL LANDS. HEARINGS . . . ON S. 2951 . . . [and] S. 3212 RELATING TO THE AUTHORITY OF THE STATES TO CONTROL, REGULATE, AND MANAGE FISH AND WILDLIFE WITHIN THEIR TERRITORIAL BOUNDARIES. 90th Cong., 2d sess. Washington, D.C.: Government Printing Office, 1968.

_____. PESTICIDES HAZARDOUS TO FISH AND WILDLIFE. HEARING . . . ON S. 3328 AND H.R. 15979. . . . 90th Cong., 2d sess. Washington, D.C.: Government Printing Office, 1968. 52 p.

_____. PROTECTION OF FISH AND WILDLIFE FROM PESTICIDES; REPORT TO ACCOMPANY S. 1251. 88th Cong., 2d sess., Senate Report no. 1053. Washington, D.C.: Government Printing Office, 1964. 28 p.

_____. PROTECTION OF FISH AND WILDLIFE FROM PESTICIDES; REPORT TO ACCOMPANY S. 1623. 89th Cong., 1st sess., Senate Report no. 169. Washington, D.C.: Government Printing Office, 1965. 11 p.

U.S. Congress. Senate. Committee on Commerce. Subcommittee on Energy, Natural Resources, and the Environment. ESTABLISHING A NATIONAL WILDLIFE REFUGE FOR THE TULE ELK. HEARING . . . ON S. 3028. . . . 91st Cong., 2d sess. Washington, D.C.: Government Printing Office, 1970. 46 p.

_____. WILDLIFE RESTORATION PROJECT AND HUNTER SAFETY PROGRAMS. HEARING. . . . 91st Cong., 2d sess. Washington, D.C.: Government Printing Office, 1970. 118 p.

U.S. Congress. Senate. Committee on Commerce. Subcommittee on Merchant Marine and Fisheries. CONSERVATION, PROTECTION, AND PROPAGATION OF ENDANGERED SPECIES OF FISH AND WILDLIFE. HEARING . . . ON S. 2217. 89th Cong., 1st sess. Washington, D.C.: Government Printing Office, 1966. 69 p.

_____. ENDANGERED SPECIES. HEARING . . . ON S. 2984 AND H.R. 11618. . . . 90th Cong., 2d sess. Washington, D.C.: Government Printing Office, 1968. 165 p.

U.S. Congress. Senate. Committee on Commerce. Subcommittee on Oceana and Atmosphere. OCEAN MAMMAL PROTECTION. HEARINGS. . . . 92d Cong., 2d sess. Washington, D.C.: Government Printing Office, 1972. Illus.

U.S. Congress. Senate. Committee on Commerce. Subcommittee on the Environment. ENDANGERED SPECIES CONSERVATION ACT OF 1972. HEARINGS . . . ON S. 249 . . . S. 3199 AND S. 3818. . . . 92d Cong., 2d sess. Washington, D.C.: Government Printing Office, 1972. 285 p.

U.S. Congress. Senate. Committee on Interior and Insular Affairs. Subcommittee on Irrigation and Reclamation. HEARING . . . ON S. 784 AND S. 795, BILLS TO PROMOTE THE CONSERVATION OF MIGRATORY WATERFOWL AND WILDLIFE RESOURCES IN THE TULE LAKE, KLAMATH, AND CLEAR LAKE NATIONAL WILDLIFE REFUGES IN OREGON AND CALIFORNIA. 88th Cong., 1st sess. Washington, D.C.: Government Printing Office, 1963. 118 p. Map.

U.S. Congress. Senate. Committee on Interior and Insular Affairs. Subcommittee on Minerals, Materials and Fuels. MARINE SANCTUARIES IN CALIFORNIA. HEARINGS . . . ON S. 1446-S. 1452. . . . 92d Cong., 1st sess. Washington, D.C.: Government Printing Office, 1972. 163 p. Illus., map.

U.S. Congress. Senate. Committee on Interior and Insular Affairs. Subcommittee on Public Lands. PROTECTION OF WILD HORSES AND BURROS ON PUBLIC LANDS. HEARING. . . . 92d Cong., 1st sess. Washington, D.C.: Government Printing Office, 1971. 193 p. Illus.

U.S. Congress. Senate. Committee on Interstate and Foreign Commerce. FISH AND WILDLIFE LEGISLATION. HEARINGS . . . ON S. 2447 . . . S. 2617 . . . AND S. 3185. . . . 85th Cong., 2d sess. Washington, D.C.: Government Printing Office, 1958. 222 p. Illus., map.

_____. PROTECTION OF NATIONAL WILDLIFE REFUGES. HEARINGS . . . ON S. 2101, A BILL TO PROTECT AND PRESERVE THE NATIONAL WILDLIFE REFUGES, AND FOR OTHER PURPOSES. 84th Cong., 2d sess. Washington, D.C.: Government Printing Office, 1956. 94 p. Tables.

_____. WILDLIFE RESTORATION. HEARINGS . . . ON S. 756, A BILL TO PROVIDE THAT THE UNITED STATES SHALL AID THE STATES IN WILDLIFE RESTORATION PROJECTS; . . . S. 757, A BILL TO AMEND THE MIGRATORY BIRD HUNTING STAMP ACT OF MARCH 16, 1934; . . . AND S. 1172, A BILL TO AMEND THE WILDLIFE RESTORATION ACT. . . . 84th Cong., 1st sess. Washington, D.C.: Government Printing Office, 1955. 77 p. Tables.

U.S. Library of Congress. Legislative Reference Service. TREATIES AND OTHER INTERNATIONAL AGREEMENTS CONTAINING PROVISIONS ON COMMERCIAL FISHERIES, MARINE RESOURCES, SPORT FISHERIES, AND WILDLIFE TO WHICH THE UNITED STATES IS PARTY. Washington, D.C.: Government Printing Office, 1965. 410 p. Map.

# FISHERIES

## Government Documents--Federal

U.S. Bureau of Sport Fisheries and Wildlife. FIFTEEN YEARS OF BETTER FISHING; THE RESULT OF FEDERAL-STATE COOPERATION UNDER THE FEDERAL AID IN FISH RESTORATION PROGRAM. Washington, D.C.: Government Printing Office, 1967. 32 p. Illus.

U.S. Congress. House. Committee on Merchant Marine and Fisheries. AUTHORIZING THE SECRETARY OF THE INTERIOR TO INITIATE A PROGRAM FOR THE CONSERVATION, DEVELOPMENT, AND ENHANCEMENT OF THE NATION'S ANADROMOUS FISH; REPORT TO ACCOMPANY H.R. 2392. 88th Cong., 2d sess., House Report no. 1768. Washington, D.C.: Government Printing Office, 1964. 15 p.

U.S. Congress. House. Committee on Merchant Marine and Fisheries. Subcommittee on Fisheries and Wildlife Conservation. ANADROMOUS FISH. HEARING . . . ON H.R. 1049 . . . [and] H.R. 9546. . . . 91st Cong., 1st sess. Washington, D.C.: Government Printing Office, 1970. 116 p. Illus., maps.

_____. ANADROMOUS FISH, 1965. HEARINGS . . . ON HUDSON RIVER SPAWNING GROUNDS. 89th Cong., 1st sess. Washington, D.C.: Government Printing Office, 1965. 213 p. Illus.

_____. BLUE CRAB SHORTAGES; COMMERCIAL FISHERIES RESEARCH LEGISLATION. HEARINGS. 90th Cong., 2d sess. Washington, D.C.: Government Printing Office, 1968. 131 p. Illus.

_____. ESTABLISHMENT OF A NATIONAL POLICY FOR COMMERCIAL FISHERIES. HEARINGS . . . ON H.R. 8001 [and others]. 84th Cong., 2d sess. Washington, D.C.: Government Printing Office, 1956. 819 p. Illus.

_____. INCREASED ASSISTANCE TO COMMERCIAL FISHERIES: ALASKA PIPELINE. HEARINGS. . . . 91st Cong., 1st and 2d sess. Washington, D.C.: Government Printing Office, 1970. 282 p.

U.S. Congress. Senate. Committee on Commerce. Subcommittee on Energy, Natural Resources, and the Environment. FISHERIES LEGISLATION, 1969-70. HEARINGS. . . . 91st Cong., 1st and 2d sess. Washington, D.C.: Government Printing Office, 1970. 358 p. Maps.

U.S. Congress. Senate. Committee on Commerce. Subcommittee on Merchant Marine and Fisheries. FISHERIES LEGISLATION, 1965: PACIFIC SALMON

CONSERVATION, FISHERY LOAN FUND EXTENSION, AND CONSERVATION AND DEVELOPMENT PROGRAM FOR ANADROMOUS FISH. HEARINGS . . . ON S. 909, S. 998 AND S. 1734. 89th Cong., 1st sess. Washington, D.C.: Government Printing Office, 1965. 189 p. Illus.

_____. MISCELLANEOUS FISHERY LEGISLATION. HEARINGS. . . . 90th Cong., 1st sess. Washington, D.C.: Government Printing Office, 1967. 130 p.

U.S. Congress. Senate. Committee on Interstate and Foreign Commerce. REG-ULATION OF FISH NETS IN ALASKAN WATERS. HEARING ON S. 456, FEBRUARY 8, 1949. 84th Cong., 1st sess. Washington, D.C.: Government Printing Office, 1955. 8 p.

U.S. Treaties. FISHERIES: CERTAIN FISHERIES OFF THE UNITED STATES COAST, SALMON FISHERIES. AGREEMENTS BETWEEN THE UNITED STATES OF AMERICA AND JAPAN, EFFECTED BY EXCHANGE OF NOTES SIGNED WASHINGTON, DECEMBER 20, 1972 WITH JAPANESE NOTE AND AGREED MINUTES. Treaties and Other International Acts Series, no. 7528. Washington, D.C.: Government Printing Office, 1973. 13 p.

_____. FISHERIES: CONSERVATION OF ATLANTIC SALMON. AGREEMENT BETWEEN THE UNITED STATES OF AMERICA AND DENMARK EFFECTED BY EXCHANGE OF NOTES SIGNED AT WASHINGTON JULY 6, 1972. Treaties and Other International Acts Series, no. 7402. Washington, D.C.: Government Printing Office, 1972. 3 p.

## Government Documents--State

Florida. State Board of Conservation. GENERAL LAWS, SALT WATER FISHER-IES AND CONSERVATION. Tallahassee: 1953. Unpaged.

Minnesota. Legislature. Outdoor Recreation Resources Commission. ACQUI-SITION OF WILDLIFE LAND IN MINNESOTA (WETLAND PROGRAM). St. Paul: 1965. xxv, 48 p. Maps.

# NATURAL RESOURCES

## Land

Brown, Londo H., and Jugar, Marlyn E. RIGHTS-OF-WAY FOR REMOVAL OF NATURAL RESOURCES FROM WEST VIRGINIA LAND: AN EXAMINATION OF EXISTING APPLICABLE LAW AND OF POSSIBLE CHANGES THEREIN. Morgan-town: Office of Research and Development, West Virginia Center for Appala-chian Studies and Development, West Virginia University, 1965. 34 p.

Bruchey, Stuart, and Bruchey, Eleanor, eds. USE AND ABUSE OF AMERICA'S NATURAL RESOURCES. New York: Arno Press, 1972-

A historically oriented collection containing forty-one separate works of which the following bear some relevance to environmental law: CIRCULAR FROM THE GENERAL LAND OFFICE SHOWING THE MANNER OF PROCEEDINGS TO OBTAIN TITLE TO PUBLIC LANDS (1899); H. Gannett, ed., REPORT OF THE NATIONAL CONSERVATION COMMISSION, FEBRUARY 1909, 3 vols.; W.T. Hornaday, WILD LIFE CONSERVATION IN THEORY AND PRACTICE (1914); J. Ise, THE UNITED STATES FOREST POLICY (1920) and THE UNITED STATES OIL POLICY (1928); J.P. Kinney, THE DEVELOPMENT OF FOREST LAW IN AMERICA (1917); R.H. Lindley, A TREATISE ON THE AMERICAN LAW RELATING TO MINES AND MINERAL LANDS, 2 vols., 2d ed. (1903); B. Moreell, OUR NATION'S WATER RESOURCES--POLICIES AND POLITICS (1956); B.M. Murphy, ed., CONSERVATION OF OIL AND GAS: A LEGAL HISTORY (1948, 1949); 60th Congress, Senate, PRELIMINARY REPORT OF THE INLAND WATERWAYS COMMISSION (1908); 58th Congress, Senate, REPORT OF THE PUBLIC LANDS COMMISSION, WITH APPENDIX (1905); 46th Congress, House, REPORT OF THE PUBLIC LANDS COMMISSION (1880); SUPPLEMENTARY REPORT OF THE PLANNING COMMITTEE TO THE NATIONAL RESOURCES BOARD (1935-42); J.F. Timmons and G.M. William, eds., LAND PROBLEMS AND POLICIES (1950); RESOURCES FOR FREEDOM: A REPORT TO THE PRESIDENT BY THE PRESIDENT'S MATERIALS POLICY COMMISSION, Vols. 1 and 4 (1952).

Callison, Charles H., ed. AMERICA'S NATURAL RESOURCES. For the Natural Resources Council of America. New York: Ronald Press Company, 1957. 211 p.

_____. AMERICA'S NATURAL RESOURCES. Rev. ed. For the Natural Resources Council of America. New York: Ronald Press Company, 1967. 220 p.

Campbell, Bruce G., and Lawlor, Timothy P., Jr. DIGEST OF FEDERAL NATURAL RESOURCE LEGISLATION, 1950-66. Department of Agriculture, Economic Research Service, ERS-355. Washington, D.C.: Government Printing Office, 1967. 62 p.

Colorado. University of. Rocky Mountain Mineral Law Foundation. NATURAL RESOURCES ENVIRONMENTAL LAW INSTITUTE MANUAL. Prepared for a special one-day Institute on Natural Resources Environmental Law, February 26, 1972. Boulder: 1972. Var. pag. Loose-leaf.

Council of State Governments. THE STATES' ROLE IN LAND RESOURCE MANAGEMENT. Lexington, Ky.: 1972. 32 p. Pap., tables.

Explains state techniques and options, current and proposed federal legislation, and various state resource management programs.

CUMULATIVE INDEX 1962-1972. The Public Land and Resources Law Digest. Boulder: Rocky Mountain Mineral Law Foundation, University of Colorado, 1975. 560 p.

Reference, or cross-references, to nearly all significant legal period - ical material published since January 1, 1962.

Fawcett, James E.S. INTERNATIONAL MEANS OF CONSERVATION OF NA-TURAL RESOURCES. London: David Davies Memorial Institute of International Studies, 1969. 20 p.

Hanson, Ivan. EVALUATING ENABLING LAWS FOR SPECIAL DISTRICTS: A CASE STUDY IN OKLAHOMA. Washington, D.C.: Department of Agriculture, Economic Research Service, 1966. 37 p. (E.A.S. 281)

Jarrett, Henry, ed. COMPARISONS IN RESOURCES MANAGEMENT: SIX NOTABLE PROGRAMS IN OTHER COUNTRIES AND THEIR POSSIBLE U.S. AP-PLICATION. Baltimore, Md.: The Johns Hopkins Press, for Resources for the Future, 1961. 217 p. Photos., maps, tables.

Essays on national parks, small forests, preservation of natural areas, water pollution abatement, local integration of programs, and regional development.

LaForest, Gerard V. NATURAL RESOURCES AND PUBLIC PROPERTY UNDER THE CANADIAN CONSTITUTION. Toronto: University of Toronto Press, 1969. 230 p.

Mayda, Jaro. ENVIRONMENT AND RESOURCES; FROM CONSERVATION TO ECOMANAGEMENT. Rio Pierdras: School of Law, University of Puerto Rico, 1968. 254 p.

Meek, W.F. ENVIRONMENTAL ANALYSIS; A GUIDE TO FEDERAL ENVI-RONMENTAL CONCERNS. Boulder: Rocky Mountain Mineral Law Foundation, University of Colorado, 1974. 120 p. Pap.

Mouzon, Olin T. RESOURCES AND INDUSTRIES IN THE UNITED STATES. New York: Appleton-Century-Crofts, 1966. 48 p. Illus., maps.

Parson, Ruben L., and Associates. CONSERVING AMERICAN RESOURCES. 3d ed. Englewood Cliffs, N.J.: Prentice-Hall, 1972. 608 p.

Paulsen, David F. NATURAL RESOURCES IN THE GOVERNMENTAL PROCESS: A BIBLIOGRAPHY SELECTED AND ANNOTATED BY DAVID F. PAULSEN. University of Arizona Institute of Government Research, American Government Studies no. 3. Tucson: University of Arizona Press, 1970. 99 p.

Resources for the Future. ENVIRONMENTAL QUALITY IN A GROWING ECONOMY: ESSAYS FROM THE SIXTH RFF FORUM, BY KENNETH E. BOULDING [and others]. Edited by H. Jarrett. Baltimore, Md.: Johns Hopkins Press for Resources for the Future, 1966. 173 p.

> Stresses resource problems of quality rather than quantity. Examines goals and values, human health, welfare economics, and public attitudes. Concludes with suggested governmental role and mechanics for improvement.

Rubino, Richard G., and Wagner, William R. THE STATES' ROLE IN LAND RESOURCES MANAGEMENT. Lexington, Ky.: Council of State Governments, 1972. 32 p.

Smith, Guy H., ed. CONSERVATION OF NATURAL RESOURCES. CONTRIBUTORS: MARION CLAWSON [and others]. 3d ed. New York: J. Wiley, 1965. 533 p. Illus., maps.

> U.S. natural resources are analyzed in terms of future productivity: soils, forests, water, minerals, wildlife. Concludes with a section on state, local, and national planning.

Thomas, Fran. LAW IN ACTION: LEGAL FRONTIERS FOR NATURAL RESOURCES PLANNING, THE WORK OF PROFESSOR JACOB H. BEUSCHER. Madison: Madison Land Economics Journal, University of Wisconsin, 1972. 93 p. Pap.

Trelease, Frank J., et al. CASES AND MATERIALS ON NATURAL RESOURCES. American Casebook Series. St. Paul, Minn.: West Publishing Co., 1965. xxi, 1,131 p. Illus.

United Nations. Secretariat. THE STATUS OF PERMANENT SOVEREIGNTY OVER NATURAL RESOURCES. United Nations Document A/AC.97/5 rev. 2, E/3511 (A/AC.97/13). New York: 1962. 245 p.

_____. THE STATUS OF PERMANENT SOVEREIGNTY OVER NATURAL WEALTH AND RESOURCES. 2 vols. Rev. ed. United Nations Document A/AC.97/5 rev. 1. New York: 1960. 674 p.

Whitaker, Joe R., and Ackerman, Edward A. AMERICAN RESOURCES: THEIR MANAGEMENT AND CONSERVATION. Use and Abuse of America's Natural Resources. New York: Arno Press, 1972 [c1951]. 497 p. Illus.

> Analysis of resource deterioration in the United States.

## GOVERNMENT DOCUMENTS

Alabama. Laws and Statutes. COAL MINING LAWS OF THE STATE OF ALA-
BAMA, AS AMENDED 1951. Birmingham: Division of Safety and Inspection,
Department of Industrial Relations, 1952. 102 p.

Massachusetts. Laws and Statutes. MASSACHUSETTS CONSERVATION LAW;
A SELECTED COMPENDIUM. Amherst: Bureau of Government Research, University of Massachusetts, 1961. 119 p.

U.S. Congress. Senate. Committee on Interior and Insular Affairs. COMMIT-
TEE'S HISTORY, JURISDICTION, AND A SUMMARY OF ITS ACCOMPLISH-
MENTS DURING THE 87TH, 88TH, 90TH, AND 91ST CONGRESSES. 92d Cong.,
1st sess. Washington, D.C.: Government Printing Office, 1971. 198 p.

_____. PROPOSED RESOURCES AND CONSERVATION ACT OF 1960. HEAR-
INGS . . . ON S. 3549, A BILL TO DECLARE A NATIONAL POLICY ON
CONSERVATION, DEVELOPMENT, AND UTILIZATION OF NATURAL RE-
SOURCES, AND FOR OTHER PURPOSES. . . . 86th Cong., 2d sess. Wash-
ington, D.C.: Government Printing Office 1960. 189 p.

_____. RESOURCES AND CONSERVATION ACT OF 1961. HEARING . . .
ON S. 239 AND S. 1415, BILLS TO DECLARE A NATIONAL POLICY ON
CONSERVATION, DEVELOPMENT, AND UTILIZATION OF NATURAL RE-
SOURCES, AND FOR OTHER PURPOSES. 87th Cong., 1st sess. Washington,
D.C.: Government Printing Office, 1961. 169 p.

U.S. Department of the Interior. Office of Information. THE RACE FOR IN-
NER SPACE: A SPECIAL REPORT TO THE NATION. Washington, D.C.:
1964. 76 p. Illus.

## Marine

Alexander, Lewis M., ed. THE LAW OF THE SEA: NATIONAL POLICY REC-
OMMENDATIONS. Kingston: University of Rhode Island Press, 1970. 583
p. Illus.

Birnie, Patricia S., et al. CRITICAL ENVIRONMENTAL ISSUES ON THE LAW
OF THE SEA. Washington, D.C.: International Institute for Environment and
Development, 1975. 57 p.

Bohme, Eckart, and Kehden, Max I., eds. FROM THE LAW OF THE SEA TO-
WARDS AN OCEAN SPACE REGIME; PRACTICAL AND LEGAL IMPLICATIONS
OF THE MARINE REVOLUTION. Hamburg, Ger.: Universtaet Hamburg, 1972.
174 p.

Papers in English and German proposing the creation, financing, and administration of an ocean regime to facilitate international regulation of the sea and the sea bed. Revised Ocean Regime Draft Statute appended.

Borgese, Elizabeth Mann, ed. PACEM IN MARIBUS. New York: Dobbs, Mead, 1973. xxxiv, 382 p.

Includes papers on law and marine resources. Selections from Pacem in Maribus Convocation in Malta, 1970, projects of the Center for the Study of Democratic Institutions, and publications of the Pacem in Maribus Institute at the Royal University of Malta.

Brown, Edward D. THE LEGAL REGIME OF HYDROSPACE. The Library of World Affairs, no. 70. London: Stevens, for the London Institute of World Affairs, 1971. xx, 236 p.

Doumani, George A. EXPLOITING THE RESOURCES OF THE SEABED. Washington, D.C.: Government Printing Office for the Subcommittee on National Security Policy and Scientific Developments of the Committee on Foreign Affairs, U.S. House of Representatives, 1971. 152 p. Illus.

English, T. Saunders, ed. OCEAN RESOURCES AND PUBLIC POLICY. Public Policy Issues in Resource Management, vol. 5. Seattle: University of Washington Press, 1973. 208 p. Figures.

Ereli, Eliezer. THE ENVIRONMENTAL REGULATION OF THE SEA AND ITS RESOURCES; CASES AND MATERIALS. Houston, Tex.: College of Law, University of Houston, 1972. 611 p.

_____. LEGAL REGIME OF THE SEA AND ITS RESOURCES, CASES AND MATERIALS. Houston, Tex.: College of Law, University of Houston, 1971. 610 p.

Henkin, Louis. LAW FOR THE SEA'S MINERAL RESOURCES. New York: Institute for the Study of Science in Human Affairs, Columbia University, 1968. 75 p.

A study of present law governing the extraction of mineral resources from the sea bed and the merits of recommended new legal arrangements.

Hood, Donald W., ed. IMPINGEMENT OF MAN ON THE OCEANS. New York: Wiley-Interscience, 1971. 738 p. Illus., maps.

Houston. University of. College of Law. Texas Law Institute of Coastal and Marine Resources. REGULATION OF ACTIVITIES AFFECTING BAYS AND ESTUARIES: A PRELIMINARY LEGAL STUDY. Houston: 1972. 22 p. Pap.

Jones, Erin B. LAW OF THE SEA: OCEANIC RESOURCES. Foreword by C.O. Galvin. Dallas, Tex.: Southern Methodist University Press, 1972. 162 p.

Knauss, John A. FACTORS INFLUENCING A U.S. POSITION IN A FUTURE LAW OF THE SEA CONFERENCE. Law of the Sea Institute Occasional Paper no. 10. Kingston: Law of the Sea Institute, University of Rhode Island, 1971. 30 p.

Law of the Sea Institute. THE LAW OF THE SEA: THE UNITED NATIONS AND OCEAN MANAGEMENT; PROCEEDINGS OF THE FIFTH ANNUAL CONFERENCE. . . . THE UNIVERSITY OF RHODE ISLAND, KINGSTON. Edited by L.M. Alexander. Kingston: University of Rhode Island, 1971. 390 p. Charts, maps.

Legg, Billy J. SEABED REGIMES AND THE LIMITS OF NATIONAL JURISDICTION. Sea Grant Technical Bulletin no. 19. Coral Gables, Fla.: University of Miami Sea Grant Program, 1971. 125 p.

National Petroleum Council. Committee on Petroleum Resources Under the Ocean Floor. PETROLEUM RESOURCES UNDER THE OCEAN FLOOR. Washington, D.C.: 1969. 107 p.

> The report includes three chapters which deal with both national and international legal aspects of oceanic petroleum resource development: "Current National Jurisdiction Over Petroleum Resources of Oceanic Areas," "Implementation of United States Policy Objectives Consistent with the 1958 Convention on the Continental Shelf," and "Regime Over Oceanic Areas Beyond Limits of Exclusive National Resource Jurisdiction."

Padelford, Norman J., ed. PUBLIC POLICY FOR THE SEAS. Rev. ed. Cambridge, Mass.: M.I.T. Press, 1970. 338 p.

> A compilation of statutes, treaties, presidential proclamations and messages, UN resolutions and other materials concerning ocean policy aspects of goals, territorial waters, the continental shelf, international law, resources and their regulation, mineral resource exploitation, pollution, safety of life at sea, future governmental models, and political processes.

Padelford, Norman J., and Cook, Jerry E. NEW DIMENSIONS OF U.S. MARINE POLICY. Massachusetts Institute of Technology, Sea Grant Project Office Report no. MITSG 71-5. Cambridge: Massachusetts Institute of Technology, Sea Grant Project Office, 1971. 250 p. Illus., maps.

SEA-BED [year]. Indexed and annotated by H.N.M. Winton. Worldmark International Documentation Series. New York: Worldmark Press, 1970-  . Annual.

> Published annually two years following the title date. Collections

of documents of international organizations within the UN designed
to provide access to documents which are otherwise difficult to obtain.

United Nations. Second Conference on the Law of the Sea, Geneva, 17 March
to 26 April, 1960. OFFICIAL RECORDS. New York: United Nations, 1962.
431 p.

In three languages. Verbatim statements of delegates on the topic
of the conference, the question of the territorial sea and fishing
limits.

United Nations. Secretariat. Legal Department. LAWS AND REGULATIONS
ON THE REGIME OF THE HIGH SEAS. New York: 1951-  . Irregular.

## GOVERNMENT DOCUMENTS

U.S. Congress. House. Committee on Foreign Affairs. Subcommittee on International Organizations and Movements. LAW OF THE SEA RESOLUTION,
H.RES. 216 AND 296. Washington, D.C.: Government Printing Office,
1973. 187 p. Pap.

The resolutions urge the Law of the Sea Conference to arrive at
an agreement upon a treaty and endorse several important principles
in the U.S. Draft Seabed Treaty. The document also includes
hearings, written statements and a long appendix which contains
statements and reports relevant to ocean law and resources development.

U.S. Congress. House. Committee on Merchant Marine and Fisheries. Subcommittee on Oceanography. COASTAL ZONE MANAGEMENT. HEARINGS
. . . ON H.R. 2492 . . . H.R. 2493 . . . [and] H.R. 9229. . . . 92d
Cong., 1st sess. Washington, D.C.: Government Printing Office, 1972.
463 p. Illus.

U.S. Congress. Senate. Committee on Interior and Insular Affairs. THE LAW
OF THE SEA CRISIS; A STAFF REPORT ON THE UNITED NATIONS SEABED
COMMITTEE, THE OUTER CONTINENTAL SHELF, AND MARINE MINERAL
DEVELOPMENT. 92d Cong., 1st and 2d sess. 2 vols. Washington, D.C.:
Government Printing Office, 1972. 335 p.

U.S. President's Science Advisory Committee. Panel on Oceanography. EF-
FECTIVE USE OF THE SEA; REPORT. Washington, D.C.: Government Printing
Office, 1966. 144 p.

U.S. Treaties. TREATIES AND OTHER INTERNATIONAL AGREEMENTS ON
OCEANOGRAPHIC RESOURCES, FISHERIES, AND WILDLIFE TO WHICH THE

UNITED STATES IS PARTY. PREPARED AT THE REQUEST OF HONORABLE WARREN G. MAGNUSON, CHAIRMAN, FOR THE USE OF THE COMMITTEE ON COMMERCE, U.S. SENATE, BY THE LEGISLATIVE REFERENCE SERVICE, THE LIBRARY OF CONGRESS. Washington, D.C.: Government Printing Office, 1971. 627 p.

## LAND USE AND OPEN SPACE

Adams, Frank T., Jr. LEGAL ASPECTS OF OPEN SPACE PRESERVATION IN VERMONT. Montpelier: Vermont Crossroads Press, 1965. 35 p.

American Bar Association. Section of Insurance, Negligence and Compensation Law. PLANNING, ENVIRONMENTAL SCIENCE, AVIATION. Proceedings of the National Institute on Environmental Litigation, vol. 1. New York: 1974. 188 p. Pap., diagrs.

American Society of Planning Officials. LAND-USE CONTROLS ANNUAL, 1971; WITH A SPECIAL SECTION CONTAINING COMMENTARY AND CRITICISM OF THE AMERICAN LAW INSTITUTE'S "A MODEL LAND DEVELOPMENT CODE." Chicago: 1972. 212 p.

The annual replaces the LAND-USE CONTROLS QUARTERLY.

Babcock, Richard F., and Bosselman, Fred P. THE CONTEST FOR PUBLIC CONTROL OVER LAND DEVELOPMENT: A ROUGH INTERGOVERNMENTAL GAME FOR THE SEVENTIES. Regents' Lecture presented at the University of California, Los Angeles, April 16, 1970. Los Angeles: Institute of Government and Public Affairs, University of California, 1970. 63 p.

Bailey, Gilbert E., and Thayer, Paul S. CALIFORNIA'S DISAPPEARING COAST: A LEGISLATIVE CHALLENGE. Berkeley: Institute of Governmental Studies, University of California, 1971. 99 p.

An examination of coastal problems through the perspective of earlier experience with development of the San Francisco Bay Conservation and Development Commission. The authors review and analyze three separate legislative proposals.

Barr, Charles W. PLANNING THE COUNTRYSIDE: THE LEGAL BASIS FOR COUNTRY AND TOWNSHIP PLANNING IN MICHIGAN. East Lansing: Michigan State University Press, 1950. 86 p. Diagrs.

Bartholomew, and Associates. LAND USE DISTRICTS FOR THE STATE OF HAWAII: RECOMMENDATIONS FOR IMPLEMENTATION OF THE STATE LAND USE LAW, ACT 187, SLH 1961. For the Department of Planning and Research and the Land Use Commission. Honolulu: 1973. 98 p. Maps, illus.

Beckman, Norman, and Langdon, Bruce. NATIONAL GROWTH POLICY: LEG-
ISLATIVE AND EXECUTIVE ACTIONS 1970-71. Washington, D.C.: Urban
Land Institute, 1972. 128 p.

A study of current urban growth policies, programs, and legislation.
Summarizes state and federal statutes and actions taken by Congress
and congressional committees. Includes a substantial annotated
bibliography of recent literature on urban and rural development
and a chart of bills proposing a land-use policy.

Berry, Brian J.L., et al. LAND USE, URBAN FORM AND ENVIRONMENTAL
QUALITY. Chicago: Department of Geography, University of Chicago, 1974.
440 p. Pap.

Bosselman, Fred P. ALTERNATIVES TO URBAN SPRAWL: LEGAL GUIDELINES
FOR GOVERNMENTAL ACTION. Washington, D.C.: National Commission on
Urban Problems, 1968. 69 p.

Approaches the problem of urban sprawl through chapters on the
planned development zone, compensative regulations, and public
land assembly.

Bosselman, Fred P., and Callies, David. THE QUIET REVOLUTION IN LAND
USE CONTROL. Washington, D.C.: Government Printing Office for the Council on Environmental Quality, 1972. 327 p. Illus.

Bowman, Wallace, and Quarles, Steven P., comps. NATIONAL LAND USE
POLICY; BACKGROUND PAPERS ON PAST AND PENDING LEGISLATION
AND THE ROLES OF THE EXECUTIVE BRANCH, CONGRESS, AND THE STATES
IN LAND USE POLICY AND PLANNING. 92d Cong., 2d sess. Washington,
D.C.: Government Printing Office, 1972. 212 p. Illus.

Branaman, Marybeth. CONTROL OF SUBDIVISIONS IN CALIFORNIA. Pre-
pared with the advice and assistance of P.F. Wendt. Berkeley: Real Estate
Research Program, Bureau of Business and Economic Research, University of
California, 1953. 43 p. Illus.

California. University of. Hastings College of Law. "California Land Use
Control." HASTINGS LAW JOURNAL 13 (February 1962): entire issue.

The entire issue is dedicated to the subject of land use controls.

Carman, Hoy F., and Polson, Jim G. THE CALIFORNIA LAND CONSERVA-
TION ACT OF 1965; LANDOWNER PARTICIPATION AND ESTIMATED TAX
SHIFTS. Information Series in Agricultural Economics, no. 71-4. Berkeley:
University of California Agricultural Extension Service, 1971. 18 p.

Carroll, Michael A. OPEN SPACE PLANNING: A SELECTED BIBLIOGRAPHY. Urbana: Bureau of Community Planning and Department of Urban Planning, University of Illinois, 1965. 59 p.

Clawson, Marion, ed. MODERNIZING URBAN LAND. Baltimore, Md.: Johns Hopkins University Press, 1973. 248 p.

Commerce Clearing House. URBAN AFFAIRS REPORTER. Chicago: 1968- . Loose-leaf.

Curtis, Virginia, ed. LAND-USE POLICIES; PAPERS PRESENTED AT THE LAND-USE POLICIES SHORT COURSE HELD AT THE 1970 AMERICAN SOCIETY OF PLANNING OFFICIALS NATIONAL PLANNING CONFERENCE. Chicago: American Society of Planning Officials, 1970. 74 p.

   The four sections are "Land Acquisition and Tax Policies," "Implementing National and Metropolitan Policies," "Retooling Land-Use Controls," "Development of New Town."

Davies, Race D. PRESERVING AGRICULTURAL AND OPEN-SPACE LANDS: LEGISLATIVE POLICYMAKING IN CALIFORNIA. Environmental Quality Series, no. 10. Davis: Institute of Governmental Affairs, University of California, 1972. 150 p.

   A study of legislative proposals from 1955 to 1970. Relates to an overall project to design a computer simulation model of land use and energy flow in human society.

Delafons, John. LAND-USE CONTROLS IN THE UNITED STATES. Cambridge: Joint Center for Urban Studies of the Massachusetts Institute of Technology and Harvard University, 1962. 100 p. Tables.

Doolittle, Fred C. LAND-USE PLANNING AND REGULATION ON THE CALIFORNIA COAST: THE STATE ROLE. Environmental Quality Series, no. 9. Davis: Institute of Governmental Affairs, University of California, 1972. 85 p.

   A history of state policy and a discussion of the various efforts to give state government a greater role in the regulation of coastal land use.

Eckbo, Dean, Austin and Williams in association with Grunwald-Crawford Associates and Baxter-McDonald and Company. STATE OPEN SPACE AND RESOURCE CONSERVATION PROGRAM FOR CALIFORNIA. For the California Legislature, Joint Committee on Open Space Lands. San Francisco: 1972. 59 p. Pap., photos., maps, tables.

   A summary of what is and what the consultants believe should be happening with respect to preservation of open space in California.

FEDERAL PUBLIC LAND LAWS AND POLICIES RELATING TO INTENSIVE AGRI-
CULTURE. 4 vols. in 1. Prepared for the Public Land Law Review Commission
by Stanley W. Kronick et al. Springfield, Va.: Clearinghouse for Federal
Scientific and Technical Information, 1969. 1,457 p.


Fellmeth, Robert C. POLITICS OF LAND: RALPH NADER'S STUDY GROUPS
REPORT ON LAND USE IN CALIFORNIA. New York: Grossman Publishers,
1972.


Greenwood, N.H., and Edwards, J.M.B. HUMAN ENVIRONMENTS AND
NATURAL SYSTEMS: A CONFLICT OF DOMINION. North Scituate, Mass.:
Duxbury Press, 1973. 429 p. Photos., illus., tables, graphs, charts.

>   An attempted synthesis of environmentalist literature. Largely non-
>   legal, but contains short sections on systems of land tenure, the
>   North American Water and Power Alliance, open space and cluster
>   development.


Gregory, David D. THE EASEMENT AS A CONSERVATION TECHNIQUE.
With the collaboration of A. Diot and H.J. Dietrich. IUCN Environmental
Law Paper no. 1. Morges, Switzerland: International Union for Conservation
of Nature and Natural Resources, 1972. 47 p. Pap.

>   A study of the conservation easement, intended to explain concepts
>   and procedures which might have application outside the originating
>   jurisdictions. One chapter on the Massachusetts Conservation Re-
>   striction Act and appendixes on French and German devices.


Guitar, Mary A. PROPERTY POWER: HOW TO KEEP THE BULL-DOZER, THE
POWER LINE, AND THE HIGHWAYMEN AWAY FROM YOUR DOOR. Garden
City, N.Y.: Doubleday and Co., 1972. 322 p.


Haar, Charles M. LAND-USE PLANNING: A CASEBOOK ON THE USE,
MISUSE AND REUSE OF URBAN LAND. Law School Casebook Series. Boston:
Little, Brown, 1959. 790 p. Illus. SUPPLEMENT I, 1966. 84 p. SUPPLE-
MENT II, 1968. 109 p.


_____, ed. LAW AND LAND: ANGLO-AMERICAN PLANNING PRACTICE.
Cambridge, Mass.: Harvard University Press and M.I.T. Press, 1964. 290 p.

>   Papers on English law and land-use controls, city planning and
>   liberty, comparison of development plans and master plans, English
>   development plans, flexibility in American zoning, planning deci-
>   sions and appeals, enforcement in England and Wales, regulation
>   and purchase as control mechanisms, compulsory acquisition in
>   England, and eminent domain in the United States.


Hagman, Donald G. URBAN PLANNING AND LAND DEVELOPMENT CON-
TROL LAW. Hornbook Series. St. Paul, Minn.: West Publishing Co., 1971.
xxvii, 539 p.

Heeter, David. TOWARD A MORE EFFECTIVE LAND-USE GUIDANCE SYS-
TEM: A SUMMARY AND ANALYSIS OF FIVE MAJOR REPORTS. Washington,
D.C.: American Society of Planning Officials, 1969. 120 p.

> The summarized reports: The Advisory Commission on Intergovern-
> mental Relations, URBAN AND RURAL AMERICA: POLICIES FOR
> FUTURE GROWTH; The National Commission on Urban Problems,
> BUILDING THE AMERICAN CITY; The American Law Institute, A
> MODEL LAND DEVELOPMENT CODE; The Canadian Federal Task
> Force on Housing and Urban Development, REPORT OF THE TASK
> FORCE ON HOUSING AND URBAN DEVELOPMENT; The Ameri-
> can Society of Planning Officials, NEW DIRECTIONS IN CON-
> NECTICUT PLANNING LEGISLATION.

Herring, Francis W., ed. OPEN SPACE AND THE LAW. Berkeley: Institute
of Government Studies, University of California, 1965. 160 p.

_____. REGIONAL PARKS AND OPEN SPACE: SELECTED CONFERENCE
PAPERS, PROCEEDINGS OF TWO CONFERENCES, JANUARY 27, 1961 AND
DECEMBER 11, 1959. Berkeley: Bureau of Public Administration, University
of California, 1961. 143 p. Illus., maps.

Higbee, Edward C. THE SQUEEZE: CITIES WITHOUT SPACE. Foreword by
F. Osborn. New York: Morrow, 1960. 348 p.

Hite, James C., and Stepp, James M., eds. COASTAL ZONE RESOURCE
MANAGEMENT. New York: Praeger, 1971. 169 p.

> Papers discuss the issues related to developing a scientific manage-
> ment system for the coastal zone. Topics relevant to legislation
> and administration are the San Francisco Bay experience, systems
> under consideration at the federal-state and state-local levels, and
> legal and institutional considerations.

International Independence Institute. THE COMMUNITY LAND TRUST: A
GUIDE TO A NEW MODEL FOR LAND TENURE IN AMERICA. Cambridge,
Mass.: Center for Community Economic Development, 1972. 180 p. Charts,
illus.

> An introduction to the community land trust as a tool that low-
> income communities can use to control development processes in
> both urban and rural neighborhoods. Covers experiments in com-
> munity land holding, organizational structure, land selection and
> acquisition, financing, land use planning, taxation, zoning, build-
> ing codes, and basic legal documents.

Krassa, Lucie G. RETAINING OPEN SPACES IN MARYLAND. College Park:
Bureau of Business and Economic Research, University of Maryland, 1961. 16 p.

Legalines, Inc. LAND USE CONTROLS. 2d ed. Los Angeles: distributed by College Book Store, 1969. 83 p.

McClellan, Grant S., ed. LAND USE IN THE UNITED STATES: EXPLOITA-TION OR CONSERVATION? The Reference Shelf, vol. 43, no. 2. New York: H.W. Wilson Co., 1971. 253 p. Bibliog.

> Part 5, "Toward a New Public Lands Policy," includes "Public Land Law Review Commission Recommendations on Public Land Use" and "A Critique of the Public Land Law Report."

Mandelker, Daniel R. GREEN BELTS AND URBAN GROWTH: ENGLISH TOWN AND COUNTRY PLANNING IN ACTION. Madison: University of Wisconsin Press, 1962. 176 p. Illus.

Meadows, Donella H., et al. THE LIMITS TO GROWTH. New York: Universe Books, 1972. 205 p. Hard. and pap.

Monaco, Grace P., and Monaco, Lawrence A., Jr. OUTLINE OF LAND USE CONTROLS (PUBLIC). Blackstone Law Summaries. Irvington-on-Hudson, N.Y.: American Legal Publications, 1969. 72 p.

National Research Council. Highway Research Board. JOINT DEVELOPMENT AND MULTIPLE USE OF TRANSPORTATION RIGHT-OF-WAY; PROCEEDINGS OF A CONFERENCE. Washington, D.C.: Highway Research Board, 1969. 198 p. Illus.

> Sections on legal aspects and current governmental policies.

_____. NATIONAL COOPERATIVE HIGHWAY RESEARCH PROGRAM REPORT 56: SCENIC EASEMENTS: LEGAL, ADMINISTRATIVE, AND VALUATION PROBLEMS AND PROCEDURES. Washington, D.C.: 1968. 175 p. Bibliog.

> A study of the legal problems involved in the acquisition and use of scenic easements, especially relative to the scenic preservation and enhancement provisions of the Highway Beautification Act of 1965. Also a proposal for legislative and administrative practices for acquiring scenic easements.

_____. NATIONAL COOPERATIVE HIGHWAY RESEARCH PROGRAM REPORT 119: CONTROL OF HIGHWAY ADVERTISING SIGNS: SOME LEGAL PROB-LEMS. Washington, D.C.: National Research Council, 1971. 72 p. Bibliog.

> A report on legal and valuation problems related to Title I of the Highway Beautification Act and on the use of police power to control roadside advertising. State legislation and a table of cases are appended.

Platt, Rutherford H. OPEN LAND IN URBAN ILLINOIS: ROLES OF THE CITI-

ZEN ADVOCATE. DeKalb: Northern Illinois University Press, 1971. 132 p. Photos.

A summary of the practice of "land advocacy" in the Chicago area.

Ploy, Stanley P. AN INVENTORY OF URBAN STUDIES CONDUCTED BY SELECTED FACULTY MEMBERS OF THE UNIVERSITY OF CALIFORNIA, LOS ANGELES. Los Angeles: Institute of Government and Public Affairs, University of California, Los Angeles, 1966. 22 p.

Bibliography which lists titles relevant to urban land use, city, county and other governments, taxation, natural resources, and reclamation.

Raymond and May Associates. ZONING CONTROVERSIES IN THE SUBURBS: THREE CASE STUDIES. Washington, D.C.: Government Printing Office for the National Commission on Urban Problems, 1968. 82 p.

Studies three types of zoning issues: the conflict between residential and industrial uses; high density structures in existing low density areas; and relative advantages of cluster zoning.

Rhea, Gordon C., et al. CALIFORNIA LAND USE PRIMER: A LEGAL HANDBOOK FOR ENVIRONMENTALISTS. Stanford, Calif.: Stanford Environmental Law Society, 1972. 79 p. Pap.

A legal guide designed for use by persons interested in influencing land-use decisions by local governments, especially relating to open space. The three parts are "The Elements of Land Use Planning," "Extent of Regulatory Powers," and "Environmental Tactics."

Rickert, John E. OPEN SPACE LAND, PLANNING AND TAXATION: A SELECTED BIBLIOGRAPHY. Prepared by Urban Land Institute for the Urban Renewal Administration, Housing and Home Finance Agency. Washington, D.C.: Government Printing Office, 1965. 58 p.

Roberts, E.F. LAND-USE PLANNING: CASES AND MATERIALS. New York: Matthew Bender, 1971. 1,269 p.

A comprehensive casebook with comment. Emphasizes planning as a process without clear "rules" but carrying with it complex implications.

Shomon, Joseph J. OPEN LAND FOR URBAN AMERICA: ACQUISITION, SAFEKEEPING, AND USE. Baltimore, Md.: Johns Hopkins Press in cooperation with the National Audobon Society, 1971. 171 p. Illus., maps.

Siegan, Bernard H. LAND USE WITHOUT ZONING. Lexington, Mass.: Lexington Books, 1972. 271 p.

Details the failures of the zoning process, advocates greater use of

the market as a land-use control mechanism and includes a number
of chapters on alternative solutions and land-use legislation.

Siegel, Shirley Adelson. THE LAW OF OPEN SPACE: LEGAL ASPECTS OF
ACQUIRING OR OTHERWISE PRESERVING OPEN SPACE IN THE TRI-STATE
NEW YORK METROPOLITAN REGION. New York: Regional Plan Associa-
tion, 1960. 72 p.

Slade, Sondra. CONSERVATION AND FLOODING EASEMENTS: A CASE
STUDY. Philadelphia: University of Pennsylvania, Institute of Environmental
Studies, 1970. 94 p. Pap.

Soil Conservation Society of America. NATIONAL LAND USE POLICY: OB-
JECTIVES, COMPONENTS, IMPLEMENTATION, THE PROCEEDINGS OF A
SPECIAL CONFERENCE. Ankeny, Iowa: 1973. 220 p.

Soong, H.M. BIBLIOGRAPHY OF LAND USE PLANNING LAW. Windsor,
Ont.: Faculty of Law Library, University of Windsor, 1973. 37 p. Mimeo.

Stanford Environmental Law Society. THE ENVIRONMENT AND CALIFORNIA'S
HIGHWAYS: GO BACK, YOU ARE GOING THE WRONG WAY. Stanford,
Calif.: Stanford University, 1972. 177 p. Charts.

> A critique of the highway building process in California in light
> of financial, environmental and political considerations, and exist-
> ing legislation.

Stanhagen, William H. HIGHWAY INTERCHANGES AND LAND USE CON-
TROLS. Washington, D.C.: Government Printing Office for the Public Roads
Bureau, 1961. 85 p.

Thomas, David. LONDON'S GREEN BELT. London: Faber and Faber, 1970.
248 p.

> Two chapters discuss the land-use controls employed to create the
> green belt.

Western Center for Community Education and Development. OPEN SPACE IN
CALIFORNIA: ISSUES AND OPTIONS. Los Angeles: 1965? 73 p. Illus.,
maps.

Whytle, William H. SECURING OPEN SPACES FOR URBAN AMERICA: CON-
SERVATION EASEMENTS. Washington, D.C.: Urban Land Institute, 1959.
67 p. Illus.

Williams, Edward A., Director. OPEN SPACE: THE CHOICES BEFORE CALI-
FORNIA; THE URBAN METROPOLITAN OPEN SPACE STUDY. San Francisco:

Diable Press, 1969. 187 p. Photos., bibliog.

> A guide to state and local governments for the planning and acqui-
> sition of open-space land in metropolitan areas. Sections that deal
> with legislation and other legal aspects are "Methods of Preserving
> Open Space" and "Pertinent Legislation."

Wisconsin Department of Resource Development and State Recreation Committee.
CONSERVATION EASEMENTS AND OPEN SPACE CONFERENCE. Proceedings
of a Conference, 13 and 14 December 1961, Madison, Wisconsin. Madison:
1961. 127 p. Illus.

> Papers on conservation easements and the law, New York's trout
> stream easements, and scenic easements for programs of the Wis-
> consin Highway Commission and Conservation departments.

Wood, Samuel E., and Heller, Alfred E. CALIFORNIA GOING, GOING:
OUR STATE'S STRUGGLE TO REMAIN BEAUTIFUL AND PRODUCTIVE. Sacramento: California Tomorrow, 1962. 63 p. Illus.

Ziebarth, Richard, and Gathe, Theodore H. THE COURT'S ASSAULT ON PRI-
VATE PRIVILEGE: A MARXIST ANALYSIS OF RECENT WASHINGTON STATE
LAND USE DECISIONS. Introductions by K. Wakayama and E. Ratner. Mos-
cow, Ida.: Teton Rising Sun Press, 1974. 322 p.

## Government Documents

California. Laws and Statutes. LAWS RELATING TO PLANNING AND RE-
SEARCH, STATE CONSERVATION AND PLANNING, AIRPORT NEEDS, OCEAN
BEACHES, BEACH AND CLIFF EROSION, BEACH EROSION CONTROL EN-
GINEER, SUBDIVIDED LANDS, SUBDIVISION MAPS, SUBDIVISION LAND
EXCLUSIONS, BASIC TOPOGRAPHIC MAPPING, STATE MAPS AND SURVEYS,
RIDING AND HIKING TRAILS, WATER RESOURCES, PROTECTION OF BEDS
OF MAPPED HIGHWAYS, STATE AID FOR LOCAL PUBLIC WORKS PLANNING,
THE LOCAL AGENCY ALLOCATION ACT, COMMUNITY REDEVELOPMENT,
PARKS, RECREATION AND PARKWAYS. Sacramento: Print Division, Docu-
ments Section, 1950. 96 p.

Northern Virginia Regional Planning and Economic Development Commission.
ACTION FOR OPEN SPACE. National Capital Open Space Program, Planning
Report no. 1. Arlington, Va.: 1965. 114 p. Maps.

U.S. Congress. House. Committee on Agriculture. Subcommittee on Conser-
vation and Credit. FEDERAL COST SHARING FOR RURAL CONSERVATION
AND DEVELOPMENT PROJECTS. HEARINGS. . . . 90th Cong., 1st sess.
Washington, D.C.: Government Printing Office, 1967. 79 p.

U.S. Federal Highway Administration. REPORT TO CONGRESS ON SECTION

109(h), TITLE 23, UNITED STATES CODE--GUIDELINES RELATING TO THE
ECONOMIC, SOCIAL, AND ENVIRONMENTAL EFFECTS OF HIGHWAY PRO-
JECTS. 92d Cong., 2d sess. Washington, D.C.: Government Printing Office,
1972. 22 p.

U.S. General Accounting Office. CONTROLS NEEDED OVER THE LEASING
OF LAND ACQUIRED UNDER THE OPEN-SPACE LAND PROGRAM [Administered
by the] DEPARTMENT OF HOUSING AND URBAN DEVELOPMENT; REPORT TO
THE CONGRESS BY THE COMPTROLLER GENERAL OF THE UNITED STATES.
Washington, D.C.: 1971. 21 p.

U.S. Lower Colorado River Land Use Advisory Committee. THE LOWER COLO-
RADO RIVER LAND USE PLAN: A REPORT. Washington, D.C.: Department
of the Interior; Government Printing Office, 1964. 187 p. Maps, illus.

U.S. National Resources Board. Land Planning Committee. USE AND ABUSE
OF AMERICA'S NATURAL RESOURCES: SUPPLEMENTARY REPORT OF THE
LAND PLANNING COMMITTEE TO THE NATIONAL RESOURCES BOARD.
New York: Arno Press, 1972. 863 p. Charts, maps, photos.

> Contains much basic data. Relevant to legal aspects in sections
> on government land policies and programs with respect to agricul-
> ture, soil, erosion, maladjustments in land use, forests, wildlife,
> recreation, and public works. The original report was issued in
> parts by the Government Printing Office, 1935-42.

U.S. Public Land Law Review Commission. PRESERVING URBAN OPEN SPACE.
Washington, D.C.: Government Printing Office, 1963. 36 p.

U.S. Urban Renewal Administration. OPEN SPACE FOR URBAN AMERICA.
Prepared by A.L. Strong. Washington, D.C.: Department of Housing and Urban Development; Government Printing Office, 1965. 154 p. Illus., maps.

Virginia. Advisory Legislative Council. PUBLIC SERVICE EASEMENTS. RE-
PORT TO THE GOVERNOR AND THE GENERAL ASSEMBLY OF VIRGINIA.
Richmond: Department of Purchases and Supply, Commonwealth of Virginia,
1965.

# PUBLIC LAND

Ashby, Andrew W. PUBLIC LANDS: AN FAO LAND TENURE STUDY. FAO
Agriculture Studies, no. 31. Rome: Food and Agricultural Organization of the
United Nations, 1956. 47 p.

Hibbard, Benjamin H. A HISTORY OF PUBLIC LAND POLICIES. Madison:
University of Wisconsin Press, 1924. 579 p.

In part, a detailed account of public land legislation from the founding of the nation until 1923.

Pyles, Hamilton K., ed. WHAT'S AHEAD FOR OUR PUBLIC LANDS? A SUMMARY REVIEW OF THE ACTIVITIES AND FINAL REPORT OF THE PUBLIC LAND LAW REVIEW COMMISSION. Washington, D.C.: Natural Resources Council of America for the Natural Resources Council of America, 1970. 343 p.

Stanford Environmental Law Society. PUBLIC LAND MANAGEMENT--A TIME FOR CHANGE? Stanford, Calif.: Stanford University, 1971. 139 p. Looseleaf.

SYMPOSIUM ON AMERICAN MINERAL LAW RELATING TO PUBLIC LAND USE; [PAPERS]. Edited by J.C. Dotson. Tucson: College of Mines, University of Arizona, 1966. 394 p. Ports.

## Government Documents

U.S. Bureau of Land Management. INFORMATION IN REGARD TO MINING CLAIMS ON THE PUBLIC DOMAIN. Washington, D.C.: 1950. 4 p.

_____. PUBLIC LANDS BIBLIOGRAPHY. Compiled by E.B. Dockens. Washington, D.C.: Government Printing Office, 1962. 106 p.

U.S. Commission on Organization of the Executive Branch of Government (1947-1949). Committee on Agricultural Activities. AGRICULTURAL FUNCTIONS AND ORGANIZATION IN THE UNITED STATES: A REPORT WITH RECOMMENDATIONS. Washington, D.C.: Government Printing Office, 1949. 112 p. (Reproduced by University Microfilms, Ann Arbor, Mich., 1968).

Study and recommendations relating to organization of regulatory functions including conservation, research, and public land and wildlife management.

U.S. Congress. House. Committee on Interior and Insular Affairs. LAND AND WATER CONSERVATION FUND ACT; REPORT TO ACCOMPANY H.R. 3846. 88th Cong., 1st sess., House Report no. 900. Washington, D.C.: Government Printing Office, 1963. 59 p. Tables.

_____. LAND CONSERVATION FUND. HEARINGS . . . ON H.R. 11172 (Aspinall) [and other] BILLS TO PROVIDE FOR THE ESTABLISHMENT OF A LAND CONSERVATION FUND, AND FOR OTHER PURPOSES. 87th Cong., 2d sess. Washington, D.C.: Government Printing Office, 1962. 14 p. Tables.

_____. LEGISLATION TO REVISE THE PUBLIC LAND LAWS. HEARINGS. . . . 92d Cong., 1st sess. Washington, D.C.: Government Printing Office, 1972. 454 p.

U.S. Congress. House. Committee on Interior Affairs. Subcommittee on the Environment. PUBLIC LAND POLICY ACT OF 1971. HEARINGS . . . ON H.R. 7211. . . . 92d Cong., 1st sess. Washington, D.C.: Government Printing Office, 1971. 476 p.

U.S. Congress. House. Committee on Interior and Insular Affairs. Subcommittee on National Parks and Recreation. LAND AND WATER CONSERVATION FUND. HEARINGS . . . ON H.R. 3846 [and others], BILLS TO ESTABLISH A LAND AND WATER CONSERVATION FUND TO ASSIST THE STATES AND FEDERAL AGENCIES IN MEETING PRESENT AND FUTURE OUTDOOR RECREATION DEMANDS AND NEEDS OF THE AMERICAN PEOPLE, AND FOR OTHER PURPOSES. 88th Cong., 1st sess. Washington, D.C.: Government Printing Office, 1963. 287 p. Diagrs., tables.

_____. LAND AND WATER CONSERVATION FUND ACT AMENDMENTS. HEARINGS . . . ON S. 1708 AND COMPANION BILLS. . . . 91st Cong., 2d sess. Washington, D.C.: Government Printing Office, 1970. 138 p.

U.S. Congress. House. Committee on Interior and Insular Affairs. Subcommittee on Public Lands. PROTECTION OF WILD HORSES ON PUBLIC LANDS. HEARINGS . . . ON H.R. 795, H.R. 5375 AND RELATED BILLS. 92d Cong., 1st sess. Washington, D.C.: Government Printing Office, 1971. 200 p.

U.S. Congress. House. Committee on Merchant Marine and Fisheries. Subcommittee on Fisheries and Wildlife Conservation. ESTUARINE AND WETLANDS LEGISLATION, HEARINGS. . . . 88th Cong., 2d sess. Washington, D.C.: Government Printing Office, 1968. 299 p.

_____. RETENTION OF LANDS AROUND JIM WOODRUFF RESERVOIR AND REGULATING HUNTING AND FISHING ON FEDERAL RESERVATIONS. HEARINGS . . . ON H.R. 11197 [and others]. Washington, D.C.: Government Printing Office, 1956. 155 p.

U.S. Congress. House. Committee on the Judiciary. PROPOSED REVISION AND CODIFICATION OF TITLE 16, UNITED STATES CODE, ENTITLED "CONSERVATION AND RECLAMATION." 83d Cong., 2d sess. Washington, D.C.: Government Printing Office, 1954. 674 p.

_____. REVISION OF TITLE 16, U.S. CODE, "CONSERVATION AND RECLAMATION." [PROPOSED] REPORT TO ACCOMPANY H.R. ____, A BILL TO REVISE, CODIFY AND ENACT INTO LAW TITLE 16, OF THE UNITED STATES CODE, ENTITLED "CONSERVATION AND RECLAMATION." Washington, D.C.: Government Printing Office, 1954. 818 p.

U.S. Congress. Senate. Committee on Interior and Insular Affairs. NATIONAL LAND USE POLICY ACT; REPORT, TOGETHER WITH SUPPLEMENTARY VIEWS TO ACCOMPANY S. 3354. 91st Cong., 2d sess., Senate Report no. 91-1435. Washington, D.C.: Government Printing Office, 1970. 115 p.

_____. NATIONAL LAND USE POLICY. HEARINGS . . . ON S. 632 . . . AND S. 992 . . . . Part 1. 92d Cong., 1st sess. Washington, D.C.: Government Printing Office, 1971. 267 p.

U.S. Congress. Senate. Committee on Interior and Insular Affairs. Subcommittee on Parks and Recreation. LAND AND WATER CONSERVATION FUND. HEARING . . . ON S. 3505. . . . 91st Cong., 2d sess. Washington, D.C.: Government Printing Office, 1970. 46 p.

U.S. Congress. Senate. Committee on Interior and Insular Affairs. Subcommittee on Public Lands. MANAGEMENT PRACTICES ON PUBLIC LANDS. HEARINGS . . . ON S. 350 . . . [and] S. 1734. . . . 3 vols. 92d Cong., 1st sess. Washington, D.C.: Government Printing Office, 1971.

_____. ONE THIRD OF THE NATION'S LAND: A REPORT TO THE PRESIDENT AND TO THE CONGRESS BY THE PUBLIC LAND LAW REVIEW COMMISSION. Washington, D.C.: Government Printing Office, 1970. 342 p.

> The report sets forth 137 recommendations for revisions in the current public land law. Proposed changes in public land policy are discussed relative to environmental quality, natural resources, agriculture, recreation, beneficial use analysis, questions of private or public ownership and occupancy, and other legal and administrative aspects.

U.S. Congress. Senate. Committee on the Judiciary. JUDICIAL PROCEEDINGS IN THE CONDEMNATION OF LANDS FOR PUBLIC PURPOSES. HEARING. Washington, D.C.: Government Printing Office, 1953. 13 p.

U.S. Library of Congress. Environmental Policy Division. PUBLIC LAND POLICY: ACTIVITIES IN THE 92D CONGRESS. By E.W. Shaw. 92d Cong., 2d sess. Washington, D.C.: Government Printing Office, 1972. 26 p.

U.S. Public Land Law Review Commission. ADMINISTRATIVE PROCEDURES AND PUBLIC LANDS. By Carl McFarland. Charlottesville: University Press of Virginia, 1969. 390 p.

U.S. Public Lands Commission. REPORT OF THE PUBLIC LANDS COMMISSION CREATED BY THE ACT OF MARCH 3, 1879, RELATING TO PUBLIC LANDS IN THE WESTERN PORTION OF THE UNITED STATES AND TO THE OPERATION OF EXISTING LAND LAWS. 46 Cong., 2d sess., Executive Document no. 46, 1880. Reprint. New York: Arno Press, 1972. 690 p. Illus.

## National Parks

Eisenbud, Robert E. EXAMINATION OF THE LAW RELATING TO THE WATER RIGHTS OF EVERGLADES NATIONAL PARK. Sea Grant Technical Bulletin, no. 21. Miami: University of Miami Sea Grant Institutional Program, 1972. 360 p.

National Parks and Conservation Association. PRESERVING WILDERNESS IN OUR NATIONAL PARKS: A PROGRAM FOR PREVENTING OVERUSE OF THE NATIONAL PARKS THROUGH REGIONAL RECREATION PLANNING OUTSIDE THE PARKS. Washington, D.C.: 1971. 122 p. Illus., maps.

## GOVERNMENT DOCUMENTS

U.S. Congress. House. Committee on Government Operations. Government Activities Subcommittee. DISPOSAL OF SURPLUS FEDERAL PROPERTY FOR PARK AND RECREATIONAL PURPOSES. HEARING . . . ON H:R. 15870. . . . 91st Cong., 2d sess. Washington, D.C.: Government Printing Office, 1970. 50 p.

U.S. Congress. House. Committee on Interior and Insular Affairs. RELATING TO THE ESTABLISHMENT OF CONCESSION POLICIES IN THE AREAS ADMIN-ISTERED BY NATIONAL PARK SERVICE; REPORT TO ACCOMPANY H.R. 5886. 88th Cong., 2d sess., House Report no. 1426. Washington, D.C.: Government Printing Office, 1964. 21 p.

_____. RELATING TO THE ESTABLISHMENT OF CONCESSION POLICIES IN THE AREAS ADMINISTERED BY NATIONAL PARK SERVICE; REPORT TO AC-COMPANY H.R. 2091. 89th Cong., 1st sess., House Report no. 591. Washington, D.C.: Government Printing Office, 1965. 14 p.

U.S. Congress. House. Committee on Interior and Insular Affairs. Sub-committee on National Parks and Recreation. GOLDEN EAGLE PROGRAM. HEARING . . . ON 2315 and RELATED BILLS. . . . 91st Cong., 2d sess. Washington, D.C.: Government Printing Office. 596 p.

_____. PARK CONCESSION POLICY. HEARINGS . . . ON H.R. 5872 [and others]. . . . 88th Cong., 2d sess. Washington, D.C.: Government Printing Office, 1964. 256 p.

U.S. Congress. House. Committee on Interior and Insular Affairs. Subcommittee on Public Lands. PROHIBITING WATER PROJECTS IN NATIONAL PARKS AND MONUMENTS. HEARINGS ON H.R. 1038, A BILL TO PRO-HIBIT THE CONSTRUCTION, OPERATION OR MAINTENANCE OF ANY PRO-JECT FOR THE STORAGE OR DELIVERY OF WATER WITHIN OR AFFECTING ANY NATIONAL PARK OR MONUMENT. 83d Cong., 1st sess. Washington, D.C.: Government Printing Office, 1953. 46 p.

U.S. Congress. House. Committee on Interstate and Foreign Commerce. Subcommittee on Transportation and Aeronautics. AIRPORTS AT NATIONAL PARKS. HEARINGS. 89th Cong., 2d sess. Washington, D.C.: Government Printing

Office, 1966. 16 p.

U.S. Congress. Senate. Committee on Interior and Insular Affairs. ESTAB-LISHING THE NATIONAL PARK FOUNDATION; REPORT TO ACCOMPANY S. 814. 90th Cong., 1st sess. Washington, D.C.: Government Printing Office, 1967. 10 p.

_____. ESTABLISHING THE SAWTOOTH NATIONAL RECREATION AREA IN IDAHO; REPORT TO ACCOMPANY S. 1267. 90th Cong., 1st sess. Washington, D.C.: Government Printing Office, 1967. 14 p.

_____. NATIONAL PARK SERVICE CONCESSION POLICIES; REPORT TO AC-COMPANY H.R. 2091. 89th Cong., 1st sess., Senate Report no. 765. Washington, D.C.: Government Printing Office, 1965. 14 p.

_____. THE ST. CROIX NATIONAL SCENIC RIVERWAY; REPORT TO AC-COMPANY S. 897. 89th Cong., 1st sess., Senate Report no. 679. Washington, D.C.: Government Printing Office, 1965. 31 p. Illus., maps.

U.S. Congress. Senate. Committee on Interior and Insular Affairs. Subcommittee on Parks and Recreation. BOUNDARY REVISION, NATIONAL PARK SERVICE. HEARING . . . ON S. 2601, S. 2650 . . . [and] S. 1878. . . . 92d Cong., 1st sess. Washington, D.C.: Government Printing Office, 1971. 43 p.

_____. CAPITOL REEF AND ARCHES NATIONAL PARKS. HEARING . . . ON S. 531 . . . [and] S. 532. . . . 91st Cong., 2d sess. Washington, D.C.: Government Printing Office, 1970. 49 p.

_____. COWPENS NATIONAL BATTLEGROUND SITE, PISCATAWAY NA-TIONAL PARK, JOHN D. ROCKEFELLER, JR., MEMORIAL PARKWAY, GULF ISLANDS NATIONAL SEASHORE, AND WOLF TRAP FARM PARK. HEARINGS. . . . 92d Cong., 2d sess. Washington, D.C.: Government Printing Office, 1972. 119 p. Maps.

_____. FEDERAL LANDS FOR PARKS AND RECREATION ACT OF 1969. HEARINGS . . . ON S. 1708. 91st Cong., 1st sess. Washington, D.C.: Government Printing Office, 1969. 33 p.

U.S. Laws and Statutes. LAWS RELATING TO THE NATIONAL PARK SERVICE. Washington, D.C.: Government Printing Office, 1950. 34 p.

_____. LAWS RELATING TO THE NATIONAL PARK SERVICE ENACTED BY THE 85TH CONGRESS, 1957-58. Washington, D.C.: National Park Service, Department of the Interior, 1959. 51 p.

U.S. National Park Service. COMPILATION OF THE ADMINISTRATIVE POLI-CIES FOR THE NATIONAL PARKS AND NATIONAL MONUMENTS OF SCIEN-TIFIC SIGNIFICANCE, NATURAL AREA CATEGORY. Washington, D.C.: Government Printing Office, 1967. 63 p.

_____. COMPILATION OF THE ADMINISTRATIVE POLICIES FOR THE NA-TIONAL PARKS AND NATIONAL MONUMENTS OF SCIENTIFIC SIGNIFI-CANCE, NATIONAL AREA CATEGORY. Rev. ed. Washington, D.C.: Government Printing Office, 1968. 138 p.

_____. COMPILATION OF THE ADMINISTRATIVE POLICIES FOR THE NA-TIONAL PARKS AND NATIONAL MONUMENTS OF SCIENTIFIC SIGNIFI-CANCE (NATURAL AREA CATEGORY). Rev. ed. Washington, D.C.: Government Printing Office, 1970. 147 p.

_____. COMPILATION OF THE ADMINISTRATIVE POLICIES FOR THE NA-TIONAL RECREATION AREAS, NATIONAL SEASHORES, NATIONAL LAKE-SHORES, NATIONAL PARKWAYS, NATIONAL SCENIC RIVERWAYS (RECREA-TIONAL AREA CATEGORY) OF THE NATIONAL PARK SYSTEM. Rev. ed. Washington, D.C.: Government Printing Office, 1968. 108 p.

_____. THE NATIONAL PARK SYSTEM PLAN. 2 vols. Washington, D.C.: 1970. Illus.

U.S. National Park System. COMPILATION OF THE ADMINISTRATIVE POLI-CIES FOR THE HISTORICAL AREAS OF THE NATIONAL PARK SYSTEM. Washington, D.C.: Government Printing Office, 1968. 116 p.

_____. FINAL STATUS OF LEGISLATION AFFECTING, OR OF INTEREST TO, THE NATIONAL PARK SERVICE, 79TH CONGRESS. By Office of the Chief Counsel, Legislative Division. Washington, D.C.: Government Printing Office, 1946. 211 p.

## Wilderness Areas

ACTION FOR WILDERNESS. A Sierra Club Battlebook, B-7. Edited by E.R. Gillette. Proceedings of the 12th Wilderness Conference, Washington, D.C., 1971. San Francisco: Sierra Club, 1972. 222 p.

WILDERNESS; THE EDGE OF KNOWLEDGE. Edited by Maxine E. McCloskey. Proceedings of the 11th Wilderness Conference, San Francisco, 1969. San Francisco: Sierra Club Books, 1970. xiv, 303 p.

WILDERNESS AND THE QUALITY OF LIFE. Edited by Maxine E. McCloskey and James P. Gilligan. Proceedings of the 10th Wilderness Conference, San Francisco, 1967. San Francisco: Sierra Club Books, 1969. xv, 267 p.

## GOVERNMENT DOCUMENTS

U.S. Congress. Conference Committees, 1964. ESTABLISH NATIONAL WIL-
DERNESS PRESERVATION SYSTEM; CONFERENCE REPORT TO ACCOMPANY
S. 4. 88th Cong., 2d sess. Washington, D.C.: Government Printing Office,
1964. 11 p.

U.S. Congress. House. Committee on Interior and Insular Affairs. BACK-
GROUND ANALYSIS AND COMPARISON OF MAJOR PROVISION: LEGISLA-
TION FOR THE ESTABLISHMENT OF A WILDERNESS PRESERVATION SYSTEM.
Committee print no. 20. Wahington, D.C.: Government Printing Office,
1964. 4 p.

_____. DESIGNATING CERTAIN LANDS AS WILDERNESS; REPORT TO AC-
COMPANY H.R. 19007. 91st Cong., 2d sess., House Report no. 91-1441.
Washington, D.C.: Government Printing Office, 1970. 24 p.

_____. NATIONAL WILDERNESS PRESERVATION SYSTEM; REPORT . . . TO
ACCOMPANY H.R. 9070. 88th Cong., 2d sess., House Report no. 1538.
Washington, D.C.: Government Printing Office, 1964. 23 p.

U.S. Congress. House. Committee on Interior and Insular Affairs. Subcommittee on National Parks and Recreation. NATIONAL SCENIC RIVERS SYS-
TEM. HEARINGS. . . . 90th Cong., 2d sess. Washington, D.C.: Government Printing Office, 1968. 547 p. Maps, illus.

U.S. Congress. House. Committee on Interior and Insular Affairs. Subcommittee on Public Lands. DESIGNATION OF WILDERNESS AREAS. HEARINGS.
. . . 91st Cong., 2d sess. Washington, D.C.: Government Printing Office,
1970. 534 p. Maps.

_____. DESIGNATION OF WILDERNESS AREAS. HEARINGS. . . . Pt. 1.
92d Cong., 1st sess. Washington, D.C.: Government Printing Office, 1972.
169 p.

_____. WILDERNESS PRESERVATION SYSTEM. HEARINGS . . . ON S. 174
[and other] BILLS TO ESTABLISH A NATIONAL WILDERNESS PRESERVATION
SYSTEM FOR THE PERMANENT GOOD OF THE WHOLE PEOPLE, AND FOR
OTHER PURPOSES. . . . 4 pts. 87th Cong., 1st sess. Washington, D.C.:
Government Printing Office, 1962. 1,762 p. Maps, tables.

_____. WILDERNESS PRESERVATION SYSTEM. HEARING . . . ON BILLS
TO ESTABLISH A NATIONAL WILDERNESS PRESERVATION SYSTEM FOR THE
PERMANENT GOOD OF THE WHOLE PEOPLE, AND FOR OTHER PURPOSES.
. . . 3 pts. 88th Cong., 2d sess. Washington, D.C.: Government Printing
Office, 1964. 1,052 p. Maps, tables.

U.S. Congress. Senate. Committee on Interior and Insular Affairs. DESIG-
NATING CERTAIN ISLANDS IN MICHIGAN, WISCONSIN, AND MAINE AS
WILDERNESS AREAS; REPORT TO ACCOMPANY S. 826. 91st Cong., 1st sess.,
Senate Report no. 91-200. Washington, D.C.: Government Printing Office,
1969. 16 p.

_____. ESTABLISHING A NATIONAL WILDERNESS PRESERVATION SYSTEM
FOR THE PERMANENT GOOD OF THE WHOLE PEOPLE, AND FOR OTHER
PURPOSES; REPORT TO ACCOMPANY S. 4. 88th Cong., 1st sess., Senate
Report no. 109. Washington, D.C.: Government Printing Office, 1963. 44 p.

_____. NATIONAL WILD AND SCENIC RIVER SYSTEM; REPORT TO ACCOM-
PANY S. 119. 90th Cong., 1st sess., Senate Report no. 491. Washington,
D.C.: Government Printing Office, 1967. 17 p.

_____. NATIONAL WILDERNESS PRESERVATION ACT. HEARING . . .
ON A BILL TO ESTABLISH A NATIONAL WILDERNESS PRESERVATION SYSTEM
FOR THE PERMANENT GOOD OF THE WHOLE PEOPLE, AND FOR OTHER
PURPOSES. 85th Cong., 2d sess. Washington, D.C.: Government Printing
Office, 1958. 218 p. Map, tables.

_____. NATIONAL WILDERNESS PRESERVATION ACT. HEARINGS . . .
ON S. 1176, A BILL TO ESTABLISH ON PUBLIC LANDS OF THE UNITED
STATES A NATIONAL WILDERNESS PRESERVATION SYSTEM. . . . 85th
Cong., 1st sess. Washington, D.C.: Government Printing Office, 1957.
444 p. Map, tables.

_____. NATIONAL WILDERNESS PRESERVATION ACT. HEARINGS . . .
ON S. 4, A BILL TO ESTABLISH A NATIONAL WILDERNESS PRESERVATION
SYSTEM FOR THE PERMANENT GOOD OF THE WHOLE PEOPLE, AND FOR
OTHER PURPOSES. 88th Cong., 1st sess. Washington, D.C.: Government
Printing Office, 1963. 276 p. Tables.

_____. NATIONAL WILDERNESS PRESERVATION ACT. HEARINGS . . .
ON S. 4028, A BILL TO ESTABLISH A NATIONAL WILDERNESS PRESERVATION
SYSTEM FOR THE PERMANENT GOOD OF THE WHOLE PEOPLE, AND FOR
OTHER PURPOSES. . . . 2 pts. 85th Cong., 2d sess. Washington, D.C.:
Government Printing Office, 1959. 1,060 p. Map, tables.

_____. NATIONAL WILDERNESS PRESERVATION ACT, 1959. HEARINGS
. . . ON S. 1123, A BILL TO ESTABLISH A NATIONAL WILDERNESS PRES-
ERVATION SYSTEM. . . . 86th Cong., 1st sess. Washington, D.C.:
Government Printing Office, 1959. 491 p. Map, tables, forms.

_____. THE WILDERNESS ACT. HEARINGS . . . ON S. 174, A BILL TO ESTABLISH A NATIONAL WILDERNESS PRESERVATION SYSTEM FOR THE PERMANENT GOOD OF THE WHOLE PEOPLE, AND FOR OTHER PURPOSES. 87th Cong., 1st sess. Washington, D.C.: Government Printing Office, 1961. 439 p. Diagrs., tables.

U.S. Congress. Senate. Committee on Interior and Insular Affairs. Subcommittee on Minerals, Materials and Fuels. THREE SISTERS WILDERNESS, OREGON. HEARINGS . . . ON S. 1784. . . . 92d Cong., 1st sess. Washington, D.C.: Government Printing Office, 1971. 95 p.

U.S. Congress. Senate. Committee on Interior and Insular Affairs. Subcommittee on Public Lands. GREAT SWAMP, PELICAN ISLAND, MONOMOY, SENEY, HURON, MICHIGAN ISLANDS, GRAVEL ISLAND, GREEN BAY, AND MOOSEHORN WILDERNESS AREAS. HEARING. . . . 90th Cong., 2d sess. Washington, D.C.: Government Printing Office, 1965. 472 p.

_____. LINCOLN BACK COUNTRY WILDERNESS AREA, MONTANA. HEARING . . . ON S. 1121. . . . 90th Cong., 2d sess. Washington, D.C.: Government Printing Office, 1968. 373 p.

_____. SAN GABRIEL, WASHAKIE, AND MOUNT JEFFERSON WILDERNESS AREAS. HEARINGS . . . ON S. 2531 . . ., S. 2630 . . ., AND S. 2751. . . . 90th Cong., 2d sess. Washington, D.C.: Government Printing Office, 1968. 308 p. Maps.

_____. WILDERNESS ADDITIONS IN ALASKA, NEW MEXICO, OREGON AND WASHINGTON. HEARINGS . . . ON S. 3014. . . . 91st Cong., 1st sess. Washington, D.C.: Government Printing Office, 1970. 234 p.

_____. WILDERNESS AREAS IN OKLAHOMA, FLORIDA, GEORGIA, AND ARIZONA; TOIYABE NATIONAL FOREST. HEARINGS . . . ON S. 3222, S. 709, AND S. 3279. . . . 91st Cong., 2d sess. Washington, D.C.: Government Printing Office, 1970. 64 p.

U.S. Department of the Interior. NATIONAL WILDERNESS PRESERVATION SYSTEM; MESSAGE FROM THE PRESIDENT OF THE UNITED STATES TRANSMITTING THE ANNUAL REPORT. Washington, D.C.: 1965- .

U.S. Library of Congress. Legislative Reference Service. THE PRESERVATION OF WILDERNESS AREAS: AN ANALYSIS OF OPINION ON THE PROBLEM. By C.F. Keyser. Washington, D.C.: 1956. 114 p.

U.S. President. Lyndon B. Johnson. SPECIAL MESSAGE TO THE CONGRESS TRANSMITTING REPORT ON THE NATIONAL WILDERNESS PRESERVATION SYSTEM. 89th Cong., 1st sess., House document no. 79. Washington, D.C.: Government Printing Office, 1965. 16 p.

## Recreation

Brockman, Christian F., and Merriam, Lawrence C., Jr. RECREATIONAL USE OF WILD LANDS. 2d ed. With two specially prepared chapters by W.R. Catton, Jr., and B. Dowdle. New York: McGraw-Hill Book Co., 1973. 329 p. Illus.

Clawson, Marion. LAND AND WATER FOR RECREATION: OPPORTUNITIES, PROBLEMS AND POLICIES. Chicago: Rand McNally & Co., 1963. 144 p. Illus.

    The chapter "Public and Private Efforts to Provide Outdoor Recreation" includes discussion of legislation, government commissions and agencies.

Doell, Charles E. ELEMENTS OF PARK AND RECREATION ADMINISTRATION. Minneapolis, Minn.: Burgess Publishing Co., 1963. 340 p. Illus.

Harris, Bryan, and Ryan, Gerard. AN OUTLINE OF THE LAW RELATING TO COMMON LAND AND PUBLIC ACCESS TO THE COUNTRYSIDE. London: Sweet & Maxwell, 1967. xxxii, 270 p. Illus., forms, tables.

Illinois. Department of Conservation. OUTDOOR RECREATION MANAGEMENT; AN ANNOTATED BIBLIOGRAPHY. Springfield: 1971? 133 p.

Shurtleff, Flavel. DIGEST OF LAWS RELATING TO STATE PARKS. Washington, D.C.: National Conference on State Parks, 1955. 256 p.

Storey, Edward H. A DIGEST OF BASIC PROVISIONS OF ILLINOIS LAWS RELATED TO PARKS AND RECREATION. Urbana: Field Service, Department of Recreation and Municipal Park Administration, University of Illinois, 1962. 14 p.

Truxal, Andrew G. OUTDOOR RECREATION LEGISLATION AND ITS EFFECTIVENESS: A SUMMARY OF AMERICAN LEGISLATION FOR PUBLIC OUTDOOR RECREATION, 1915-1927, TOGETHER WITH A STUDY OF THE ASSOCIATION BETWEEN RECREATION AREAS AND JUVENILE DELINQUENCY IN MANHATTAN, 1920. Studies in History, Economics, and Public Law, no. 311. New York: AMS Press, 1968. 218 p. Maps.

Van der Smissen, Margaret Elizabeth. AN ANALYSIS OF THE STATE LAWS PERTAINING TO THE ESTABLISHMENT OF PUBLIC PARK AND RECREATION BOARDS. La Crosse, Wis.: Northern Engraving and Manufacturing Co., 1956. Microfilm, Indiana University Library.

## GOVERNMENT DOCUMENTS

Great Britain. Laws and Statutes. THE LAW OF PARKS AND RECREATION GROUNDS. By Roland J. Roddis. London: Shaw, 1953. 155 p.

Maine. Laws and Statutes. LAWS RELATING TO FORESTS, PARKS, LAKES, AND RIVERS. AS AMENDED BY PUBLIC LAWS OF 1965. Augusta: Maine Forest Service, 1965. 68 p.

Minnesota. Legislature. Outdoor Recreation Resources Committee. MORRC LEGISLATIVE AND APPROPRIATION RECOMMENDATIONS. St. Paul: 1967. 29 p. Map.

_____. PUBLIC ACCESS IN MINNESOTA. St. Paul: 1965. 78 p. Maps.

Nevada. Laws and Statutes. LAWS RELATING TO HIGHWAYS AND STATE PARKS. Issued by H.D. Mills, State Highway Engineer. Carson City: State Printing Office, 1953. 107 p.

Tennessee. General Assembly. Legislative Council Committee. STUDY ON BOND FINANCING OF PARKS AND RECREATIONAL FACILITIES. Nashville: 1968. 77 p.

Texas. Laws and Statutes. TEXAS PLANNING, ZONING, HOUSING, PARK AND AIRPORT LAWS. Austin: The Bureau of Municipal Research, University of Texas, 1946.

U.S. Bureau of Outdoor Recreation. FEDERAL ASSISTANCE IN OUTDOOR REC-REATION AVAILABLE TO STATES, THEIR SUBDIVISIONS, ORGANIZATIONS, INDIVIDUALS. Rev. ed. Washington, D.C.: Government Printing Office, 1966. 83 p.

_____. FEDERAL OUTDOOR RECREATION PROGRAMS AND RECREATION-RELATED ENVIRONMENTAL PROGRAMS. 1st rev. ed. Washington, D.C.: Government Printing Office, 1970. 226 p.

U.S. Congress. House. Committee on Interior and Insular Affairs. FEDERAL WATER PROJECT RECREATION ACT; REPORT TO ACCOMPANY H.R. 9032. 88th Cong., 2d sess. Washington, D.C.: Government Printing Office, 1964. 20 p.

_____. FEDERAL WATER PROJECT RECREATION ACT; REPORT TO ACCOM-PANY H.R. 5269. 89th Cong., 1st sess., House Report no. 254. Washington, D.C.: Government Printing Office, 1965. 28 p.

U.S. Congress. House. Committee on Interior and Insular Affairs. Subcommittee on Irrigation and Reclamation. RECREATION ALLOCATION POLICY. HEARINGS . . . ON H.R. 9032, A BILL TO PROVIDE UNIFORM POLICIES WITH RESPECT TO RECREATION AND FISH AND WILDLIFE BENEFITS AND COSTS OF FEDERAL MULTIPLE-PURPOSE WATER RESOURCE PROJECTS, AND PROVIDE THE SECRETARY OF THE INTERIOR WITH AUTHORITY FOR RECREATION DEVELOPMENT OF PROJECTS UNDER HIS CONTROL. . . . 88th Cong., 1st sess. Washington, D.C.: Government Printing Office, 1964. 126 p.

U.S. Congress. House. Committee on Interior and Insular Affairs. Subcommittee on National Parks and Recreation. LAND AND WATER CONSERVATION FUND ACT AND RELATED PROGRAMS. HEARINGS . . . WITH RESPECT TO DEVELOPMENT WITHIN THE NATIONAL PARK SYSTEM. 92d Cong., 2d sess. Washington, D.C.: Government Printing Office, 1972. 127 p.

_____. PROPOSED AMENDMENTS TO THE LAND AND WATER CONSERVATION FUND ACT. HEARINGS . . . ON H.R. 6730 AND RELATED BILLS. . . . 92d Cong., 1st sess. Washington, D.C.: Government Printing Office, 1971. 353 p. Illus.

U.S. Congress. Senate. Committee on Interior and Insular Affairs. FEDERAL WATER PROJECT RECREATION ACT; REPORT TO ACCOMPANY S. 1229. 89th Cong., 1st sess., Senate Report no. 149. Washington, D.C.: Government Printing Office, 1965. 31 p.

_____. LAND AND WATER CONSERVATION FUND. HEARING . . . ON H.R. 3846, AN ACT TO ESTABLISH A LAND AND WATER CONSERVATION FUND TO ASSIST THE STATES AND FEDERAL AGENCIES IN MEETING PRESENT AND FUTURE OUTDOOR RECREATION DEMANDS AND NEEDS OF THE AMERICAN PEOPLE, AND FOR OTHER PURPOSES. 88th Cong., 1st sess. Washington, D.C.: Government Printing Office, 1964. 115 p.

_____. LAND AND WATER CONSERVATION FUND. HEARINGS . . . ON S. 859, A BILL TO ESTABLISH A LAND AND WATER CONSERVATION FUND TO ASSIST THE STATES AND FEDERAL AGENCIES IN MEETING PRESENT AND FUTURE OUTDOOR RECREATION DEMANDS AND NEEDS OF THE AMERICAN PEOPLE, AND FOR OTHER PURPOSES. 88th Cong., 1st sess. Washington, D.C.: Government Printing Office, 1963. 242 p. Tables.

_____. LAND AND WATER CONSERVATION FUND ACT; REPORT TO ACCOMPANY H.R. 3846. 88th Cong., 2d sess., Senate Report no. 1304. Washington, D.C.: Government Printing Office, 1964. 39 p.

_____. LAND AND WATER CONSERVATION FUND ACT AMENDMENTS. HEARINGS. . . . 90th Cong., 2d sess. Washington, D.C.: Government Printing Office, 1968. 358 p. Map.

_____. NATIONWIDE SYSTEM OF TRAILS. HEARINGS . . . ON S. 827. 90th Cong., 1st sess. Washington, D.C.: Government Printing Office, 1967. 185 p.

_____. PROVIDING PROTECTION, DEVELOPMENT, AND ENHANCEMENT OF PUBLIC RECREATION VALUES OF PUBLIC LANDS; REPORT TO ACCOMPANY S. 3389. 91st Cong., 2d sess., Senate Report no. 91-1256. Washington, D.C.: Government Printing Office, 1970. 6 p.

_____. WATER PROJECT RECREATION ACT. HEARING . . . ON S. 1229. 89th Cong., 1st sess. Washington, D.C.: Government Printing Office, 1965. 66 p.

_____. WILD AND SCENIC RIVERS. HEARINGS. . . . 90th Cong., 1st sess. Washington, D.C.: Government Printing Office, 1967. 242 p. Maps.

_____. WILD RIVERS SYSTEM. St. CROIX WATERWAY. HEARINGS. . . . 2 vols. 89th Cong., 1st sess. Washington, D.C.: Government Printing Office, 1965. 620 p. Illus., maps.

U.S. Congress. Senate. Committee on Public Works. EVALUATION OF RECREATIONAL BENEFITS FROM RESERVOIRS. HEARINGS . . . ON S. 1164, A BILL TO MAKE THE EVALUATION OF RECREATIONAL BENEFITS RESULTING FROM THE CONSTRUCTION OF ANY FLOOD CONTROL, NAVIGATION, OR RECLAMATION PROJECT AN INTEGRAL PART OF THE PROJECT PLANNING. . . . 85th Cong. Washington, D.C.: Government Printing Office, 1957. 153 p. Tables.

U.S. Congress. Senate. Committee on Public Works. Subcommittee on Public Roads. HIGHWAY BEAUTIFICATION AND SCENIC ROAD PROGRAM. HEARINGS. . . . 89th Cong., 1st sess. Washington, D.C.: Government Printing Office, 1965. 537 p. Illus., maps.

U.S. National Park Service. LIST OF AGENCIES ADMINISTERING STATE PARKS AND RELATED RECREATION AREAS. Rev. ed. Washington, D.C.: Department of the Interior, National Park Service, Division of Recreation Resource Planning, 1959. 16 p.

U.S. The Presidents Council on Recreation and Natural Beauty. FROM SEA TO SHINING SEA: A REPORT ON THE AMERICAN ENVIRONMENT--OUR NATURAL HERITAGE. Washington, D.C.: Government Printing Office, 1968. 304 p. Pap., photos.

 The report includes sections in government actions and state, local and federal agencies.

Virginia. Laws and Statutes. LAWS RELATING TO THE VIRGINIA OUTDOORS

PLAN, AS ENACTED BY THE 1966 GENERAL ASSEMBLY. Richmond: Commission of Outdoor Recreation, 1967. 21 p.


Washington. Laws and Statutes. WASHINGTON STATUTES RELATING TO PARK BOARDS AND/OR RECREATIONAL FACILITIES IN CITIES AND TOWNS. Seattle: Recreation Division, Washington State Parks and Recreation Commission, 1956? 18 p.


_____. WASHINGTON STATUTES RELATING TO PARKS AND RECREATION, WITH ANNOTATIONS. Prepared by E.H. Campbell and H.D. Ambers. Seattle: Bureau of Governmental Research and Service, University of Washington, 1954. 121 p.


## Forests


Falk, Harry W. TIMBER AND FOREST PRODUCT LAW. Berkeley, Calif.: Howell-North, 1958. 365 p.


Freeman, Orville L., and Frome, Michael. THE NATIONAL FORESTS OF AMERICA. New York: Putnam, 1968. 191 p. Illus., maps, ports.


Gordon, William A. THE LAW OF FORESTRY. London: H.M. Stationery Office, 1955. 574 p. Maps, tables, diagrs.


Kinney, Jay P. THE DEVELOPMENT OF FOREST LAW IN AMERICA, INCLUDING FOREST LEGISLATION IN AMERICA PRIOR TO MARCH 4, 1789. Use and Abuse of America's Natural Resources Series. New York: Arno Press, 1972. 405 p.


Myren, Richard A. LAW ENFORCEMENT IN FOREST FIRE PREVENTION. Chapel Hill: University of North Carolina, Institute of Government, 1956. 77 p.


National Association of State Foresters. FORESTS AND FORESTRY IN THE AMERICAN STATES; A REFERENCE ANTHOLOGY. Edited by Ralph R. Widner. Missoula, Mont.: 1968. xx, 594 p. Illus., map, ports.


Shaw, Elmer W. AN ANALYSIS OF FORESTRY ISSUES IN THE FIRST SESSION OF THE 92D CONGRESS. Washington, D.C.: Government Printing Office, 1972. 64 p.

Prepared at the request of Henry M. Jackson, Chairman, Committee on Interior and Insular Affairs, United States Senate.


Society of American Foresters. Division of Silviculture. Committee on Forest Practices. FOREST PRACTICES DEVELOPMENTS IN THE UNITED STATES, 1940 TO 1955; REPORT, JANUARY, 1956. Washington, D.C.: 1956. 39 p.

Stanford Environmental Law Society. CALIFORNIA'S PRIVATE TIMBERLANDS: REGULATION, TAXATION, PRESERVATION. Edited by C. Johnson et al. Stanford, Calif.: 1973. 97 p.

> Consists of two chapters. The first is a history and evaluation of the California Forest Practice Act and the California Supreme Court decision which voided the act's rule-making procedure. The second chapter is "Factors To Be Considered When Drafting New Forest Practice Legislation."

Stevens, James. GREEN POWER: THE STORY OF PUBLIC LAW 273. Seattle, Wash.: Superior Publishing Co., 1958. 95 p. Illus.

Western Forestry and Conservation Program. FOREST LAWS OF OREGON, HISTORY OF FOREST AND FIRE LAWS, SUMMARY OF FOREST CONSERVATION ACT. Portland, Ore.: 1952. 36 p. Map.

## GOVERNMENT DOCUMENTS

Alabama. Laws and Statutes. FORESTRY AND FORESTRY RELATED LAWS. Compiled and edited by C.H. Barnes. Montgomery: State of Alabama, Forestry Commission, 1971? 63 p.

Connecticut. Laws and Statutes. CONNECTICUT LAWS RELATING TO PARKS, FORESTS AND FORESTRY. Hartford: Connecticut State Park and Forest Commission, 1962. 49 p.

Great Britain. Laws and Statutes. AN ACT FOR THE PRESERVATION OF WHITE AND OTHER PINE TREES IN HER MAJESTIES COLONIES OF NEW HAMPSHIRE AND MASSACHUSETTS-BAY FOR THE MASTING OF HER MAJESTIES NAVY, 1710. Waltham, Mass.: Arlington Publishing Co., 1949.

Maine. Laws and Statutes. LAWS RELATING TO FORESTS, PARKS, LAKES AND RIVERS AS AMENDED BY THE PUBLIC LAWS OF 1965. Augusta: Maine Forest Service, 1965. 68 p.

Maryland. Laws and Statutes. MARYLAND LAWS AND REGULATIONS RELATING TO FORESTS AND PARKS, JUNE 1, 1963. Annapolis: Department of Forests and Parks, 1963. 95 p.

Minnesota. Division of Forestry. Department of Conservation. A HISTORY OF FORESTRY IN MINNESOTA, WITH PARTICULAR REFERENCE TO FORESTRY LEGISLATION. Compiled by E. Bachman. St. Paul: 1965. 109 p. Map.

Montana. Laws and Statutes. LAWS RELATING TO FORESTRY. Compiled by R. Parker. Missoula: Office of the State Forester, 1954. 120 p.

North Carolina. Laws and Statutes. LAWS RELATING TO FORESTRY FROM GENERAL STATUTES OF NORTH CAROLINA. Rev. ed. Raleigh: Office of the State Forester, 1963. 30 p.

U.S. Congress. House. Committee on Agriculture. Subcommittee on Forests. COOPERATIVE FOREST MANAGEMENT AND FIRE PROTECTION, AND URBAN ENVIRONMENTAL FORESTRY PROGRAM. HEARINGS. . . . 92d Cong., 1st sess. Washington, D.C.: Government Printing Office, 1971. 139 p.

_____. FOREST LAW ENFORCEMENT. HEARING. . . . 92d Cong., 1st sess. Washington, D.C.: Government Printing Office, 1971. 18 p.

_____. FORESTRY INCENTIVES ACT OF 1972. HEARING. . . . 92d Cong., 2d sess. Washington, D.C.: Government Printing Office, 1972. 59 p.

_____. MISCELLANEOUS FOREST LEGISLATION. HEARING . . . ON H.R. 8898 [and others], JUNE 14, 1956. 84th Cong., 2d sess. Washington, D.C.: Government Printing Office, 1956. 163 p. Illus.

U.S. Congress. House. Committee on Government Operations. WHETHER RESERVOIR LANDS SHOULD BE ACQUIRED BY EXCHANGE OF TIMBERLANDS; FOURTH REPORT. Washington, D.C.: Government Printing Office, 1959. 23 p. Pap.

U.S. Congress. Senate. Committee on Agriculture and Forestry. ENFORCE-MENT OF FOREST AND GRASSLAND REGULATIONS; REPORT TO ACCOM-PANY H.R. 7588. 88th Cong., 2d sess., Senate Report no. 1447. Washington, D.C.: Government Printing Office, 1964. 5 p.

U.S. Congress. Senate. Committee on Agriculture and Forestry. Subcommit-tee on Environment, Soil Conservation, and Forestry. FORESTRY PROGRAMS. HEARING . . . ON S. 3105 . . . AND S. 3459. . . . 92d Cong., 2d sess. Washington, D.C.: Government Printing Office, 1972. 57 p.

U.S. Congress. Senate. Committee on Commerce. EXPORT CONTROLS ON BLACK WALNUT LOGS. HEARINGS. 2 vols. 89th Cong., 1st sess. Washington, D.C.: Government Printing Office, 1965–66. 253 p. Illus.

U.S. Laws and Statutes. THE PRINCIPAL LAWS RELATING TO THE ESTAB-LISHMENT AND ADMINISTRATION OF THE NATIONAL FORESTS AND TO OTHER FOREST SERVICE ACTIVITIES. Compiled by H. Irion, Administrative Assistant, Forest Service. Washington, D.C.: Government Printing Office, 1951. 80 p.

_____. THE PRINCIPAL LAWS RELATING TO THE ESTABLISHMENT AND AD-

MINISTRATION OF THE NATIONAL FORESTS AND TO OTHER FOREST SERVICE ACTIVITIES. U.S. Department of Agriculture, Handbook no. 20. Rev. ed. Washington, D.C.: Government Printing Office, 1964. 127 p.

U.S. Treaties. Canada, June 1, 1971. FOREST FIRE PROTECTION: ALASKA-YUKON BOUNDARY AREA. AGREEMENT BETWEEN THE UNITED STATES OF AMERICA AND CANADA, EFFECTED BY EXCHANGE OF NOTES SIGNED AT WASHINGTON JUNE 1, 1971. . . . Treaties and Other International Acts Series, 7132. Washington, D.C.: Government Printing Office, 1971. 8 p.

West Virginia. Laws and Statutes. WEST VIRGINIA CONSERVATION, GAME, FISH AND FORESTRY LAWS. Charlottesville, Va.: Michie Co. for Conservation Commission of West Virginia, 1953. 94 p.

## Soil Conservation and Erosion

Held, R. Burnell, and Clawson, Marion. SOIL CONSERVATION IN PERSPECTIVE. Baltimore, Md.: The Johns Hopkins Press, 1965. 344 p.

Includes discussion of various past and present federal soil conservation programs.

Otte, Robert C. LOCAL RESOURCE PROTECTION AND DEVELOPMENT DISTRICTS. STATUTORY FUNCTIONS AND POWERS AS RELATED TO THE WATERSHED PROTECTION AND FLOOD PREVENTION ACT. Washington, D.C.: Government Printing Office, 1957. 12 p. Illus.

Roddis, Roland J. THE LAW OF COAST PROTECTION. WITH AN EXPLANATION OF THE COAST PROTECTION ACT, 1949, AND ITS RELATIONSHIP WITH OTHER BRANCHES OF THE LAW RELATING TO COAST PROTECTION, ETC. London: Shaw, 1950. 159 p.

Analyzes coastal protection in Great Britain.

Simms, D. Harper. THE SOIL CONSERVATION SERVICE. New York: Praeger, 1970. 238 p.

Explains the history, organization, programs, and responsibilities of the Soil Conservation Service.

Soil Conservation Society of America. PROCEEDINGS OF ANNUAL MEETINGS. Ankeny, Iowa: 1948- .

To date, there have been twenty-eight annual meetings. Recent publications of proceedings include:

1970: TURNING POINTS IN TIME. 185 p. Legal papers on land tenure, land policies, and regional government.

1971: THE SHAPE OF THINGS TO COME. 262 p. Relevant

papers on land-use planning in the Carribean, in metropolitan areas and in Connecticut, floodplain land use, land-use controls at different governmental levels, the President's National Land Use Policy Proposal, liability and public use of private lands, federal regulation of surface mining and the roles of local and state governments, and land-use regulation based on soil and water conservation facts.

1972: THE EARTH AROUND US. 242 p. Relevant papers on land-use planning for Lake Tahoe, Idaho, and recreation, the Western U.S. Water Plan, and the Iowa Conservancy District Law.

## GOVERNMENT DOCUMENTS

U.S. Congress. House. Committee on Agriculture. Subcommittee on Conservation and Credit. AMENDMENTS TO WATERSHED PROTECTION AND FLOOD PREVENTION ACT. HEARINGS . . . ON H.R. 6146 AND H.R. 6148. 84th Cong., 1st sess. Washington, D.C.: Government Printing Office, 1955. 56 p.

_____. AMENDMENT TO WATERSHED PROTECTION AND FLOOD PREVENTION ACT. HEARINGS . . . ON H.R. 6687 [and others]. 84th Cong., 2d sess. Washington, D.C.: Government Printing Office, 1956. 82 p.

U.S. Congress. House. Committee on Public Works. Subcommittee on Rivers and Harbors. BEACH EROSION, EXTENSION OF FEDERAL AID TO PRIVATE AS WELL AS PUBLIC PROPERTY. HEARINGS . . . ON H.R. 4470 [and others] TO AMEND THE ACT ENTITLED, AN ACT AUTHORIZING FEDERAL PARTICIPATION IN THE COST OF PROTECTING THE SHORES OF PUBLICLY OWNED PROPERTY, APPROVED AUGUST 13, 1946. 84th Cong., 1st sess. Washington, D.C.: Government Printing Office, 1956. 79 p.

_____. RIVER AND HARBOR AND BEACH EROSION OMNIBUS BILL (TITLE I, H.R. 12080). HEARINGS . . . ON H.R. 12080, A BILL AUTHORIZING THE CONSTRUCTION, REPAIR AND PRESERVATION OF CERTAIN PUBLIC WORKS ON RIVERS AND HARBORS FOR NAVIGATION, FLOOD CONTROL, AND FOR OTHER PURPOSES. 2 vols. 84th Cong., 1st and 2d sess. Washington, D.C.: Government Printing Office, 1956. 581 p. Tables.

_____. RIVER AND HARBOR, BEACH EROSION, AND FLOOD CONTROL PROJECTS. REPORT ON H.R. 12080, A BILL AUTHORIZING THE CONSTRUCTION, REPAIR, AND PRESERVATION OF CERTAIN PUBLIC WORKS ON RIVERS AND HARBORS FOR NAVIGATION, FLOOD CONTROL, AND FOR OTHER PURPOSES. 84th Cong., 2d sess., House Report no. 2639. Washington, D.C.: Government Printing Office, 1956. 75 p. Tables.

_____. RIVER AND HARBOR, BEACH EROSION CONTROL, AND FLOOD CONTROL PROJECTS. REPORT . . . ON H.R. 12955, A BILL AUTHORIZING THE CONSTRUCTION, REPAIR, AND PRESERVATION OF CERTAIN PUBLIC

WORKS ON RIVERS AND HARBORS FOR NAVIGATION, FLOOD CONTROL, AND FOR OTHER PURPOSES. 85th Cong., 2d sess. Washington, D.C.: Government Printing Office, 1958. 135 p. Tables.

_____. RIVER AND HARBOR, BEACH EROSION CONTROL, AND FLOOD CONTROL PROJECTS. REPORT ON H.R. 7634, A BILL AUTHORIZING THE CONSTRUCTION, REPAIR, AND PRESERVATION OF CERTAIN PUBLIC WORKS ON RIVERS AND HARBORS FOR NAVIGATION, FLOOD CONTROL, AND FOR OTHER PURPOSES. 86th Cong., 1st sess. Washington, D.C.: Government Printing Office, 1959. 54 p. Tables.

U.S. Laws and Statutes. COMPILATION OF STATUTES RELATING TO SOIL CONSERVATION, MARKETING QUOTAS AND ALLOTMENTS, CROP INSURANCE, SUGAR PAYMENTS AND QUOTAS, COMMODITY CREDIT CORPORATION, AND RELATED STATUTES AS OF JANUARY 1, 1955. U.S. Department of Agriculture Handbook no. 79. Washington, D.C.: Government Printing Office, 1955. 193 p.

_____. COMPILATION OF STATUTES RELATING TO SOIL CONSERVATION, MARKETING QUOTAS AND ALLOTMENTS, CROP INSURANCE, SUGAR PAYMENTS AND QUOTAS, PRICE SUPPORT, COMMODITY CREDIT CORPORATION, AND RELATED STATUTES AS OF JANUARY 1, 1957. U.S. Department of Agriculture Handbook no. 113. Washington, D.C.: Government Printing Office, 1957. 275 p.

U.S. Soil Conservation Service. Planning Division. FACTS ABOUT THE WATERSHED PROTECTION AND FLOOD PREVENTION ACT. U.S. Department of Agriculture publication no. PA-298. Washington, D.C.: Government Printing Office, 1957. 14 p.

U.S. Soil Conservation Service. Watershed Planning Branch. HOW TO GET HELP UNDER THE WATERSHED PROTECTION AND FLOOD PREVENTION ACT. U.S. Department of Agriculture publication no. PA-276. Washington, D.C.: Government Printing Office, 1955. 13 p. Illus.

_____. SMALL WATERSHED PROJECTS UNDER THE WATERSHED PROTECTION AND FLOOD PREVENTION ACT. U.S. Department of Agriculture publication no. PA-392. Washington, D.C.: Government Printing Office, 1959. 14 p. Illus.

U.S. Treaties. TECHNICAL COOPERATION: EROSION CONTROL AND SOIL CONSERVATION PROGRAMS IN THE BRITISH CARIBBEAN AREA. AGREEMENT BETWEEN THE UNITED STATES OF AMERICA AND THE UNITED KINGDOM OF GREAT BRITAIN AND NORTHERN IRELAND, EFFECTED BY EXCHANGE OF NOTES SIGNED AT WASHINGTON JANUARY 12 AND 20, 1954, ENTERED INTO FORCE JANUARY 20, 1954. U.S. Department of State publication no. 5529. Washington, D.C.: Government Printing Office, 1955. 6 p.

# Appendix A

## SELECTED PERIODICALS

AIR AND WATER POLLUTION. New York: Pergamon Press, October 1958- .
Irregular. Illus.

AIR POLLUTION CONTROL ASSOCIATION JOURNAL. Louisville, Ky.: July
1951- . Monthly.

ALL CLEAR. Paramus, N.J.: All Clear Publishing, 1969- . 10/year.

AMERICAN FORESTS. Washington, D.C.: American Forestry Association,
1895- . Monthly.

AMERICAN INSTITUTE OF PLANNERS JOURNAL. Baltimore, Md.: Port City
Press, 1925- . Bimonthly.

ANNUAL CLEAN AIR CONFERENCE. Brighton, Sussex, Engl.: National Society for Clean Air, 1924- . Annual.
   Publications of conference presentations include papers on the legal
   aspects of air pollution, especially legislation.

ATMOSPHERIC ENVIRONMENT. Oxford, Engl. and Long Island City, N.Y.:
Pergamon Press, 1967- . Bimonthly, illus.

AUDUBON MAGAZINE. New York: National Audubon Society, 1899- .
Bimonthly.

CAHNERS CRITICAL ISSUE REPORT. Boston: Cahners Publishing Co., 1969- .
Quarterly, illus.

CALIFORNIA WATER POLLUTION CONTROL ASSOCIATION BULLETIN. Duarte,
Calif.: Bulletin Committee, California Water Pollution Control Association,
1964- . Quarterly.

CLEAN AIR. Brighton, Engl.: National Society for Clean Air, Spring 1971- .
Quarterly.

CLEAN AIR AND WATER NEWS. New York: Commerce Clearing House, January 1969- . Weekly.

> Information about government programs, legislation, court cases, environmental organizations, and politics.

COAL AGE. New York: McGraw-Hill Book Co., 1911- . Monthly.

CONSERVATION NEWS. Washington, D.C.: National Wildlife Federation. 1938- . Semimonthly.

CONSERVATIONALIST. Albany: New York Department of Environmental Conservation. Bimonthly.

THE CONSERVATIONIST. Madison: Wisconsin Conservation Department, 1947- . Monthly (irregular).

CRC CRITICAL NEWS IN ENVIRONMENTAL CONTROL. Cleveland: Chemical Rubber Co., 1970- . Quarterly, illus.

CRY CALIFORNIA. San Francisco: California Tomorrow, 1965- . Quarterly.

EARTH LAW. Leiden, Holland: Sijthoff International Publishing, 1974- . Journal of international and comparative environmental law. Quarterly.

ECOLOGY. Durham, N.C.: Ecological Society of America, Duke University Press. 1920- . 6/year.

ECOLOGY LAW QUARTERLY. Berkeley: School of Law, University of California, 1971- . Quarterly.

ENVIRONMENTAL ACTION. Washington, D.C.: Environmental Action, 1970. Biweekly.

ENVIRONMENTAL AFFAIRS. Brighton, Mass.: Environmental Law Center, Boston College Law School, April 1971- . Quarterly.

ENVIRONMENTAL HEALTH AND POLLUTION CONTROL. Amsterdam, Netherlands: Excerpta Medica Foundation, 1971. Monthly.

ENVIRONMENTAL LAW. Portland, Ore.: Northwestern School of Law, Lewis and Clark College, 1970- . Semiannual.

ENVIRONMENTAL LETTERS. New York: Mercel Dekker, 1971- . Quarterly.

ENVIRONMENTAL POLICY AND LAW. Lausanne, Switzerland: International Council of Environmental Law, 1975- . Quarterly.

ENVIRONMENT & PLANNING. London: Pion Limited, 1969- . Quarterly, illus.

ENVIRONMENT LAW REVIEW. Albany, N.Y.: Sage Hill Publishers, 1970- . Annual.

IUCN BULLETIN. Morges, Switzerland: International Union for Conservation of Nature and Natural Resources, 1952- . Monthly.

JOURNAL OF ENVIRONMENTAL MANAGEMENT. New York: Academic Press, 1973. Quarterly.

JOURNAL OF ENVIRONMENTAL QUALITY. Madison, Wis.: American Society of Agronomy, 1972- . Quarterly.

JOURNAL OF FORESTRY. Washington, D.C.: Society of American Foresters, 1902- . Monthly.

JOURNAL OF SOIL AND WATER CONSERVATION. Ankeny, Iowa: Soil Conservation Society of America, 1946- . Bimonthly.

JOURNAL OF WILDLIFE MANAGEMENT. Washington, D.C.: Wildlife Society, 1937- . Quarterly.

LIVING WILDERNESS. Washington, D.C.: Wilderness Society, 1935. Quarterly.

MARINE FISHERIES REVIEW. Washington, D.C.: U.S. Department of Commerce, available from Government Printing Office, 1939. Monthly.

MARINE POLLUTION BULLETIN. London: Macmillan Journals, 1970- . Monthly, illus., maps.

MARINE RESOURCES DIGEST. Mt. Arlington, N.J.: Girard Associates, 1968- . Monthly.

MINING CONGRESS JOURNAL. Washington, D.C.: American Mining Congress, 1915- . Monthly.

NATIONAL FISHERMAN. Camden, Me.: Journal Publications, 1904- . Monthly.

NATIONAL PARKS & CONSERVATION. Washington, D.C.: National Parks & Conservation Association, 1919- . Monthly.

NATION'S CITIES. Washington, D.C.: National League of Cities, 1963- . Monthly.

NATURALIST. Minneapolis: Natural History Society of Minnesota, 1950- . Quarterly (irregular).

NATURAL RESOURCES JOURNAL. Albuquerque: School of Law, University of New Mexico, 1961- . Quarterly.

NATURAL RESOURCES LAWYER. Chicago: American Bar Association, Section of Natural Resources Law, 1968- . Quarterly.

NATURE AND RESOURCES. Paris: UNESCO, 1958- . Quarterly.

NEWSLETTER. New York: Natural Resources Defense Council, 1971- . Quarterly.

NEW YORK FISH AND GAME JOURNAL. Albany: New York Department of Environmental Conservation, 1954- . Semiannual. Illus., diagrs.

NOT MAN APART. San Francisco: Friends of the Earth, 1970- . Monthly.

NUCLEAR NEWS. Hinsdale, Ill.: American Nuclear Society, 1959- . Monthly.

OCEAN DEVELOPMENT AND INTERNATIONAL LAW JOURNAL. New York: Crane, Russak and Co., 1973- . Quarterly.

OCEAN MANAGEMENT. Amsterdam, Netherlands: Elsevier Scientific Publishing Co., 1973- . Quarterly.

OCEANS. Menlo Park, Calif.: Oceans Magazine Co., 1969- . Bimonthly.

102 MONITOR. Washington, D.C.: Council on Environmental Quality, 1971- . Monthly.

OUTDOOR AMERICA. Arlington, Va.: Izaak Walton League of America, 1922- . Monthly.

PARKS & RECREATION. Arlington, Va.: National Recreation and Park Association, 1903- . Monthly.

PLANNING MAGAZINE ASPO. Chicago: American Society of Planning Officials, 1943- . Monthly.

POLLUTION ABSTRACTS. La Jolla, Calif.: Paul Janensch, 1970- . 6/year. Illus.

PROFESSIONAL SANITATION MANAGEMENT. Clearwater, Fla.: Environmental Management Association, 1969- . Quarterly.

THE PUBLIC LAND AND RESOURCES LAW DIGEST. Boulder: Rocky Mountain Mineral Law Foundation, University of Colorado, 1970- . Semiannual.

PUBLIC ROADS. Washington, D.C.: Bureau of Public Roads, available from Government Printing Office, 1918- . Bimonthly.

PUBLIC UTILITIES FORTNIGHTLY. Washington, D.C.: Public Utilities Reports. Biweekly.

PUBLIC WORKS. Ridgewood, N.J.: Public Works Journal Corp., 1896- . Monthly.

REAL ESTATE LAW JOURNAL. Boston: Warren, Gorham, & Lamont, 1972- . Quarterly.

REAL ESTATE REVIEW. Boston: Warren, Gorham & Lamont, 1971- . Quarterly.

RECLAMATION ERA. Washington, D.C.: Bureau of Reclamation, U.S. Department of the Interior, available from Government Printing Office, 1908- . Quarterly.

SHORE AND BEACH. Miami, Fla.: American Shore and Beach Preservation Association, 1923- . Semiannual.

SIERRA CLUB BULLETIN. San Francisco: Sierra Club, 1893- . Monthly.

SOIL CONSERVATION. Washington, D.C.: Soil Conservation Service, U.S. Department of Agriculture, available from Government Printing Office, 1935- . Monthly.

SOLID WASTES MANAGEMENT. New York: Communication Channels. 1958- . Monthly.

STATE COASTAL REPORT. Sacramento: California Research, 1973- . Bi-weekly.

WATER, AIR, AND SOIL POLLUTION. Dordrecht, Holland: D. Reidel Publishing Co., 1971- . Quarterly, illus.

WATER CONTROL NEWS. Chicago: Commerce Clearing House, 1966- . Monthly.

 News about water and its availability, pollution, and treatment.

WATER RESOURCES BULLETIN. Urbana, Ill.: American Water Resources Association, 1965- . Bimonthly.

WPCF JOURNAL. Washington, D.C.: Water Pollution Control Federation, 1928- . WPCF. Monthly.

# Appendix B
## SELECTED LIST OF LAW LIBRARIES

The libraries listed below have been selected as possible sources for books and government documents published since the compilation of this bibliography and for other materials such as court decisions and legislation. The mailing address and telephone number of each listed library is given. The fact that a library is listed below does not suggest that one has unrestricted access to it. It is suggested that one intending to visit a particular library first write or telephone there and inquire as to what restrictions, and in some instances charges, are involved. Many of the items listed in this bibliography are also available in public libraries. If not, some public libraries offer interlibrary loan service reaching law libraries, so that specified books may often be obtained without the necessity of leaving one's local area. Finally, there are many law libraries throughout the country not listed below. These can be identified in the biennial compilation, DIRECTORY OF LAW LIBRARIES, published for the American Association of Law Libraries by Commerce Clearing House. The most recent volume is the 1974 edition. Copies may be found in all of the law libraries listed below.

ALABAMA

    Alabama Supreme Court Library
    Judicial Building-Capitol
    Montgomery, Ala. 36104
    (205) 269-6623

    University of Alabama
    School of Law Library
    P.O. Box 6205
    University, Ala. 35486
    (295) 348-5925

ALASKA

    Alaska Court Libraries
    941 4th Avenue
    Anchorage, Alaska 99501
    (907) 274-8611

ARIZONA

    Arizona State University
    Law Library
    Tempe, Ariz. 85281
    (602) 965-6141

# List of Law Libraries

University of Arizona
College of Law Library
Tucson, Ariz. 85721
(602) 884-1547

## ARKANSAS

University of Arkansas
Law Library
Fayetteville, Ark. 72701
(501) 575-5604

## CALIFORNIA

University of California
School of Law Library
Berkeley, Calif. 94720
(415) 642-4044

University of California
Law Library
Davis, Calif. 95616
(916) 752-3322

Los Angeles County Law Library
301 West First Street
Los Angeles, Calif. 90012
(213) 629-3531

University of California
Law Library
405 Hilgard Avenue
Los Angeles, Calif. 90024
(213) 825-7826

San Diego County Law Library
1105 Front Street
San Diego, Calif. 92101
(714) 236-2231

## COLORADO

University of Colorado
Law Library
Boulder, Colo. 80302
(303) 443-2211 ext. 7536

University of Denver
Law Library
200 West 14th Avenue
Denver, Colo. 80204
(303) 753-3405

## CONNECTICUT

Connecticut State Library
231 Capitol Avenue
Hartford, Conn. 06115
(203) 566-4601

Yale Law Library
127 Wall Street
New Haven, Conn. 06520
(203) 436-2215

## DELAWARE

Delaware Law School Law
Library
P.O. Box 1624
Wilmington, Del. 19899
(302) 658-8531

## DISTRICT OF COLUMBIA

Environmental Law Institute
1346 Connecticut Avenue, N.W.
Washington, D.C. 20036
(202) 659-8037

George Washington University
National Law Center Library
716 20th Street
Washington, D.C. 20006
(202) 676-6647

Georgetown University Law
Center
Fred O. Dennis Law Library
600 New Jersey Avenue, N.W.
Washington, D.C. 20001
(202) 624-8260

Library of Congress
Law Library
10 First Street, S.E.
Washington, D.C.   20540
(202) 426-5056

## FLORIDA

University of Miami
Law Library
P.O. Box 8087
Coral Gables, Fla.   33124
(305) 284-2250

University of Florida
Law Library
Gainesville, Fla.   32611
(904) 392-0418

## GEORGIA

University of Georgia
Law Library
Athens, Ga.   30602
(404) 542-1922

Georgia State Library
301 Judicial Building
Atlanta, Ga.   30334
(404) 656-3468

## HAWAII

Hawaii Supreme Court Library
P.O. Box 779
Honolulu, Hawaii   96808
(808) 548-7434

University of Hawaii
Law Library
Honolulu, Hawaii 96822
(808) 948-7966

## IDAHO

Idaho State Law Library
Supreme Court Building
451 West State Street
Boise, Idaho  83720
(208) 384-3317

University of Idaho
Law Library
Moscow, Idaho  83843
(208) 885-7950

## ILLINOIS

University of Illinois
Law Library
Champaign, Ill.   61820
(217) 333-2913

Cook County Law Library
2900 Chicago Civic Center
Chicago, Ill.   60602
(312) 321-5423

Northwestern University
School of Law Library
357 East Chicago Avenue
Chicago, Ill.   60611
(312) 649-8451

University of Chicago
Law Library
1121 East 60th Street
Chicago, Ill.   60637
(312) 753-3421

Illinois State Library
Centennial Building
Springfield, Ill.   62756
(217) 525-2994

INDIANA

Indiana University
Law Library
Bloomington, Ind.   47401
(812) 337-9666

Indiana University
Indianapolis Law School Library
735 West New York Street
Indianapolis, Ind.   46202
(317) 264-4028

IOWA

Iowa State Law Library
State House
Des Moines, Iowa   50319
(515) 281-5125

University of Iowa
Law Library
Iowa City, Iowa   52242
(319) 353-5968

KANSAS

University of Kansas
Law Library
Lawrence, Kans.   66045
(913) 864-3025

State Law Library of Kansas
State House
Topeka, Kans.   66612
(913) 296-3257

KENTUCKY

Kentucky State Law Library
Capitol
Frankfort, Ky.   40601
(502) 227-7417

University of Kentucky
Law Library
Lexington, Ky.   40506
(606) 258-8686

LOUISIANA

Louisiana State University
Law Library
Baton Rouge, La.   70803
(504) 388-8802

Law Library of Louisiana
100 Supreme Court Building
New Orleans, La.   70112
(504)   527-8268

MAINE

Law & Legislative Reference
Library
State House
Augusta, Maine   04330
(207)   289-2754

University of Maine
Law Library
246 Deering Avenue
Portland, Maine   04102
(207)   775-5691

MARYLAND

Maryland State Library
Court of Appeals Building
361 Rowe Boulevard
Annapolis, Md.   21401
(301)   267-5395

University of Maryland
School of Law Library
500 West Baltimore Street
Baltimore, Md.   21201
(301) 528-7270

MASSACHUSETTS

Boston University
Pappas Law Library
765 Commonwealth Avenue
Boston, Mass.  02215
(617) 353-3151

State Library of Massachusetts
341 State House
Boston, Mass.  02133
(617) 727-2590

Harvard Law School Library
Langdell Hall
Cambridge, Mass.  02138
(617) 495-3174

MICHIGAN

University of Michigan
Law Library
Ann Arbor, Mich.  48104
(313) 764-9322

Wayne State University
Law Library
Detroit, Mich.  48202
(313) 577-3925

Michigan State Library Law
Division
P.O. Box 1237
Lansing, Mich.  48904
(517)  373-0630

MINNESOTA

University of Minnesota
Law Library
Minneapolis, Minn.  55455
(612) 373-2737

Minnesota State Law Library
117 University Avenue
St. Paul, Minn.  55155
(612) 296-2775

MISSISSIPPI

Mississippi State Law Library
Carroll Gartin Justice Building
P.O. Box 1040
Jackson, Miss.  39205
(601) 354-7113

University of Mississippi
School of Law Library
University, Miss.  38677
(601) 232-6511

MISSOURI

University of Missouri
Law Library
Columbia, Mo.  65201
(314) 882-6096

University of Missouri-Kansas
City
Law Library
Kansas City, Mo.  64110
(816) 276-1650

St. Louis University
Law Library
3700 Lindell Boulevard
St. Louis, Mo.  63108
(314) 535-3300 ext. 355

Washington University
Law Library
Lindell & Skinker Boulevards
St. Louis, Mo.  63130
(314) 863-0100 ext. 4355

# List of Law Libraries

MONTANA

Montana State Law Library
State Capitol
Helena, Mont. 59601

University of Montana
Law Library
Missoula, Mont. 59801
(406) 243-5603

NEBRASKA

University of Nebraska
College of Law Library
Tenth & R Streets
Lincoln, Nebr. 68508
(402) 472-3548

Creighton University
Law Library
2500 California Street
Omaha, Nebr. 68178
(402) 536-2872

NEVADA

Nevada Supreme Court Library
Supreme Court Building
Carson City, Nev. 89701
(702) 882-7056

NEW HAMPSHIRE

New Hampshire State Library
Supreme Court Building
Concord, N.H. 03301
(603) 271-3777

NEW JERSEY

Rutgers--The State University
Law Library
Fifth and Penn Streets
Camden, N.J. 08102

Rutgers--The State University
Law Library
180 University Avenue
Newark, N.J. 07102
(201) 648-5675

New Jersey State Law Library
185 West State Street
Trenton, N.J. 08625
(609) 292-6230

NEW MEXICO

University of New Mexico
School of Law Library
1117 Stanford Drive, N.E.
Albuquerque, N. Mex. 87131
(505) 277-6236

Supreme Court Law Library
Supreme Court Building
P.O. Drawer L
Santa Fe, N. Mex. 87501
(505) 827-2515

NEW YORK

New York State Law Library
Education Building
Washington Avenue
Albany, N.Y. 12224
(518) 474-5957

State University of New York
Law Library
Buffalo, N.Y. 14260
(716) 636-2043

Cornell University
Law Library
Myron Taylor Hall
Ithaca, N.Y. 14850
(607) 256-4236

Columbia University
Law Library
435 West 116th Street
New York, N.Y. 10027
(212) 280-3737

New York University
Law Library
40 Washington Square South
New York, N.Y. 10003
(212) 598-3071

Appellate Division Law Library
525 Hall of Justice
Rochester, N.Y. 14614
(716) 454-7200

Syracuse University
Law Library
Syracuse, N.Y. 13210
(315) 423-2527

NORTH DAKOTA

North Dakota Supreme Court
Law Library
Capitol Building - 2d Floor
Bismark, N. Dak. 58501
(701) 224-2227

University of North Dakota
School of Law Library
Grand Forks, N. Dak. 58201
(701) 777-2204

OHIO

University of Akron
Law Library
Akron, Ohio 44325
(216) 375-7330

University of Cincinnati
Law Library
Cincinnati, Ohio 45221
(513) 475-3021

Cleveland State University
Cleveland-Marshall College of
Law Library
Euclid Avenue & East 24th
Street
Cleveland, Ohio 44115
(216) 687-2250

Ohio State University
College of Law Library
1659 North High Street
Columbus, Ohio 43210
(614) 422-6691

University of Toledo
College of Law Library
Toledo, Ohio 43606
(419) 537-2733

OKLAHOMA

University of Oklahoma
Law Library
630 Parrington Oval
Norman, Okla. 73069
(405) 325-4311

University of Tulsa
College of Law Library
3120 East Fourth Place
Tulsa, Okla. 74104
(918) 939-6351

OREGON

University of Oregon
Law Library
Eugene, Oreg. 97403
(503) 686-3088

Lewis and Clark College
Northwestern School of
Law Library
10015 S.W. Terwilliger
Boulevard
Portland, Oreg. 97219
(503) 244-1181

# List of Law Libraries

PENNSYLVANIA

State Library of Pennsylvania
Law Library Bureau
Box 1601, Education Building
Harrisburg, Pa. 17126
(717) 787-7343

University of Pennsylvania
Law Library
3400 Chestnut Street
Philadelphia, Pa. 19174
(215) 594-7478

University of Pittsburgh
Law Library
Pittsburgh, Pa. 15260
(412) 624-6213

Villanova University
Law Library
Garey Hall
Villanova, Pa. 19085
(215) 527-2100

PUERTO RICO

Catholic University of Puerto Rico
College of Law Library
Ponce, P.R. 00731
(809) 842-4150 ext. 218

University of Puerto Rico
Law Library
P.O. Box L
San Juan, P.R. 00931
(809) 764-0000 ext. 424 545

RHODE ISLAND

Rhode Island State Law Library
Providence County Court House
Providence, R.I. 02903
(401) 331-1363

Rhode Island State Library
State House
Providence, R.I. 02903
(401) 277-2473

SOUTH CAROLINA

University of South Carolina
Law Library
Columbia, S.C. 29208
(803) 777-5942

SOUTH DAKOTA

University of South Dakota
Law Library
Vermillion, S. Dak. 57069
(605) 677-5259

TENNESSEE

University of Tennessee
Law Library
Knoxville, Tenn. 37916
(615) 974-4381

Memphis State University
School of Law Library
Memphis, Tenn. 38152
(901) 454-2421

Vanderbilt University
Law Library
Nashville, Tenn. 37203
(615) 322-2568

TEXAS

University of Texas
Law Library
2500 Red River
Austin, Tex. 78705
(512) 471-3238

Southern Methodist University
Law Library
Dallas, Tex. 75275
(214) 692-3258

University of Houston
Law Library
3801 Cullen Boulevard
Houston, Tex. 77004
(713) 749-3191

Texas Tech University
School of Law Library
Lubbock, Tex. 79409
(806) 742-6124

UTAH

Brigham Young University
Law Library
Provo, Utah 84602
(801) 374-1211 ext. 3296

University of Utah
Law Library
Salt Lake City, Utah 84112
(801) 322-6594

VERMONT

Vermont Department of Libraries
Library and Supreme Court Building
Montpelier, Vt. 05602
(802) 828-3268

VIRGINIA

University of Virginia
Law Library
Charlottesville, Va. 22901
(703) 924-3384

Washington and Lee University
Law Library
Lexington, Va. 24450
(703) 463-3157

Virginia State Law Library
Supreme Court Building
1101 East Broad Street
Richmond, Va. 23219
(804) 770-2075

WASHINGTON

Washington State Law Library
Temple of Justice
Olympia, Wash. 98504
(206) 753-6524

University of Washington
Law Library
Seattle, Wash. 98195
(206) 543-4089

WEST VIRGINIA

West Virginia State Law Library
State Capitol Building
Charleston, W. Va. 25305
(304) 348-2607

West Virginia University
College of Law Library
Morgantown, W. Va. 26506
(304) 293-2701

WISCONSIN

University of Wisconsin
Law Library
Madison, Wis. 53706
(608) 262-1151

Marquette University
Law Library
1103 West Wisconsin Avenue
Milwaukee, Wis. 53233
(414) 224-7031

# List of Law Libraries

WYOMING

Wyoming State Library, Law
Division
Supreme Court Building
Cheyenne, Wyo.  82002
(307) 777-7509

University of Wyoming
Law Library
Laramie, Wyo.  82070
(307) 766-5175

# Appendix C
# SELECTED ENVIRONMENTAL ACTION ORGANIZATIONS

The organizations listed below are concerned with environmental research, dissemination of information, and promotion of ecological concerns. These organizations frequently have available for distribution brochures, annual reports, and other publications describing their aims, work, and accomplishments. Additional organizations can be found listed in the ENCYCLOPEDIA OF ASSOCIATIONS (10th ed. 3 vols. Detroit: Gale Research Company, 1976). Volume 1 lists and describes more than 14,000 organizations. The index should be consulted starting with the entry "Environment" for references to appropriate organizations. Volume 2 lists all organizations alphabetically by state and also separately lists the executives of the organizations alphabetically by last name. Volume 3, NEW ASSOCIATIONS AND PROJECTS, is a periodical publication in loose-leaf form which supplements information in Volume 1. Another source of information is the DIRECTORY OF CONSUMER PROTECTION AND ENVIRONMENTAL AGENCIES (1st ed. Orange, N.J.: Academic Media, 1973). Both publications are generally available in reference departments of university libraries and large public libraries.

American Shore & Beach Preservation
Assn.
10812 Admirals Way
Potomac, Md.  20854

American Water Resources Assn.
206 E. University
Urbana, Ill.  61801

Environmental Action
1346 Connecticut Ave., N.W.
Suite 731
Washington, D.C.  20036

Environmental Clearinghouse, Inc.
124 E. 39th Street
New York, N.Y.  10016

Environmental Law Institute
1346 Connecticut Ave., N.W.
Suite 614
Washington, D.C.  20036

Environmental Management Assn.
1710 Drew Street
Clearwater, Fla.  33515

Environmental Research Institute
P.O. Box 156
Moose, Wyo.  83012

Friends of the Earth
529 Commercial Street
San Francisco, Calif.  94111

National Audubon Society
950 Third Avenue
New York, N.Y. 10022

Soil Conservation Society of America
7515 N.E. Ankeny Road
Ankeny, Iowa 50021

National Parks and Conservation Assn.
1701 18th Street, N.W.
Washington, D.C. 20009

Wilderness Society
1901 Pennsylvania Avenue, N.W.
Washington, D.C. 20006

National Wildlife Federation
1412 16th Street, N.W.
Washington, D.C. 20036

Wildlife Society
3900 Wisconsin Avenue
Suite S-176
Washington, D.C. 20016

Sierra Club
1050 Mills Tower
San Francisco, Calif. 94104

In addition to the above organizations, there are several recently organized public interest law firms that devote all or a substantial portion of their activity to environmental law problems. Some of the more widely known firms are listed below. These firms may have annual reports, brochures, or other publications describing the kinds of environmental cases handled either as completed litigation or as pending matters. Some of these firms are funded through the Ford Foundation and are described in an excellent forty-one page pamphlet, THE PUBLIC INTEREST LAW FIRM; NEW VOICES FOR NEW CONSTITUENCIES, a report published in 1973 by the Ford Foundation. Copies may still be available from the Ford Foundation, 320 East 43 Street, New York, N.Y. 10017, or kept as part of the permanent collection in law libraries and public libraries.

Center for Law & Society Policy
1751 N Street, N.W.
Washington, D.C. 20036

Pacific Legal Foundation
455 Capitol Mall
Sacramento, Calif. 95814

Center for Law in the Public Interest
10203 Santa Monica Boulevard
5th Floor
Los Angeles, Calif. 90067

Project/International
1751 N Street, N.W.
Washington, D.C. 20036

> An outgrowth of the Center for Law and Social Policy, concerned with questions of international scope.

Environmental Defense Fund
162 Old Town Road
East Setauket, N.Y. 11733

Public Advocates
433 Turk Street
San Francisco, Calif. 94102

Natural Resources Defense Council
15 West 44th Street
New York, N.Y. 10036

# AUTHOR INDEX

This index lists writers, editors, and compilers. Also listed are authors of articles included either as main entries or as contributors.

# Author Index

# Author Index

# Author Index

MacDonald, James B.  5, 45
McEvoy, James III  43
McGovern, George  3, 6
Mack, Leslie E.  45
Mackintosh, Douglas R.  32
McKnight, Allan D.  25
McLoughlin, James  25
McNairn, Colin H.  61
McNeil, Richard J.  75
McNickle, Roma K.  45
McPhee, John A.  84
Magill, Paul L.  32
Maloney, Frank E.  45
Mandelker, Daniel R.  105
Marks, Herbert S.  67
Marquis, Ralph W.  11
Martin, Roscoe C.  45
Maryland.  University of.  School of Law  46
Maryland.  Water Resources Commission  58
Massachusetts.  Division of Water Pollution Control  58
Massachusetts.  General Court. Senate.  Select Committee Established to Investigate and Study Water Pollution in Rivers and River Networks in Massachusetts  58
Massachusetts.  Legislative Research Council  14
Massachusetts.  Office of Comprehensive Health Planning  14
Matthews, E.S., Jr.  20
Mayda, Jaro  94
Meadows, Donella H.  105
Meek, W.F.  94
Meetham, A.R.  32
Mellanby, Kenneth  75
Merriam, Lawrence C., Jr.  119
Merrill, Maurice H.  64
Mersky, Roy M.  39
Meyers, Charles J.  5
Mills, Clarence A.  32
Michigan.  Laws and Statutes  59
Minnesota.  Division of Forestry. Department of Conservation  124
Minnesota.  Legislature.  Outdoor Recreation Resources Commission  92, 120

Missouri.  Air Conservation Commission  38
Missouri.  University of.  Air and Water Pollution Conference  46
Mitchell, John G.  11
Monaco, Grace P.  105
Monaco, Lawrence A., Jr.  105
Moreell, B.  93
Morgis, G.G.  28
Morrisey, Thomas J.  11
Morton, Ruvelle S.  83
Mouzon, Olin T.  94
Murphy, B.M.  93
Murphy, Earl Finbar  11, 46
Murphy, George H.  14
Mylroie, Gerald R.  11
Myren, Richard A.  84, 123

# N

Nader, Ralph  4
Nash, A.E. Keir  46
National Academy of Sciences.  Environmental Studies Board.  Committee for International Environment Programs  19
National Agricultural Chemicals Association  75
National Association of Counties Research Foundation  46
National Association of State Foresters  123
National Center for Resource Recovery  79
National Institute for Petroleum Landmen  25
National Parks and Conservation Association  113
National Petroleum Council.  Committee on Petroleum Resources Under the Ocean Floor  98
National Research Council.  Highway Research Board  105.  See also U.S. Department of Health, Education and Welfare
Nebraska.  Environmental Control Council  38
Nestle, Manuel E.  2
Nevada.  Commission of Environmental Protection  38

# Author Index

# TITLE INDEX

Titles of articles, periodicals, and journals are not included.

## A

Acquisition of Wildlife Land in Minnesota 92

Act for the Preservation of White and Other Pine Trees in Her Majesties Colonies of New Hampshire and Massachusetts-Bay for the Masting of Her Majesties Navy, An 124

Action for Environmental Quality 56

Action for Open Space 108

Action for Wilderness 115

Administration of Pesticide Laws and Regulations 76

Administration of the National Environmental Policy Act 15

Administrative Procedures and Public Lands 112

Administrative Rule Making in Wisconsin Conservation 8

AEC Licensing Procedure and Related Legislation 70

AEC Omnibus Bills for 1963 and 1964 69

Agreements Registered with the International Atomic Energy Agency 67

Agricultural Functions and Organization in the United States 110

Air and Water Pollution 29, 39

Air Pollution 29, 30

Air Pollution: A Bibliography 28

Air Pollution, An Annotated Bibliography 28

Air Pollution--1966 36

Air Pollution--1968 36

Air Pollution--1969 36

Air Pollution--1970 36

Air Pollution: The Emissions, the Regulations and the Controls 34

Air Pollution, Volume III: Sources of Air Pollution and Their Control 34

Air Pollution and Its Control 34

Air Pollution and the Regulated Electric Power and Natural Gas Industries 37

Air Pollution and Urban Planning 29

Air Pollution Control 31

Air Pollution Control: Guidebook for Management 33

Air Pollution Control: Hearings 36

Air Pollution Control, Part 2 34

Air Pollution Control and Solid Wastes Recycling 35, 80

Air Pollution Control Field Operations Manual 34

Air Pollution Control Regulations on the State of North Dakota 38

Air Pollution Handbook 32

Air Pollution in California 38

Air Pollution in the Iron and Steel Industry 32

Air Pollution Publication 28

# D

# E

# Title Index

# Title Index

## O

## P

# Title Index

# Title Index

# SUBJECT INDEX

Underlined numbers refer to main entries within the book.

# Subject Index

# Subject Index

# Subject Index

## R

Radiation. See Pollution
Radioactivity. See Pollution
Ralph Nader Study Group 30, 42, 103
Rat Extermination Act of 1967, report 77
Recreation 119-23
Reform, environmental 2
Refuse Act 24
Refuse Act of 1899, hearing 51
Regional approaches 13, 29, 43, 44, 48, 94
Remedies 4, 5, 6, 7, 61
  marine pollution 48
  oil pollution 46
  private 6
  water pollution 47
Resource Recovery Act of 1969, hearings 81
Resources and Conservation Act of 1967, hearing 96
Resources management 94
Resources Recovery Act of 1970, report 80, 81
River and Harbor and Beach Erosion Omnibus Bill 127
Rivers and Harbors Act of 1899 5
Rulings, air pollution 30

## S

San Francisco Bay 11, 40, 43, 47, 48, 87, 100, 104
Scotland 83
Soil conservation and erosion 12, 126-28
Solid waste. See Pollution, solid waste
Sonic boom 61
South Carolina 27
Sovereignty, permanent, over natural resources 95
Soviet Union, water resources law 43
SST. See supersonic transport plane
Standard setting 2, 4, 47
Standing, law of 3, 5
State parks, laws relating to 119
States' roles 13, 24
  land resource management 93, 95, 102
  soil erosion 127
Substantive rules 5
Suits 3, 4, 11, 43
Supersonic transport plane 11

## T

Tax 17
  California timberlands 124
  depreciation allowances 14
  energy and subsidies 64
  exempt status 4
  incentives 14, 31, 59
  land conservation 101
  means of control 14
  policies 56, 102
  urban land use 104, 106
Technological growth, curb on 11
Tennessee 39, 62
Texas 9, 27
  air pollution 29
  Clean Air Act 27
  laws and statutes, urban planning 120
  Solid Waste Disposal Act 27
  state agencies 15
  water quality 12, 59
Tort liability 12, 61, 66
Toxic Substances Control Act of 1971, hearings 28
Transportation 31, 56, 60
Treaties 58, 90
  atomic radiation 66
  fisheries 92
  forestry 126
  oil pollution 39
  sea 98, 99
  soil conservation 128
  wildlife 84

## U

United Nations 19
  fisheries 84
  law of the sea 98
U.S. President, messages
  energy 70
  environment 17